On the Fringe

CONFESSIONS OF A MAVERICK ANTHROPOLOGIST

Edward C. Green

Black Rose Writing | Texas

First printing

Some names and identifying details have been changed to protect the privacy of individuals.

ISBN: 978-1-68513-296-5
PUBLISHED BY BLACK ROSE WRITING
www.blackrosewriting.com

Printed in the United States of America
Suggested Retail Price (SRP) $22.95

On the Fringe is printed in Garamond Premier Pro

*As a planet-friendly publisher, Black Rose Writing does its best to eliminate unnecessary waste to reduce paper usage and energy costs, while never compromising the reading experience. As a result, the final word count vs. page count may not meet common expectations.

This book is dedicated to the Matawai people
of the Suriname rainforest.

Also, great thanks to those friends and colleagues who helped shape this book: H. Russell Bernard, Charles Good, John Janzen, John Lenoir, John Lozier, Dan McNeill, Donald A. Ranard, Peter Rousmainere, Paul Salstrom, Janice Shay.

Praise for

On the Fringe

"Medical anthropologist Ted Green's memoir is a deeply moving, reflective, and indeed soul-baring account of his prominent family's history and its far-reaching effects on his life's extraordinary journey. Through the global reach of his consulting, applied field research, and numerous highly regarded publications Green earned prominence as a scholar and keen observer of health conditions and needs of developing societies, especially in East and Southern Africa and the Middle East. His work on HIV/AIDS prevention in Uganda challenged standard (condom centered), well-funded approaches that ultimately led to his research posts at Harvard School of Public Health and membership on the President's Advisory Council on HIV/AIDS in 2003. Green's uncommonly fearless approach to his autobiography may encourage other professionals to dig deeper and more honestly."
–Charles Good, Professor emeritus, Virginia Tech

"In this equally disturbing and uplifting book, Ted Green lays bare the self-doubt that dogged his decades of high-powered and highly effective public health consulting. Green's body of written and consulting work has influenced the response to public health emergencies by governments across the world -- from Bangladesh's program to reduce the incidence of childhood diarrhea to the U.S. government's response to HIV/AIDS. And now, in this unique autobiography, Green's clear writing about his peripatetic career is yet another of his many contributions to the social science canon."
–H. Russell Bernard, Professor emeritus of anthropology, University of Florida; Director, Institute for Social Science Research at Arizona State University

"Edward Green has written a courageous self-revealing anthropological memoir that combines his various anthropological undertakings, especially his remarkable career in public health advocacy, with the vivid details of an adventurous personal life. If reading this work leads even a few young aspiring anthropologists entering the field to overcome their fears and self-doubts to undertake creative, original, daring initiatives— to become mavericks--this tell-all memoir will have succeeded in fulfilling its author's stated intention for writing it."
–John M. Janzen, University of Kansas emeritus professor of anthropology

"Dr. Green brings the reader along on a fascinating and intimate journey from rebellious dropout to his considerable accomplishments as an anthropologist. Hardly a rags-to-riches tale, Green finds his own way despite the privilege of a Kennedy-like family. The reader gets an inside view of the anthropologist at work, from ethnography with the Matawai in Suriname to applied medical anthropology among traditional communities in Southern and West Africa, Asia, the Middle East, and beyond."
–JD Lenoir, PhD, JD, US Dept. of Justice

"Edward C. Green's engrossing life story *On the Fringe* shares the intimate texture of his life in applied medical anthropology. His book is a precious gift to all his fellow seekers."
–Paul Salstrom, author, *Appalachia's Alternative to Mainstream America (2021)*, Professor Emeritus of History, Saint Mary-of-the-Woods College.

"Dr. Green says so much in just one book! This is definitely a guide book for applied anthropology and transculturalism, because after a few pages it ceases to be about him and more about everyone who wants to know what it means to be human in our complex world. Green confronts the negative noises in our heads that frame failure and success according to parental or societal "gospel," showing that there are other ways of living a truthfully meaningful life. This is not a memoir of a self-obsessed person trying to ride on his "celebrity currency" but of an accomplished and brave world explorer who carried out an awful lot of transformative work around the world. His scope is amazing and he successfully uncovers the humanity of the "Other" by dispelling past, present and probably future stereotypes."
–Dr. Regina Kessy Wilkinson (PhD) Research Director: Transcultural Foundation (UK), Founder, Global HARMONY Foundation, Founder; Tuko Sawa Harmony Society of Tanzania

"(Green's) story dwells on remarkable career success in "freelance anthropology." This came after an extended youthful rebellion against elite prestige educational opportunities and expectations. He has much to say about psychology and mental health, sibling birth order, imposter syndrome, substance addiction, depression, nature-nurture, etc. He also offers a number of "paranormal" experiences, his own and others, involving faith-healing, synchronicity, and out-of-body experience, etc. Much of this book challenges conventional academic practice in research and publication. This book deserves to be widely read and reviewed.
–John Lozier, PhD University of Minnesota, 1969; Assistant Professor West Virginia University 1969-78; Adjunct Professor of Agricultural Education, WVU College of Agriculture, 1995-2005

"I can say with confidence that the reader will find in these pages the lively memoir of a rogue anthropologist who dared to defy the given rules. This book captures not only the essence of Dr. Green's brilliant career, including accounts of successfully applied but divergent anthropology, but also the human side of a scientist dealing with love, inspiration, fear, anxiety, loss, and defiance in his family, and the long-time friends who helped him get through difficult times."
–Elaine Murphy, PhD., Professor of Public Health at George Washington University (ret.) and Visiting Scholar at the Population Reference Bureau, Washington, DC

Author's Note

I started this memoir by promising myself—and by extension you, the reader—that I would be honest in revealing my fully human, highly flawed life, the outer and the inner, the lows as well as the highs, the good, bad, and ugly, the paranormal, the ontological, and the downright embarrassing.

When I had finished writing, I had to wonder if I really wanted to tell the world all these personal things? Patti Davis (Ronald Reagan's daughter) wrote an opinion piece about Prince Harry's just-out memoir and observed, "Not every truth has to be told to the entire world." At least in my book, I do not try to settle any scores, or get even. I do try to prove to my (late) mother that she was wrong when she told me I was destined to a life of failure. This was on the occasion of my expulsion from an elite boarding school where my father had excelled, and where my brother was an upperclassman at the time. She repeated her prediction often. A life of failure, I thought? *You ain't seen nothing!*

There followed years of enhanced adolescent rebellion, during which I slipped almost entirely off the academic ladder. When years later I found myself at Harvard taking an unpopular position on AIDS, I figured: I am still a rebel, a marginal character, a maverick. But things aren't that clear-cut because, well, how did I even get to a place like Harvard, the pinnacle of the establishment?

I found myself attracted to anthropology in college, and I discovered a fellowship of fellow nonconformists (many of us) who don't fit neatly into their own cultures and who, in the words of anthropologist Walter Goldschmidt, "distrust all sources of power, influence, and wealth. We loathe authority—indeed, we shrink from the prospect of finding ourselves in positions of authority. Our 'escapist tendencies' find expression in xenophilia, the romanticization of all things foreign.…" In other words, we hope to have a transformative experience by living for a couple of years in a society very different from our own, but find we do not really fit there either. So yes, I am a marginal character, but so are many others in my field. Yet I am not sure what

I would have done with my life had I not found refuge in a field—a whole profession—of nonconformists like myself.

I still have trepidation about revealing so much of myself, perhaps even seeming self-absorbed, which maybe one has to be to even undertake a memoir. I have encountered few memoirs by professionals that delve into career setbacks, disastrous job interviews, fears and failures, anxiety and depression, deeply rooted feelings of being an imposter. I hope that this book might be useful for especially younger people entering public health, anthropology, international development, or allied fields in order to know about my struggles and not feel so alone, different, and isolated if they have experienced life events and feelings like my own.

On the Fringe

Contents

Chapter 1
Trespassing in the Tropics, Armed with Contract

I was flying to Dar es Salaam one night in 1993, and was sitting next to a Malawian official named Dr. Banda. He was proud of his recent year at Harvard's John F. Kennedy School of Government, confiding that everyone in his class had been "set up for life" by mere acceptance into the prestigious one-year program. No need to graduate. I thought about it. You could argue that I was set up for life right at birth, yet if so, I had trashed the gift and discovered my own path through this world.

The official and I were seated in business class, and I put a mask over my eyes and tried hard to sleep. Laying there, I thought about a colleague who asked a couple of days earlier if I was excited about my coming assignment in Tanzania, a new country for me. I was, but despite years of experience, anxiety was marring the anticipation. It always did. Old fears and doubts poked out of well-worn neural pathways and whispered, "*This* assignment will finally be the time you totally fail, when you will be exposed as a professional imposter who doesn't know a damned thing."

Everyone knows the stereotype of those plagued by inadequacy: the shy, bland character fearful of a frown, much less a real adventure. Me? In my teens, I co-founded a street gang and challenged a teacher to a fistfight in class. I have now traveled to the most disease-ridden countries on earth, and to hidden places tourists have no inkling of. Being an anthropologist, I've immersed myself deep in special populations, seen and worked with their issues, and known the world as even great travel writers can't. I have been deemed a pioneer in medical anthropology, written nine books and about 500 scholarly articles and similar pieces, and given advice to a US president. My rebelliousness has carried me like a magic carpet to remarkable places and people all over the earth, and given me the lift of contribution and deep-core professional satisfaction.

I worried about failing before every project, in Africa and elsewhere. My life has been a quest to silence that persistent whispery voice.

I had taken my first consulting job in 1980 Sudan (before it broke into North and South Sudan), six years after earning my PhD. It was a USAID program to control schistosomiasis, a water-borne disease in which tiny flatworms penetrate the skin of people swimming, wading, or washing in contaminated water, and lay eggs. After several years, victims can suffer damage to their kidneys, liver, and other organs. Even today, it infects over 200 million people, most of them in Africa. There was much we didn't know about it back then. Treatment with the drug praziquantel was just coming on the market and, in any case, it cost far than most Africans could afford.

Self-doubt competed with excitement, according to my journal entries. I knew too little of the region, the country, the health sector, the parasitic disease sub-sector, and much else. Even under these circumstances, the Americans I worked with usually seemed brimming with self-confidence. Perhaps engineers and agricultural economists feel they possess special knowledge and skills they can easily export all over the world. Drip irrigation may be the same everywhere. The study of people and their health is not.

In Sudan, the men (and one woman, our team leader) were all beyond retirement age. Right from the start, I would hear one old-timer remark, "Well, you clearly haven't read my latest book on integrated pest management," which would prompt our team's physician to object, "Of course, we were doing that in Borneo in the early '60s," whereupon the snail man would rejoin, "Indeed, I made the same point in 1958 at the international conference on... ." Occasionally I tried to add something anthropological-sounding, but not too often. The physician on our Sudan team held two additional PhDs, and juggled multiple faculty appointments at apparently six universities on three continents. Although German was his native tongue, he lectured in three languages, and could probably curse like a bandit in a dozen.[1]

When we were first introduced, this M.D/PhD/DRPH/MPH seemed to sense my unease, not to mention my inexperience, if not incompetence. So he took me aside and asked me sympathetically where I had worked with schistosomiasis. Well, the truth was, I'd only worked "professionally" in obscure Suriname, and schistosomiasis... actually, I'd only worked on a *proposal* for a schisto project on behalf of a consulting agency. He looked at me with frank disbelief. (Panic! Exposed as a fraud!)

Later that afternoon, he sat me down in the coffee shop of our hotel and for an hour and a half tried to teach me about schistosomiasis. After I listened carefully this whole time and took notes, he pronounced judgment: I seemed to be a "keen observer" and a hard worker. I don't know how he reached this conclusion, but it restored a tiny modicum of my self-confidence.

I had no way to catch up with this first team. But as I flew south in 1993, I now had far more experience, and I was on my way to assist Tanzanian sex workers, most of them infected with HIV. Again, I felt the same apprehension as in Sudan.

Virtually from birth, I had been expected to further the long line of privilege I came from. I descended from Governor John Winthrop of Massachusetts Bay Colony, as well as from the first Episcopal bishop of the United States, Samuel Seabury, who gazed down on us from the often-invoked family pantheon, along with four fellow colonial governors. My parents had laid out a Life Plan for me, and it differed little from that for my well-behaved elder brother: Groton, Yale, then one or more graduate degrees, whereupon noblesse oblige nudged us away from Wall Street (making money is so *vulgar*, my mother reminded us) and toward the Foreign Service, an Ivy League professorship, or an Episcopal bishophood. So, in order to become my own person, I had to rebel against all the above, as most psychologists would agree.

Indeed, I left a trail of controversy from that first assignment in Sudan. I kept a diary there because I thought I might never again have such an unusual experience in a faraway country I knew nothing about. I later showed it to a friend just to amuse him. He happened to be the editor of *Human*

Organization, a major journal in my field, and I guess he thought it would be a lark to publish it. This thought gave me pause. I had criticized the USAID Mission Director, and this piece might end any USAID-related career in international health before it even began. But an article in this journal would be pretty cool. And would I even have a career at USAID? This Sudan job seemed like a onetime gig. So I allowed the diary article to be published in the Spring 1981 issue, under the title "Have Degree Will Travel: A Consulting Job for AID in Africa."

Almost at once, the USAID/Sudan Mission director threatened to sue *Human Organization* for my criticism of him. My unflappable editor friend dared the director to try: the publicity would just show an even wider audience what a jerk this guy was. I won't reproduce the really critical parts here. I wasn't out for shaming anyone, and still am not. I just wanted to tell my academic colleagues what it was like to do a consulting job like this one—especially when you, the anthropologist, had specialized in a very different part of the world, yet had to become a culture area specialist on the fly, within a couple of weeks. I confessed in an international, peer-reviewed journal—totally unprofessional, I know—that I felt thoroughly intimidated during this first consulting gig, that I found myself in way over my head. Five years later, I published a second diary-style article in the Letters section of the *American Anthropologist*, [II] and one critic wrote, "Puerility oozed from every pore." Ouch. I was invited to write a rejoinder to defend this type of honest reporting, which I did.

Twenty years after that first job, when I lay sweltering in an apartment in Maputo, Mozambique, negative thoughts again overwhelmed me. They often flooded my brain even at the beginning of short assignments, and now I was beginning a two-year gig with higher stakes. I couldn't dispel the obsessive thoughts or unknot my stomach. A Valium would, though. I had one emergency Valium that I had carried around for years in case I really started to lose my sanity, in an ultimate panic attack from which I might never recover. I remember thinking that there was something wrong with my brain, some *defect* in brain chemistry that caused me to suffer needless, highly destructive, debilitating self-doubt and anxiety. Depression was part of the pattern too. In fact, when I thought about it...I had a *bad brain*! I needed anti-depressants, tranquilizers, stabilizers, euphorics—something. Yet I had nothing.

My life seemed to be an obstacle course, one of dark pits. I haven't escaped them, but now they are rarer and shallower. And over the years I've discovered surprises about them, and new mysteries as well.

Chapter 2
Born to Rebel: Sweden, Boarding Schools, and South Korea

I grew up all over the world. My brothers and I were raised in a Foreign Service family, so we moved around every few years. My earliest memories are of life near Wellington, New Zealand's capital. I am happy to report that I remember quite a bit of this beautiful bayside town, even though we left New Zealand before I had turned three. We had a Māori nanny named Molly who used to shampoo my hair.

I was the second of three sons. I had an older brother, Mark, and a younger one, Brampton, born in our flat in Stockholm. In theories of male sibling birth order, the first-born is the center of love and delight for parents. When Son #2 arrives he quickly sees he must compete for the parents' attention. To be noticed, he had to rebel against the established order, represented by Son #1. He becomes the Eternal Rebel. He is more intellectually flexible than the first-born, who is a Defender of the Established Order, from which he benefits. By the time a third boy arrives, the roles of Defender of the Established Social Order and Eternal Rebel are occupied, and so to get attention in families (especially dysfunctional ones), Son #3 becomes The Clown, one who uses mocking humor to make everyone embarrassed, and to show that he has insight about what is behind all family roles. I summarized this idea to my father one day, and his reaction was, "My God! This perfectly describes you three boys! Who is this author?" He was fascinated, and perhaps a bit relieved that it might have been sibling dynamics and not anything he or my mother did or failed to do that got me

kicked out of Groton where he had excelled, or landed Son #3 in various troubles.

My main source for this theory was *Born to Rebel: Birth Order, Family Dynamics and Creative Lives,* by Harvard's Frank Sulloway, who made a scholarly study of historical characters while looking for evidence that supports this theory—therefore some confirmation bias is probably at work, as his critics were quick to point out. Nonetheless, his book received endorsements from the likes of biologist E.O. Wilson and sociologist Robert K Merton. The concept had circulated in pop psychology circles for years prior to Sulloway's attempt to bring scientific rigor to it.

Of course, as an anthropologist with a cross-cultural perspective, I wonder how universally the theory of sibling birth order applies, given how much families differ from one another when viewed cross-culturally. Putting that concern aside, it seems to at least offer some explanatory power in my own family, society, and culture.

Between my father's assignments, I lived either overseas or in Washington, except when I was in boarding schools. Our peripatetic lifestyle meant my friendships usually lasted only a couple of years. Except for Sweden.

Life in an Igloo

Before we departed for the frozen north, I asked my brother Mark where Sweden was and what it was like there. He was then 7 and I was 5, and he told me that for starters we'd be living in a tiny house made of snow and ice called an *igloo,* and it would mostly be dark all day. Instead, we dwelt in a flat on Strandvägen, one of Stockholm's most elegant, prestigious boulevards, overlooking a small park with a duck-filled pond, the delightful harbor with its slow-moving boats. It was an enormous apartment, and there was no more sharing a bedroom with my brother, as I now had a spacious room of my own.

I made a couple of close friends at the English (or International) School in Stockholm, and one was Michelle. She was my age, and she became my first girlfriend. Her father worked for the British airline—then called BOAC—and he would often be away on weekends, and leave her to stay with us. My bedroom was pretty isolated and the guest room was too, so she would often come and jump in bed with me in the wee hours, for company. It was very innocent and non-sexual. Then one summer in about 1952, her parents invited me to join their family to stay on a tiny nudist island in the Baltic Sea. I remember feeling embarrassed to find myself running around naked among girls and—egad—a couple of ancient parents who must have been close to 30. Yuk. What I remember most from Nudist Island is painful sunburn and ubiquitous mosquitoes.

But the main thing about her is that we got along well, and told each other everything and anything. She was like a best friend. I think this friendship may be why I have never been accused of being unable to share intimate thoughts or feelings with women in later life. Unlike a lot of American men, women have confided in me.

However, peer rules operated then as now, and boys as young as I—I was under ten—simply didn't have girlfriends. I had to warn Michelle not to approach me at school, because if she did, I would pretend she was just a pesky girl trying to bother me, and no friend of mine. She went along with this make-believe, but then on weekends we had all kinds of unsupervised adventures throughout Stockholm, that great, beautiful, and surprisingly safe city for adventurous, hyperactive kids.

I wonder what became of her—and if she is alive, how she remembers our friendship.

The Vodka Glass and the Commie Upstairs

The future of all life on Earth depends on the vodka glass in the hands of a man in Russia. That's what my mother told me casually one day when I was perhaps seven, adding that his name was Stalin. I had never heard the words "vodka" or "Stalin." My mother explained that this man was the dictator ("like a ruthless king with too much power") of Soviet Russia, and that he had atom bombs ready to destroy America and the world, depending on whether he was drunk or sober. I didn't know about these alternatives either.

I was confused and alarmed. Was this news the origin of my chronic insecurity? Maybe, but it might also have occurred when I was three or four after my brother Mark told me what death was. He explained I would be "all alone, permanently" after our parents died. They would be gone forever and ever, as if they had never even lived. I lay in my bed that night and tried to imagine Death. I still remember tossing and turning, and tears.

Our building housed diplomatic families from all over, and a Bulgarian bachelor lived right above us. My mother told me he was a Communist who worked for the unstable vodka guzzler Stalin, and I'd better watch out and never speak with him because he'd likely kidnap me and send me to Siberia. Siberia was a backward land of slave labor where it was always dark, freezing, and snowing. Al Capp drew cartoons of it, calling it Lower Slobovia. Sweden was cold enough in winter; I sure didn't want to end up in Lower Slobovia.

The Bulgarian guy's bedroom was just above mine, and I often heard him practicing his saxophone. He seemed to know only one (Western, decadent) tune: "Tea for Two," which seemed harmless enough to me. My bedroom was off in one corner of our big home, far from my brother and our nanny. Sometimes I got scared knowing that I was all alone, and the Bulgarian might descend from a drop-ladder and pack me off to Lower Slobovia. My parents' room was not too far away, but they were frequently out at diplomatic dinner parties. I felt secure only when they came home at perhaps 11 p.m., and I would hear my father playing a Chopin *étude* on the piano.

My father was a good, decent man and unusually popular in the Foreign Service, where his intelligence, Yale pedigree, sense of humor, and love of puns carried him far, to ambassadorships and to Assistant Secretary of State for East Asia and Pacific Affairs. He died in 1998, and not long after I found myself at a party with friends I had worked with in Mozambique. My friend's son had a wind-up toy that would play well-known Chopin melodies. After hearing a few of these I was seized with grief, and was afraid I would break down in front of the guests.

Enter My Bodyguard

The English (language) School of Stockholm was the center of my life, at first. Mark had been shipped off to Groton School as a 7th grader (or First Former), and even though he and I fought constantly, life felt boring after he was no longer around for me to torment. My mother came up with what turned out to be a brilliant idea for hyperactive #2 Son: send him to horseback riding lessons.

I fell completely in love with riding and horses, and soon my daily routine became: Come home from school at about 4 p.m., in a world already dark in the winter. Vacuum down a peanut butter and jelly sandwich, jump on my bike (which generated a headlight from my front wheel's spin), zip over to the stables a mile or so away, and hang with my new Swedish friends of all ages. My first Swedish friend was a boy about my age: Bertil Kampf, who lived just off Karlaplan, a mini-park with a fountain that spurted water during summer months. I began to pick up colloquial Swedish more and more, and life seemed good, rich, and intense, even during those endless, dark winter months. I hardly saw my family any more, and I suppose even my girlfriend Michelle had to find something else to do on her weekends.

I should mention Gary Haskell, the school bully, a tough, beefy Welsh kid with red cheeks who seemed to have it in for me. Gary and I were on opposite sides in our frequent war games. He routinely and unapologetically broke unspoken norms and rules, for example, by putting rocks inside snowballs. Once we were told we were soon to have a new student from Africa. Gary started to organize a little Ku Klux Klan reception for our first Black student, saying "We don't want blacks in our school!" My friends and I decided to organize a welcoming committee in direct opposition to Gary. What did Gary do? He told our teacher, Miss Johnson, that I was the one behind the racist reception. I was forced to stay after school for two days and write "Manners Are Essential in Everyday Life," 200 times on the blackboard. Manners? How did that relate to my alleged racist views, which were really Gary's, about an incoming African student?

When I was about 8, Yakov Salmon arrived as a new boy. He had red hair, just like mine, and now there would be two redheads. But he was a year older, so I didn't know if we might become friends. On his first day, during the long hour and a half recess after lunch, at the edge of woods that belonged to the Swedish Royal Family, Yak came right over to me, looked at my hair, and said, "Well, I guess we're going to have to be friends." Yes, indeed!

He asked for a rundown on who was who among the kids. So I obliged, and when I got to Gary the bully, Yakov said, "Let's go over and see just how tough this kid is."

So we went up to Gary and Yak said, "So I hear you're the tough guy around here. Let's see how tough you really are," and he pushed Gary around, then twisted his arms and legs into knots, forcing him to beg for mercy. Well, okay, I might be exaggerating. It's been almost 70 years since the incident, let's say Gary politely *requested* mercy.

In a single act, Yakov established himself as Top Dog in the schoolyard, and as my new best friend, my redheaded brother.

Yak was the son of an Israeli diplomat named Avram, or Abraham Salmon, who was unusually kind and involved with his only child's life. He would drive Yak and me to wonderful places like the Tivoli amusement park or Skansen, the open-air museum and zoo on the island of Djurgården, if it was summer. Yak's mother was pale and sickly. She had been in a TB sanitorium. I knew nothing about Israel, the country Mr. Salmon represented. My mother just told me it was a "new country," whatever that meant.

I remember Mr. Salmon would make his own coca cola by mixing carbonated water with syrup, thereby saving money. I thought that was pretty cool, but what stays with me is how much he was part of his son's life, how much time he spent with his son, unlike my dad who seemed forever busy at work—and only got busier as his career took off during our years in Stockholm and beyond.

Purgatory

By 1955, when I was ten, I was living a life of independence and cross-cultural immersion in Sweden, and I was used to it. My Nordic existence suited me. Then my parents moved back to America and life flip-flopped.

I was sent to a pre-prep boarding institution, Fay School in Southborough, Massachusetts. I hated it from the start. I had been dropped into a suffocating, totalitarian "total institution" of the fascist variety where dyspeptic planners programmed every minute of the day and night, and prescribed each article of clothing, and—if they had their way—every thought in our heads. We all wore numbers on our suit jackets, announcing to the world the precise degree of conformity to which we would submit. If a "1" could be seen on our jacket, it meant we were fully indoctrinated, whereas a "4" signified only marginal brainwashing. No number at all meant we were beyond redemption. The school awarded numbers at the end of each school term, based on grades achieved, an absence of punitive black marks, and the amount of school spirit we exhibited, a quality that surely defied quantification. And there were rewards supporting this Orwellian system: with a low number, a boy could get one weekend home, if his family happened to be nearby, and not in faraway DC.

This regimentation was all the more galling after my life of largely unsupervised freedom in Stockholm. Kids sent away to boarding school at tender ages—Fay started with third grade—tended to come from divorced or highly mobile families. Think of actor Henry Fonda moving from set to set, occasionally overseas. His son would become the 1960s icon Peter Fonda, who was three forms ahead of me. How ironic that he became the face of rebellious Sixties Youth, as Captain America in *Easy Rider*. He candidly records his Fay boarding school experiences in his memoir *Don't Tell Dad*.

I was at Fay because my earlier education at an international school in Stockholm might not have prepared me for Groton, my father's alma mater, and the secondary school my brothers and I were expected to attend. Or so my parents carefully planned, without consulting me. I felt lonely and alienated. I didn't know about American sports such as football and baseball, which put me at a disadvantage from the start, plus I believe I had a slight British accent. Any quirk or quality that set a boy apart from other kids set someone up for teasing, or worse. I did have one thing in my experience that helped, namely experience with horses. In the 1950s, Fay offered horseback riding, and I was already a good rider at ten and was therefore taken on as a groomer and manure shoveler by Miss McCartney, our mannish riding instructor. I do have a few good memories of taking rides on cold, frosty mornings, on trails that wound through snow-laden boughs, and led away from school and thus to freedom.

There was chapel every day, and even in study hall they sometimes set aside time for singing hymns. We sang "Onward Christian Soldiers." We also sang "Oh God Our Help in Ages Past," which contains the lines, "Time like an ever-rolling stream bears all its sons away; they fly forgotten as a dream, dies at the opening day." I liked that, and committed the words to memory.

But I was lonely and miserable at Fay School. All the forced Christianity around me made me wonder if God existed. It occurred to me that maybe God was testing me. And if that were really so, it changed everything. I knew I could pass the test, but first I needed to know if God was truly there.

One late November night in my little cubicle, I gazed out the window at the cold harvest moon and asked God to give me a sign. If He were actually omnipotent, He could turn every other person's eyes elsewhere at the precise moment I thought the word "Now!" Then God could have the moon perform, say, a back flip, for my eyes only. Then I would know that there was a purpose to my suffering, and I would work hard and be a good Christian.

I gave God several chances to perform a little miracle in the sky on that frigid, lonely November night, but a sign never came. I concluded there was no purpose behind my suffering.

One warm day in late spring, with summer vacation looming and hope in the air, I was sitting in Mr. Baker's English class. I was near an open window, thinking about Holden Caulfield and escape, when Mr. B made an arresting statement: "You boys are all from good families or you wouldn't be here. That means you will likely go on to graduate from good senior prep schools and then from Ivy League colleges. And *that* means most of you will go on to have good jobs and interesting careers. You will become doctors and teachers and explorers and scientists and wealthy businessmen, and some of you will be artists and writers and musicians and philanthropists...

just think of the sheer *potential* right here in *this room*! It's staggering, *extraordinary*! Do you boys think ever about your *futures*?"

Our other masters never said anything so encouraging, so his remark made a serious impression. Wow, I thought, maybe even I would have an interesting life as an adult... if I ever survived this purgatory. Occasionally at dinner I would hold my knife up where I could see the overhead lights reflected in the glittering blade. I would squint my eyes and imagine I could glimpse into my future when there would be parties and chandeliers and music; or maybe I'd be on a ship anchored in a tropical harbor somewhere, and Fay School would be nothing but a troubled memory. Much later I would actually meet a Fay old boy at a yacht club in Lagos, Nigeria. I would also sit next to an exotic woman at a lunch in Hong Kong. Her husband had gone to Fay School, and he suffered from a recurrent dream that he was back at Fay because he had failed a course and still had to make it up.

Fay, Groton, and virtually all these boys' boarding schools went co-ed in the 1970s. In 1981, the daughter of my friend and colleague Bill Hoadley came to Africa for her first vacation—from Fay School to Swaziland. And she loved Fay! In the years to come I would meet females who were at, or had gone to, formerly boys' New England prep schools, and they were all pretty much happy with their experiences. Going co-ed was probably the best thing that ever happened to these schools.

The Sewer Rats

In 1955, due to my hyperactivity and general misbehavior, I was placed in a summer camp in Wells, Maine, a half hour from where the rest of my family stayed in the summer. Most the kids were Jewish and from New York, but my family didn't know this. I experienced culture shock... and I fell in love with my first—but not last—dark curly-haired Jewish girl.

Meanwhile, I ran into Yakov scarcely a year after we left Sweden, and in 1957 he and I co-founded a street gang in Washington we called The Sewer Rats. We had switchblades, black leather jackets with our names on the back, Elvis haircuts—the works. I began smoking cigarettes at 12, got a police record for a switchblade incident which I would tell tales about for years to come, so I'd better say more about it now. I was arrested for threatening a kid from St. Anne's high school with my show-off blade. I wasn't planning to hurt him—it was all for show, for the benefit of the Sewer Rats and wannabe hoodlums present—but someone took me seriously enough to call the cops, who visited my parents that very day. Now, it happened that the Chief Justice of the juvenile court was a good friend of my parents. He handled my case, and I was told that if I never got in trouble again, by age 18 my arrest record would be "expunged," a lovely word I was hearing for the first time in 1957. But that summer of '57. I reveled in the youthful rebellion. I was the black sheep of the family and was mighty proud of it.

The Sewer Rats would last until when Yak left DC and returned to Israel, although there were rumors of kids roaming the subterranean sewers of that city at least a generation later, and carrying on our gang's name.

Yakov was with me in my last summer at the camp. It happened that an older camper was bullying me one day. I tried out a little jujitsu maneuver I must have seen in a movie or on TV. It actually worked, and, unfortunately, I broke the bully's arm. He happened to be the camp director's son, so I was expelled from camp. There was only a week or so left in that camp season, so Yakov called his dad and Mr. Salmon decided on the spot to drive to Maine and pick up Yak and me. He secured my parents' permission to pick me up early, and we three took a drive through the White Mountains of New Hampshire for a week until it was time for camp to be over. My parents never found out about the camp director's son and his broken arm.

I practiced hitchhiking during the earlier summer of 1957. I had recently read *Catcher in the Rye*. During my last semester at Fay, Bill Hopper slipped me a copy of a book he said was "forbidden" because it described a boy running away from school. Of course! That was the solution to my problem—run away! I was about to enter the First Form at Groton. If I ran away by hitchhiking, I first had to discover if people would pick up a 12-year-old boy. So I practiced hitchhiking on Route 1 around Rehobeth Beach, Delaware, where we were spending the last month of summer vacation in 1957. My first ride was with a family, with the dad driving. He warned me that it was dangerous for a boy my age to be hitchhiking. I agreed, and gave a dubious explanation for why I was doing it—a special circumstance that required immediate travel. Soon I got off and hitched back to where we were staying.

Hitchhiking could actually work, I decided.

Speaking of hitchhiking, my mother was driving me home from my meeting with the DC juvenile court over the switchblade thing late that same summer of 1957, when a kid I knew put his thumb out for a ride near our home. I told my mother this was Brit Hume, a nerdy, goody-goody kid from St. Albans school (later the popular conservative anchor at Fox News), and so, of course, she stopped and we picked him up. He charmed her with his good manners, and after we dropped him off, my mother asked me why I couldn't act and, indeed, dress more like this nice Hume boy? He wore his ironed khakis a few inches above his waist, that's why.

Runaway

I'd been living a freewheeling hoodlum life during vacations, and arriving at Groton in 1957 was quite a shock. On my first day there, a boy in my form came up to me and said, "Hey, did you hear the one about Winston Churchill?"

I hadn't.

"Well, so Churchill's secretary came up to him and said, 'Sir, is it true that one cannot end a sentence with a verb?' To which Churchill replied, 'My dear, that is the sort of nonsense up with which I will not put!'"

I agreed that was a real knee-slapper, and thought more seriously about running away and rejoining the Sewer Rats.

Groton looked like a world apart. The renowned landscape architect Frederick Law Olmsted, creator of Central Park, had designed its 480 acres of campus, with forests and meadows, for just a few hundred students. Its first headmaster in 1884 was the Reverend Endicott Peabody, the model for the titular character in *The Rector of Justin*, a novel about Groton (written by my dad's roommate at Yale). The school was based on the so-called public—meaning private—schools of England, and they promoted a philosophy known as physicality, or muscular Christianity, which aimed at promoting *mens sana in corpore sano* (a healthy mind in a healthy body). In his biography of C.S. Lewis, Alister McGrath defines the pervasive British public school ideology of athleticism as essential to the cultivation of manliness and the development of character, which was necessary to produce and reproduce members of the ruling class. There was a sense that WASP aristocrats were becoming effeminate by the 1880s; indeed, a character in Henry James' *The Bostonians* makes this very accusation. So the young, newly ordained Episcopal minister Endicott Peabody felt the need to start his own boarding school, one dedicated to the cultivation of manliness. Unlike boarding schools like Exeter or St. Marks, Groton boys would live a carefully choreographed, spartan way of life—sleeping in bare cubicles under a common ceiling, then up each morning for cold showers and having one's room inspected for tidiness.

I knew nothing about trends in the late 19th century America; I simply saw football and other mandatory sports as an obvious tool of brainwashing boys to make us conform. Just as the Brits like to say that World War I was won on the playing fields of Eton, so it was at Groton, where football rather than rugby was the tool used to force-feed uniformity. I would resist, I promised myself. After my five years in Sweden and a couple of months in the Sewer Rats, I was my own person, and would not be molded into anything. But also, given the years I spent out of the country, I was still relatively unfamiliar with American sports like football and baseball. Boys at both Fay School and Groton had shown off by reciting carefully memorized football statistics and baseball batting averages. I knew none of these things, and didn't care to try to catch up with my peers.

Boys at Groton quickly caught on to my lack of school spirit, and my failure to stand in awe of football. My muscular Christianity was more like muscular dystrophy. My failure to fit in came to a head early in my First Form year, in the fall of 1957, after I suppose I had made a snide remark about both football and school spirit. A Third Form boy named Toby H. turned to me frothing with rage, which caught me by surprise. He cried out, "Green, if you disrespect football *one more time*, I will kick your ass!"

To which I replied curtly, "Fine. Let me say one more time, I disrespect football."

Unexpectedly, he asked that I look at the cast on his arm. I looked and— *wham!* He hit me on the bridge of my nose with his heavy cast. I saw stars and fell to the ground. Toby then jumped on me, pinned my shoulder to the grass, and proceeded to beat me more times on my face and head with his cast. There were other boys present, but none intervened.

It occurred to me that this kid might really want to kill or permanently disfigure me, so in desperation, I did what they called in these schools a "spaz out." I screamed at the top of my lungs and went briefly psychotic. I somehow managed to get out from under Toby, and even on top of him. But before I could inflict even the first real retaliatory blow, other boys and the football coach pulled me away. So in the end, I was all bloody and beaten and Toby, of course, was completely unharmed, and was considered by all present to be in the right, even though he was about three inches taller than me. Oh, the supreme unfairness of life!

He did try to apologize later that year. He invited me into his study room and showed me his harp-guitar, an unusual instrument the likes of which I would not see again for years. Fifth Former Tom Rush had recently shown me how to graduate from playing my baritone ukulele to a full-sized guitar. Tom became a preeminent folk music revivalist, and I have been able to go through life proudly mentioning that Tom Rush showed me my first guitar chords.

One October Sunday morning, early that first semester, I decided it was time to make my break and run away from school. There would be no roll call until dinner, so I had several hours for my getaway. I dressed in nerdy fashion and walked off campus so I could start hitchhiking far enough from school that I'd be unlikely to have anyone recognize me. I had thought up a cover story. I would name myself Henry Allison (what hoodlum would give himself an effeminate name?), and if I could get to the train station 13 miles away at Fitchburg and board a train, my story would be that I was visiting my aunt and, well shucks, I seem to have lost my ticket! I was heading to DC, and if I got there and my parents tried to send me back to Groton, I'd hitchhike to San Francisco. There I would seek out beatniks in coffee shops, and hopefully they would adopt me as a mascot. I could dust off their bongo drums between poetry readings or whatever they needed.

I got a couple of rides that took me to Fitchburg, with warnings from drivers about how unwise it was for a kid my age to be hitchhiking. It turned out later that I, indeed, had quite a few relatives in Fitchburg, but I didn't know this at the time, nor would they likely have helped me escape from school. I boarded the train, and a half hour later the conductor started to work his way down the aisle to check tickets. I slipped into the toilet inconspicuously and locked the door. After time elapsed, I went back to my seat and thought I was okay, but no, the conductor came back and asked for my ticket. I performed my cover story and he seemed to accept it. But when the train pulled into the South Boston station, a cop boarded and said he was arresting me as a runaway. Damn! Turns out the train got occasional runaways, and when my conductor reported me, someone called ahead so a cop could snare me.

I still remember the avuncular cop telling me that protocol required that he handcuff me as we crossed the crowded station to his waiting police car. He said it would look awkward for us both so, if I *promised* him not to bolt, I could just walk beside him, unattached. And so with no fuss, I let myself be taken to his police precinct. By now, it was late Sunday afternoon and I was with a bunch of cops with Irish names. My bright red hair had them thinking I was a good Irish Catholic boy. They asked me if I had eaten that day. I hadn't, so someone sent out for a hamburger and a chocolate milkshake. They gave me the Sunday comics section of the *Globe* to read. Then they asked me questions about the school, wanting to understand why I had run away. I told them about the horrors of boarding school, and since I was new at Groton, I mostly related tales from Fay where a classmate had hanged himself. I was gradually winning over their sympathy.

My parents were called. I learned later they were seeing a double-feature movie with Jack and Caroline Service. Jack was an old China Hand, among the best-known victims of Joseph McCarthy's accusations of Communists in government, and his case went to the Supreme Court. I heard that the movie was interrupted with a public announcement that Marshall and Lisa Green should report at once to the manager's office. Of course, they were greatly alarmed and thought that one of their boys had died. They were told that little Teddy was at a police station in Boston and that he had run away from school. The cops called Groton, and about an hour later my dorm master, Mr. Abry, showed up wearing his clerical collar, whereupon the cops became deferential, thinking him a priest. They told him, "The little lad here has been telling us some rather tall tales, Father."

Mr. Abry drove us back to Groton in virtual silence through the dark, rainy fall night. The next day, I was called in to see Mr. Wright, who I found out was the assistant headmaster and a decent guy. As I recall, his first question was whether I had timed my running away on a day when the headmaster, Reverend Crocker, would be away. I told him I had no idea of Reverend Crocker's schedule. Mr. Wright then genuinely sought to understand what would motivate a boy to run away from Groton. How could I throw this great privilege away? For what? I told him that I didn't fit in there and I missed my friends in Washington. I just wanted to be a day student, like a normal kid.

I think we had a couple of meetings to get at the heart of my 12-year-old angst. Mr. Wright had known my father, who had been a football hero and prefect of Hundred House. How could I besmirch this legacy? How could I be so different? Father and son were both redheads. He sincerely wanted to understand. A few days later Rev. Crocker returned and, well, they didn't seem to know what to do with me because no one had ever run away before. There was no precedent for punishment.

My parents, of course, were summoned to the school. After much wringing of hands, my mother made a deal with me: if I could work hard and make the honor roll, it would prove that I wasn't "too stupid" to be a student at Groton and having proved that—if I could—she would allow me to transfer to St. Albans in Washington. This is the school Al Gore and Gore Vidal (and Brit Hume) attended. I proceeded to invent clever study habits and I worked my ass off, and, by God, by the second semester of First Form year, I had made the honor roll. My mother was ecstatic, confiding to me that my dad had only ascended to the less exclusive merit roll. In fact, I was doing so well by now, and was so well adjusted that "it would be a *crime* to take Teddy out of Groton."

What? I was flabbergasted. Deceived by my own mother. I should have known better. That well-adjusted Teddy was just a pose, a sham. After that cruel betrayal, I never put much effort into schoolwork.

During my years at Groton, starting with First Form year (so, at age 12), I did much of my best reading after "lights out," under my bed covers, with a flashlight. As long as the book was not assigned in any course I was taking, I was keen to read it. And, except for the odd Erskine Caldwell novel with a lurid cover, I read books that nowadays doubtless *are* assigned in English classes, including *Catcher in the Rye* and any book by Steinbeck, Hemingway, or Richard Wright. I remember feeling deeply and emotionally involved in *Native Son*. I swore to myself that I would always oppose capital punishment, if only because a person could be completely innocent of murder, and yet still be sent to the electric chair. I was outraged at the injustice doled out to Bigger Thomas. And I was charmed by the poetry of the "thee and thou" language spoken by Mexican immigrant grape pickers in *Sweet Thursday* and *Cannery Row*. And I couldn't wait until lights out, until I could return to another chapter or two of the picaresque *Grapes of Wrath*. And I was moved to tears at the ending of *Mice and Men*, when George has to shoot Lenny while telling him about how the two friends would find paradise on earth, and live off the fat of the land. The fact that I cannot remember any reading material assigned by my English teachers speaks volumes, although it probably boils down to my chronic insubordination.

Groton Farewell

As in England, New England prep schools offered six forms, corresponding to the 7th through 12th grades. By the time a boy became a Sixth Former, he was granted considerable power. All Sixth Formers were made prefects, and they could get younger boys into serious trouble. A grandnephew—perhaps—of Teddy Roosevelt, whom we all called Rosey, showed how power could corrupt a well-regarded, all-around nice fellow. Because no sooner had he become a prefect, assigned to my own dorm, than he became a dreaded and much-resented Nazi, at least among misbehavers like me. "Rosey! What have you become?" I was tempted to cry out more than once. "You are a nice, genial guy deep down. Drop this act—we miss the real, uncorrupted, inner you."

When I was a Third Former, my brother Mark was a Sixth former. To show me he didn't take this role too seriously; he and his friend Jim Gaver took me to the woods at the beginning of that year, and we smoked cigarettes (had this been 10 years later, I suppose this would have been pot). What an act of wanton rebellion! This was most satisfying and among my better memories of the school. What could be finer on a warm fall afternoon than to be in the woods breaking school rules with two prefects? It happened to be a Sunday when we had a window of free time, so a dodge to the woods was possible.

That evening, as dinner was concluding, the headmaster announced that a small fire had broken out in the woods, down by the river near the boathouse, not far from where the three of us had been smoking. The headmaster invoked the honor code (um, we *had* one?), and asked that any boys come forward with information that might help explain what was probably *not* a spontaneous combustion event. I cast a glance over to the table where Mark and Jim sat, and they glanced back uneasily at me. Nobody came forward, and we breathed a sigh of relief. But the next morning in study hall, when the whole student body was assembled as usual, the headmaster asked each boy to take a piece of paper and write down exactly where he had been and with whom, and exactly what he had been doing in the late afternoon of the previous day.

Oh God, we wouldn't be able to coordinate our lies! But whatever Gaver and the Green brothers wrote, we were never found out.

It was said of Andover Academy, "Boys are free to do whatever they want, tempered by (threat of) expulsion." Groton offered precious little freedom (there was actually more in earlier and later times), and they did use expulsion as the ultimate sanction. Short of that, they used a system of black marks which boys had to serve off by doing meaningless chores on Saturday afternoon, the one time of the week when we were permitted to walk into the village of Groton and buy things like candy and, if we could get away with it, cigarettes.

Unlike even repressive Fay School, we were not allowed to access the extramural world by owning radios, magazines, or newspapers. I was often serving off black marks and so did not get to town often. I do have a memory of sharing a pack of Lucky Strikes under a railroad bridge with Grenville Clark on one or two outings. My closest friend was Don Chauncey, although I don't remember now if he was a smoker.

I went through the fall semester in 1959, not caring about studying much anymore. I wished I could be a day student in Washington. My school spirit was abysmal and my attitude was negative, and this did not go unnoticed. The final straw came when a group of boys had a fight in the cavernous basement of Hundred House, where I spent First Form year in the dorm upstairs. Jugs of apple cider were hurled, and there was said to be abundant broken glass. Just the kind of thing Ted Green would instigate, only I had not even heard about this caper. I went home to Washington for Christmas vacation of 1959, and my mother asked me odd questions: Did the Reverend Crocker shake hands with me and say goodbye (as he did to every boy)? Did he look me in the eye when he said it? I said yes. My mother sighed with relief.

A week later, he expelled me.

In the letter, Crocker said he felt it best if I went with my family to Seoul, Korea, and resume my studies with whatever might be available there. I was described as having a "chronic, negative attitude," and then there was the riot in the basement that they were pretty sure I masterminded, although I wasn't even there. And I probably smoked cigarettes, although they could not prove it. There was a faculty vote, and all voted to expel me save two masters, Messrs. O'Brian and Beebe. How do I know all this? Unbeknownst to me, three boys in my form had rigged a tape recorder and a couple of microphones in the headmaster's study. This diabolically clever scheme was discovered soon after my expulsion, and the boy who served as lookout, Victor Ashe, wrote to me and supplied these interesting details of my expulsion. For instance, the school was well aware that I was influencing other boys to be anti-Groton. Therefore I had to go.

My mother was devastated. **She told me that I was a failure and *would always be a failure*, words that stuck in my heart and are there even today.** "The only career open to a boy who has been *expelled* (she spat the loathsome word out) is the *army* (another loathsome word). But if you've been expelled," she continued, "you can never be an officer, so *at best* you will retire at age 60 as a private first class." Hell, my dad went to Groton, not my mother. Why was *she* the one so undone? I remember her saying to my dad more than once, "And he (the headmaster) didn't even have the guts to tell me that Teddy wasn't coming back! What a coward." She remained bitter and resentful for the rest of her life. But then she never forgot any real or imagined slight.

Still, as a favor to the family, my expulsion was to be expunged from the official record. They altered it to show that I'd withdrawn from Groton voluntarily to go to Seoul, where my dad had just been assigned. And as I think about my behavior decades later, I find myself wishing I had stayed at Groton a few more years. Not all my crippling self-doubt is psychogenic, without justification, because there are definitely major gaps in my general knowledge foundation.

When in later years, I was asked to write an article in the Groton School Quarterly about the role of Groton "boys" in World War II, I mentioned that while many graduates (and the odd expellee) went into high finance or law, quite a few entered public service including the foreign service. Indeed, "service" is in Groton's Latin motto, *Cui Servire est regnare,* which translates "to serve is to reign," or more loosely, "service is perfect freedom."

My father was one such product of his school and social class, and I guess for all my rebelliousness, I absorbed the idea that a meaningful life required some type of service to make the world a better place.

Band, Brothel, and Blackmail

When I first arrived in Seoul, Korea, with a rebellious attitude on a freezing day in early January 1960, we moved into a fancy house that had belonged to a high Japanese colonial functionary. It had paper-thin sliding doors and a few servants. I was to attend the US military school on the Eighth US Army base.

January 1960 · Korea

Arriving in Seoul, Korea

Arthur was a bit older than I, and a sophomore, while I was a freshman. Nevertheless, we became instant friends. He had been living in Cambodia and was what we'd today call "home-schooled," supplemented by college-level correspondence courses that the University of Maryland had set up for soldiers who wished to continue their college education while serving abroad. He was definitely much smarter and more cosmopolitan than the average high school kid. He had diverse interests that included Buddhism, philosophy, photography, opera, math, and physics. As an example of his prowess in advanced physics, he informed me that "the angle of the dangle is directly proportional to the heat of the meat, according to the mass of the ass."

One frozen day in February we walked past the school auditorium as the newly formed rock band was having one of its first rehearsals. I wanted to watch, whereas Arthur wanted to split. When the lead guitarist went to the bathroom, I asked if I could pick up his guitar and play along on "Tequila," which they had been rehearsing. I happened to have worked out an interesting counter-point melody on my Sears & Roebuck Silvertone guitar. I was asked to join the band right then and there. I am pretty sure Fred, the former lead guitarist, never forgave me for displacing him. He dropped out altogether a few weeks later, in a dark mood.

That same day, one of the band members, Dave, advised me strongly that I shouldn't be hanging out with nerds, weirdos, or inner-directed nonconformists like Arthur. I'm afraid that I took his advice, and my friendship with Arthur ended that same day. I felt ashamed of myself because of my behavior, even at that time, but between peer influence and the opportunity for acceptance by older guys considered ultra-hip by prevailing high school standards, Dave's dictum won out.

Early in my freshman year—still in 1960—our band was playing at a Korean nightclub downtown—and our manager Mr. Lee received an urgent call from the principal of our high school. The principal had gotten himself into a situation in a brothel where he had been relieved of his wallet and money, and most of his clothes. Mr. Lee needed to grab a taxi ASAP, find the principal and collect him. I happened to be in the taxi when we retrieved the principal in boxer shorts and wrapped in a blanket. You can imagine his embarrassment.

Now about this principal: when I arrived midyear as a transfer from Groton, I immediately felt much older and worldlier than the "children" in 9th grade. How to remedy this? I went to the principal and argued that I should be advanced a grade, and for justification I used examples such as second and third year Latin at Groton that ought to count as a high school level courses.

But no dice. The principal wouldn't budge on this. So I was to be thrown in with the earnest, callow Lilliputians of the 9th grade. Not a hoodlum in the lot, at least until I corrupted a fellow prep school expellee, Don, later that year. Don, who became a lifelong friend, feels that perhaps it was he who corrupted me.

I waited a discreet week after the brothel incident, and then went to see the principal about moving ahead a year. This time he decided, now that he thought about it anew, that several courses I had taken at Groton might well be considered high-school level, therefore I had probably earned enough credits to leap ahead from freshman to junior. No mention of the brothel incident.

Hoodlum in History Class

In 1961 the roles available in high school were pretty much limited to squares, nerds, jocks, and hoodlums. I was a hood with an Elvis haircut, black leather jacket, a curled-lip and menacing sneer which I perfected in front of a mirror. It mattered little that this school happened to be in Korea and it was for army brats. We were as American as anyone in, well, Tecumseh, Nebraska.

That happens to be where my teacher, Mr. William D. Hervey, came from. I see in my 1961 yearbook that he graduated from a place called Peru State Teachers College, also in Nebraska. He was a fair-haired, well-meaning, thirty-something man whom I nevertheless resented as an authority figure. I paid no attention in class, or so I thought, and I remember passing the time dozing off the previous night's hangover, or writing suggestive notes to several of the more appealing girls in class, especially those brimming with school spirit who were completely beyond the reach of lowlifes like myself.

Mr. Hervey began each class by reviewing the daily cartoon strip *Peanuts*. "What a totally *pathetic* attempt to ingratiate himself to the class," I sneered to fellow hoodlum Wayne. Wayne was actually meant to be a jock—he was on varsity football, after all—but I took him with me to the bars and off-limits neighborhoods of Seoul, and before long he was an anti-social fellow miscreant, becoming my close friend in the 11th grade.

Mr. Hervey was an animated teacher. He paced, he waved his arms, his voice rose and fell, and he generally bounced around the room, behavior I recall as starling and disturbing to a student used to dozing, and occasionally nursing a crushing hangover headache.

One day we had a surprise quiz. Mr. H. handed out a page of test questions, and told us that he'd leave us alone for the next 20 minutes while we wrote the answers. About five minutes into the test, my eyes drifted over to the busily writing scholar to my right. I hadn't meant to exactly cheat, but somehow my eyes just went of their own accord to the test paper next to me.

Suddenly, Mr. Hervey came charging into the room from the back door and announced that he'd caught me cheating red-handed! I immediately put on a great show of shock and indignation. Me? How dare this wimp of a man accuse *me* of *cheating*? So I said, "If you think I'm a cheater, why don't you and I just step outside and we can settle this *like men*?"

I proposed it in my most menacing voice, also probably rehearsed in front of a mirror. I somehow sensed that Mr. Hervey had been a nerd back in his own school days in Nowhere, Nebraska, and was certainly not the kind of guy to get into a fistfight with the likes of me at age sixteen.

It seemed like no one breathed for a few minutes. I knew I *had* him.

Mr. Hervey ended up backing down. I should have felt triumphant, but I actually felt ashamed of myself, sorry about the whole situation. I sensed this might be the low point of my secondary school career.

Now we fast-forward a few weeks. We called our high school rock-'n-roll band The Silvertones after my cheap, brown, Sears & Roebuck, solid-bodied electric guitar, and we were performing at our first high school dance. We started off with the then-famous Champs instrumental, "Tequila." During the break after our first set, Mr. Hervey, who I guess was there as a chaperone, came up to me and quietly asked if the band could play "Tequila" a second time, and this time he could join us, because, as a matter of fact, he happened to have his tenor sax in the trunk of his car.

I was surprised this man would even talk to me. I mean, what if I had said no and sneered at him? What would he have done? Big loss of face if anyone happened to hear the exchange. But I consulted the band and they thought it was a cool idea, and so we performed "Tequila," but this time with the great sax part heard on the Champs' recording. Mr. H. knew his rock 'n roll.

One night that summer Wayne and I were having a late-night beer and our last cigarette under the stars at a baseball field at the American army base in Teagu. Wayne looked up at the sky and had an inspiration: "Hey, why don't we dedicate our lives to science?" I didn't know what that really meant, but it sounded noble and self-sacrificing. So I agreed, but with the provision that we not tell anyone, in case we didn't in fact go on to dedicate our lives to science.

We left Korea at different times, and Wayne went on to get a PhD in geology and I got my PhD in anthropology, to the great relief of both our anxious mothers. Mine had been reminding me during high school on nearly a daily basis that I would end up as a "perpetual private" in the army "at best," since to be an officer I'd have to have gone to college. And then there was that business about me being kicked out of Groton prior to my hasty exile to Korea.

Now here's the ironic part. In the years since high school, whenever something related to American history comes up, I have vivid memories of Mr. Hervey explaining, dramatizing, *acting out, romancing* some chapter of American history. For example, as the world slides deeper into the great post-1929 economic depression, so details of FDR's depression-busting programs come to mind, along with visions of giant locusts gobbling up crops... the Oklahoma Dust Bowl hobos riding the rails and living in Hoovervilles... FDR's fireside chats... Woody Guthrie capturing the zeitgeist in his ballads... eight million jobs created through the WPA.... And somehow in my mind, Mr. Hervey still dances excitedly around all this pageantry. Yet he also described darker chapters in the American past, such as the systematic dispossession of the lands of indigenous people by White settlers. Or the horrific story of how at least one White, Jeffrey Amherst, commander of British forces in North America, advocated giving a group of native people blankets deliberately contaminated with smallpox.

My memories of history and Hervey somehow never dim with the passing of years.

Many years after high school, when search engines were first becoming powerful, I tried to see if Mr. Hervey was still alive. I wanted to apologize for my churlish behavior, and to thank him for putting up with me, and for teaching me so much valuable history in spite of myself. A few years ago, I noticed in my yearbook that he had *signed* it: "William 'Uncle Fred' Hervey." (Did his peers call him Fred?). I never found him, but I confirmed that he died around the time I wrote down this story. But perhaps a descendant in Tecumseh, Nebraska, will read this account and know that Mr. Hervey made a deep impression on someone. If I, the worst kid in American history, learned so much, I can only imagine the overflowing memories of the students who actually listened and did homework. I sent this story around via e-mail to several old classmates from that school in Korea, and it turned out that Arthur had taken a photo of Mr. H joining me with his tenor sax when we played "Tequila" that night in 1961. I had begun to wonder if that event really happened.

Mr. H. plays sax with The Silvertones

Chapter 3
My War Against the War

I was 17 when I started at City College of San Francisco. I found myself there because I had poor grades from high school, plus I had never taken the college board exams. Smoking was not allowed during the exams, and there was no way I could last hours without a cigarette, especially under stressful conditions. It was a shock for me to be back in the United States and living in California, sharing an apartment with my older brother in Berkeley. I was extremely lonely in my first months. Other than hanging out with my Ripple wine-drinking-buddy Pavloff, his friends, and my brother, I had almost no friends in California. I felt like I didn't belong with all those young Californians who all seemed to know who they were and what their purpose in life was. Me, I was living in Berkeley among elite college students, yet I was commuting to San Francisco and going to a *junior* college. From superficial interactions with Berkeley folk, I felt, well, second-class, inferior, uninformed, ignorant, stupid. I felt I had wasted my high school years (all three of them) and had learned precious little. A couple of girls who lived downstairs from my brother and me invited us to a party one night. I was talking with one of the girls, perhaps trying to impress her with my expertise on a topic I really knew nothing about. She looked at me with mild amazement and said, "God, you really *are* stupid," as if someone else had made this charge, and she had foolishly defended me.

Monica and the Mental Hospital

Later that night in bed I found myself thinking. *God, I really AM stupid. My mother was right: I'm a complete failure.* I'd made almost no friends at City College. I just didn't fit in. I was in no way a Californian. Perhaps it was just a coincidence, but almost immediately after I decided to move on from Pavloff and his pals in San Francisco, the girl my brother was dating suggested that it would be good therapy for me to hang out with more wholesome people. He and Melissa Farley had been discussing my steady consumption of Ripple wine and were growing concerned. Melissa was a student at Mills College, and one Saturday she invited me to drive up to Napa State (Mental) Hospital and join her group of Mills and UC Berkeley student volunteers for a project supported by the American Friends Service Committee (AFSC). These volunteers were engaged in something called recreational therapy with the mental patients. They also brought along guitar, banjo, and an autoharp, and they played folk and country music on some of the wards. This seemed like a perfect fit since I loved folk music. I first heard the beautiful, earthy, haunting Carter Family songs from Melissa and the trio. With me, we became a quartet.

Plus, I was starting to study abnormal psychology to find clues about why I felt so different from others my age in the great state of California. What better place for me than a mental hospital—especially if I didn't have to be a patient. I could pass for some sort of staff at the hospital. I imagined that I would gain insights into my alienation. In later years, I would find that people who are attracted to abnormal (now called clinical) psychology had their own personal reasons for going into the field.

There was more to Melissa's plan for improving my life. She happened to know another lost soul like me, a fellow Mills student and a potential girlfriend for me. So the day we first drove up to Napa was the day I met Monica, from an old, respectable Massachusetts family with a trust fund and a dad who had graduated from Harvard, but had suffered from "shell shock" (the old name for PTSD) from World War II. She had long hair that she let cover her entire face when she wanted to retreat from the world. She seemed quite the mysterious girl. I tried to impress her with stories of my exploits in

Korea, and she pulled a sticker off a Chiquita banana and stuck it on my forehead, without comment. This seemed promising. Before long, I began to have an interest and a purpose in my life. I began to look forward to my Saturdays at the mental hospital.

Margie and Bobby

We continued working at Napa, and got to know a catatonic schizophrenic patient named Margie. She was in her 30s, dressed as a man, sported a crewcut, and chewed tobacco, spitting the dark, viscous cud into an ashtray. She didn't seem to think she was a woman. But she began to respond remarkably to our Carter Family country music, sung by Melissa and accompanied by our improvised string band. We learned that Margie was from Appalachia and from a poor family. Furthermore, she had been sexually abused—probably raped—in a men's room at a Kentucky diner.

Around Monica, Melissa, and me, Margie slowly grew more animated and, well... sane. She told us she loved Hank Snow, Hank Williams, Hank Locklin, and just about every Hank in country music. She began to request songs and tried to sing along with us. We had not heard about music therapy, but in retrospect that is what we were providing, and the results were astonishing. Nowadays music therapy is an established, allied health profession, and there is even an American Music Therapy Association.

As we were witnessing her steady transformation, one day she asked Monica for one of her hand-me-down Levi skirts. Before long, Margie was beginning to look like a woman. After several months, she even attracted a boyfriend, an older, tubercular, good ol' country boy named Russ. In some ways, this state hospital could have been the model for *One Flew Over the Cuckoo's Nest*. This was in 1962–63, not long after powerful neuroleptic drugs became available, and so patients were heavily medicated instead of being put in straightjackets and subject to other restraints and therapies that seem inhumane today. Yet a nice thing happened. The nurses and technicians on Margie's ward chipped in from their meager salaries and bought her an 8-bar autoharp. I gave her lessons and her progress continued.

Meanwhile, I still remember two boys on the child and adolescent ward. One was severely autistic. He lived in his private world, and no stimulus could penetrate it. I could make a loud noise right next to his ear, and he'd show zero response. What he would do—his sole *raison d'etre* it seemed— was to very slowly loosen screws from door frames, until eventually he could get a door to fall off its hinges. Then he would go work on the next door.

The other patient I remember far better. He was a boy of about 12 named Bobby who seemed quite normal. He grew fond of Monica and me, and we liked him. Why was he in a mental hospital? Pyromania. It seems he had predilection for burning down houses, such as that of his parents, allegedly twice. He drew lurid paintings of men and horses, both sporting super-sized penises. Melissa heard from a staff member that he had been sexually abused. He had that in common with Margie.

One Saturday about a year into my volunteer work there, the administrator of the hospital asked to see us. He informed us that Bobby had run away from the hospital. They apprehended him on the highway jogging towards Berkeley, and he explained that he wanted to go and "live with Monica and Ted." This meant we had crossed certain professional boundaries that we didn't know about—they had never been discussed. But this incident meant the suspension of our AFSC volunteer program for up to a whole year. There would be an "emotional cooling-off period," the administrator informed us, and when and if our program resumed, we were not to let patients became emotionally attached to us.

Monica and I came back after the "cooling-off" period, and we went at once to find Margie. We found her in a state of catatonia, about where she was when we first met her. She didn't recognize us, or anyone. She was reduced to a state of *cerea flexibilitas*, a name I later learned in an abnormal psych course. It meant keeping one's arms, legs, and body rigidly in the last position anyone put them in. Perhaps we *had* become too involved with two patients, but Margie at least had made great strides toward improved mental health. I wish this could have been documented by an authoritative clinician.

The Second Force

My life at 18 and 19 seemed to be going nowhere. But rebellion was only one of the two forces that shaped my life. The other was more or less its opposite: a yearning for conventional respectability and achievement. For all was not right with my alternative, defiant life. My mother had drummed into my head that I was a *failure* and would always be a failure, unlike my faultless older brother. Part of me needed to prove my mother wrong. I could be as good as my older brother—if I cared to. I just didn't for a number of years. But what if I changed my mind later on? I realized I shouldn't cut off my options entirely.

So the whole time I was a hoodlum, and later a hippie and drug indulger, I was also quietly working on a degree or a postdoc or writing an article or a book. Most of my friends didn't know about my secret life. The Vietnam War fed into this dualism. As tens of thousands of people in my generation died overseas, and the question "Why are we in Vietnam?" stumped the officials who had been deeply involved in the war (including my father, by 1969 the Assistant Secretary of State for East Asian and Pacific affairs), I spent those war years in antiwar activism.

I dropped out after two years at City College, and after a semester at UC Berkeley in a non-degree program, I transferred to George Washington University in DC. I was determined to have a normal college experience before it was too late. My expectations of it came almost entirely from Max Shulman's comic novel *Barefoot Boy with Cheek*, wherein our hero as a student at the University of Minnesota must decide between a respectable sorority girl, named Noblesse Oblige, and her beatnik, Communist counterpart, Yetta Samovar. Also, as it happened, the only person I knew at GWU was Claudia Chaille, president of what I was told was the leading sorority on campus. I'd met Claudia in Korea, where we became close friends, and now at GWU she urged me to pledge the fraternity Sigma Alpha Epsilon. There was the promise of free beer, wild off-campus parties, and unfettered access to plentiful, beautiful, mini-skirted, obliging sorority girls like... like... *noblesse oblige*! Why not? Otherwise, absolutely no social life, right? I remember being so lost, lonely, and friendless at City College of San Francisco. I wanted to be popular again, as I had been in Korea.

That summer I went to SAE parties and frolicked with Pi Beta Phi sorority girls. But with fall, official pledge season arrived. New guys became pledges and had to go through demeaning initiations in my presence. No one made me do anything because I was a junior and I played guitar well, and I was a special friend with the President of Pi Beta Phi, our official... I don't remember the word for our special relationship. Let's say Harvard was to Radcliffe as SAE was to Pi Beta Phi. By the fall of 1965, my transfer year, my current girlfriend Linda was not only not a Pi Phi girl, she was not even a student. She worked as a secretary, *très déclassé*.

It was suggested to me discreetly that I lose secretary Linda. Plus, I was generally more attracted to Yetta Samovar-type girls (we used "girls" back then, and they called themselves the same, because they were young, by God, and not yet "women"). I was growing increasingly anti-war, and I attended meetings of SDS and the Young Socialist League, whereas frat boys were probably headed for military service, and then to respectable professions. Also I went to Jewish folk dances, where Yettas were to be found.

My misgivings all came to a climax one night, during the final initiation ceremony for pledges. They all had to line up in the well-decorated frat house living room, and the Brothers yelled orders at them: "Stand at attention! Get that smirk off your face! Get down on the floor! Do 20 push-ups! Do 50 sit-ups! Faster!"

The only acceptable answer was "Yes, sir!"

God, it was like boarding school, or the fucking army. I didn't belong there. I was a beatnik, or an independent, or a Neo-Marxist—not a frat boy. Finally, I couldn't just stand there with the Brothers bullying the pledges. I broke though the line of debased newbies, strode over to the fireplace, picked up the sacred SAE bugle, and blew it with all my lung power. Everything came to a standstill. I said, "Fuck all this!" and stormed out.

About a week later, a SAE senior bound for Vanderbilt med school was given the unpleasant task of coming to my apartment—which I shared with an SAE brother—and informing me that I was asked to leave. I made the assignment easy for him. I told him some guys just weren't cut out for the Greek life and I held no grudges against anyone, especially against him. We shook hands, and that was that.

When I had transferred to George Washington, I was leaning toward clinical psychology, through which I hoped to gain insights into why I felt generally alienated from the human race. But before long, I discovered an entire academic field of study—a whole *profession*— peopled by the alienated: anthropology. The literary theorist Susan Sontag had recently published an enticing essay called "The Anthropologist as Hero," about the brave journeys into exotic unknowns that anthropologists take. Professors in this field wore dusty cowboy boots or sandals, sported beards when most professors were clean-shaven, offered courses in arcane subjects like Magic, Witchcraft, and Religion, opposed the Vietnam War (the American Anthropological Association was the first scientific professional association to formally take a stand against it), and smoked pot with their students. It was hard to resist.

I transferred to anthropology, and I found offbeat professors like Patrick Gallagher who seemed to be educating a generation of nonconformists, and who assured us there was a marvelous world out there that we could interpret any way we liked. I also became (lifelong) friends with Ray Roberts-Brown, who also changed his major to anthropology. We later shared a group house on K St. NW, where we had some memorable parties. I should also mention Willard Caldwell in Psychology. These professors treated students as *peers*; they made us feel that we could come up with ideas every bit as original and important as their own. This did wonders for my self-esteem (well, temporarily), and it put me in the habit of questioning accepted wisdom ever since. Is there any worthier objective of a university education?

In 1967, two years later, I had a BA in anthropology, I had been accepted at five good graduate schools, one that offered a full fellowship, and I was engaged to Shannon, a beautiful young lady I had met in Survey of Western Art. Somehow George Washington University proved to be the place to give me direction in life, and to tease out the potential that a few of my earlier guidance counselors assured my anxious mother surely lay somewhere beneath all my defiance and rebellion.

Flying Back to Monica

Now let me go back to my arrival at GWU as a junior. My first undeniable out-of-body experience happened in that summer of 1965. I had just moved into a dorm, and Monica was staying at my parents' house while they were away in Indonesia, where my father was US ambassador.

I was lying in the upper berth of a double-decker bed in the dorm room that had two such beds. I hadn't closed my eyes for long when I began looking around the room with growing interest. It dawned upon me that I was lying on my right side, my head facing the wall... so how could I be observing the room? My vision would have been blocked. What was happening? Fear gripped me and I tensed up. But then a voice kicked in and told me that this could be the wished-for mystical experience that my Berkeley friend Howard and I talked about at length before I left California. I should try to put my fear aside, and let this experience happen.

Presently I rolled out of bed and began moving across the floor, while my body was still on the upper berth facing the wall. I examined the wooden floorboards and the tiny bits of dust on the floor, , realized the dust and the floor were actually beautiful to behold. What I would later call my astral body—once I had learned terminology to describe out-of-body experiences—moved all around the room with growing excitement. I wondered if I could pass through the walls of the dorm. So I practiced it and discovered that I could, indeed. Then I wondered if I could go over to my parents' house about four miles away and share this wondrous experience with Monica.

And so I did. Putting fear of the unknown aside, I flew through the air and presently I found Monica asleep, wearing a blue nightgown. I stared into her eyes, and telepathically (I suppose), told her: *Look: we can exist outside of and without our physical bodies! Think of the staggering implications. Aren't you excited? Aren't you thrilled to be alive in a world that now has meaning? We now know we are immortals!*

Monica communicated back to me that she was excited as I was. We stared into one another's eyes for several minutes, not saying much because I had just said it all, and demonstrated that we both (and all of us?) have astral bodies, although I was not to learn that term until I had dipped into the literature on psychic phenomena. We grew happier and happier, ever more excited. Finally, it became just too much to bear and I knew it was time to go back to my physical body. I did this in a flash and then immediately sat up, climbed out of the dorm bunk, and went to the bathroom to have a glass of water and look at myself in the mirror. I *knew* this had not been a dream.

I heard the dorm room lock being opened, and my new roommate entered and introduced himself as someone from Fairfield, Connecticut, here at George Washington for summer school. I started to babble about the amazing experience I had just had, but he began to look alarmed so I changed the subject after saying that I'd probably just had a very realistic dream. But I now call it my Paranormal Experience #1.

The next day I went to my parents' house and saw Monica. I asked her if she'd by any chance had a dream the previous night. She said she had, but it was tricky to describe. I asked her to try. She remembered that she and I were sitting on a bed, staring deeply into each another's eyes and not saying much, just getting happier and happier for a reason she could not conjure.

I told her it wasn't a dream and explained what I've just related. More inexplicable, anomalous, or "transpersonal" experiences were to come. Even at the risk of having this book dismissed as the work of someone mentally unbalanced, I feel I need to faithfully record key events my life, the Inner no less than the Outer, the mystical as well as the everyday.

I later read William James's *The Varieties of Religious Experience* and found he used "ineffable" to express what I am trying to *effing* express. Reading further, I realized I had experienced an OOBE (Out-Of-Body Experience), this one involving telepathy.

My War Against the War

Some of us had déjà vu as we witnessed the US making a hasty, chaotic retreat from Afghanistan in 2022, at the end of a 22-year war carried out by an all-volunteer American military. If we still had military conscription, would the war have ended years earlier? Henry Kissinger once remarked that we lost the Vietnam war because the sons of the elite turned against it. The lesson for the military was to get rid of the draft, so we can fight wars unimpeded by pesky protesters and their influential families. As a result, we have "forever wars" that rely solely on volunteers, mostly from lower-income homes.

I myself qualified as the son of an elite. My dad was Assistant Secretary of State for East Asia and the Pacific (he was "Yale, Male, and Pale," part of the Old Boys' network that still prevailed in the latter 1960s). In fact, a Communist newspaper circulating at the January 1969 Counter-Inaugural rally in DC called Marshall Green one of the "nine most dangerous custodians of the imperialist establishment."

We had the draft in 1965, and the Selective Service was taking young men from their communities and sending them to kill or be killed in Vietnam. I was 20 when my "Greetings" were received from President Lyndon Johnson. I had just hitchhiked from Boston to DC on that frozen New Year's Eve of 1965. I so wanted to reach DC before midnight because I had a party to go to. But I had only gotten a series of short rides and some of the drivers were drunk, so I finally arrived in Washington in the first hour of 1966. The first thing I saw in my apartment was an official-looking letter from the Selective Service that my roommate had perversely placed right on my pillow. I tore it open with foreboding. I was directed to report two weeks later to Fort Holabird, Baltimore for a "pre-induction" physical. My heart sank. "Pre-induction" sounded like an official, unalterable first step toward the war in Vietnam.

I was conflicted. I didn't want to go, but I had little idea how to avoid the draft. Wasn't it the law? I sensed I might yield and sign up.

As soon as that Christmas vacation ended, I went for draft counselling at George Washington University, where I was a student. Sympathetic counsellors in their small, hectic, paper-cluttered office told me that if I could claim that I had already paid tuition for the spring semester at GWU, I could probably get a 2-S-C deferment until the end of that period.

The written rule for a 2-S stipulated that the student had to be making "normal progress" toward his degree. This rule would mean I was drafted—and I still had to take that physical—but I could legally delay the date when I reported for induction. However, if a student had happened to take a semester off to Seek Enlightenment on the Road to Damascus, as I did with my best buddy Don—although we got no further east than Genoa—the Selective Service could immediately revoke the 2-S. Guys from less affluent backgrounds who needed jobs to pay their college fees could not make "normal progress," so they were drafted and faced threats like tripwires, flag bombs, and the pits lined with sharp punji sticks.

Well, I took the 2-S-C. If I had not gotten it, and had reported to the induction center at age 20, I might well have wound up in live combat. And the end of that semester at GW, I heard nothing from my draft board, so I applied for another 2-S-C and I can't remember all these years later if I got a response. But I kept applying for a 2-S-C for five semesters, right through completion of my master's degree, and somehow I kept getting these postponements. This was not kosher, but my draft board for some reason left me alone—had forgotten me, I hoped—between December 1965 and June 1968.

Soon, the government introduced a national lottery for the draft, designed, I suppose, to make selective service less selective, fairer, more random—but also to get younger recruits. As the *Harvard Crimson* observed about the draft in 1967:

If the Administration wins approval for the lottery, it will almost certainly shift to the 19-year old age group. However, even without this approval the step might be taken in a year's time, according to Defense Department officials.

The Department has continually emphasized that it wants to keep the age of induction low—between 19 and 21.

Well, of course it does. Get 'em while they are still too young to think critically about what they are signing up for. If I had been drafted at 18, in 1963, I would have dutifully gone in. But by mid-1968, I had educated myself about the war in Vietnam. As a college student, I had access to draft counselling as well as organizations that offered a variety of viewpoints on war and peace, and on the war in Vietnam in particular. I was attracted to the American Friends Service Committee (AFSC), the Quaker pacifist group. I already had a connection with the AFSC because it had organized the volunteer work I did at Napa State Hospital in 1963-64. The AFSC published a White paper in 1969 that documented the terrible destruction that the United States was inflicting on Vietnam, which, after all, was struggling to throw off the yoke of colonialism from the French and become an independent nation. Ho Chi Minh was an admirer of the American War of Independence, and saw himself as something of a latter-day George Washington. Some streets in Hanoi were named after left-leaning American authors, such as Ernest Hemingway and Jack London.

Why was the United States taking over from the French and trying to squash Vietnamese independence? The rationale was that if all Vietnam went Communist, with Red China pulling the strings, the neighboring nations would fall like dominoes. Liberal intellectuals criticized the falling dominoes theory, which ignored the nationalism energizing the Vietnamese and assumed other nations were helpless against Communism. But no one, to my limited knowledge, predicted that before the 1970s were over Vietnam and China would actually be in a shooting war with each other. The Vietnam domino was falling backwards. And Communism was not monolithic.

I had also read earlier AFSC reports. They all started from a pacifist perspective regarding all wars, but they made me think about the great damage we—Americans—were inflicting on "distant, brown-skin people who do not live or look like us," 10,000 miles from our safe homeland, to quote and paraphrase war correspondent Martha Gellhorn. She added, "Where's the honor in that?"

On a trip back to Berkeley in early 1968, I picked up more books on conscientious objection, including a guide for draft resisters published by the Central Committee for Conscientious Objectors (CCCO), a Quaker organization well-known among male college students. I read all my materials non-stop on the flight back to Washington, and I couldn't wait to tell my fiancée Shannon that I had reached my decision. Maybe my draft board had forgotten about me, but if not, I would register as a CO. I still have the form today, and I see I registered as a CO in April 1968.

My fiancée thought I was unpatriotic. My plan was reckless. Where could it lead? Her reaction reflected her background and her dad's values, but nonetheless we intended to get married after graduation, and then her life and mine would be inextricably bound.

My mother was also opposed. She made the curious comment that I would be depriving myself of a "man's greatest life experience: war."

Shannon and I did get married after graduation, and off I went to Northwestern University, near Chicago. Our first apartment was on West Columbia in a poor neighborhood of Appalachian migrants, Italians, Poles and others. I don't know how our Rogers Park neighborhood has changed since the late 1960s, but the one group of locals I got to know slightly was country boys, mostly from Kentucky and West Virginia. There were a couple of bars where the men drank Pabst Blue Ribbon beer after work, and one night I somehow found a guitar in my hands. I sensed I was being tested. Was I some damned hippie, or was I a good ol' boy? I was soon leading some guys in singing Johnny Cash's "Ring of Fire." I ended up bringing a few of these guys home that night to my apartment, where we sang country songs and drank more beer. Shannon was a good sport about me bringing these men home late in the evening, disturbing her homework. She was finishing up her last undergraduate year at the brand-new University of Illinois Chicago Circle campus, celebrated for its futuristic architecture. I became a semi-regular at that bar, until the night of the riots following the assassination of Martin Luther King Jr. There were reports of fires set deliberately and looting by Blacks, and as I was walking back home from the el station, a carload of my beer-guzzling, blue collar buddies called out, "Hey Red, let's go downtown shoot us some (n-word)!" That ended my superficial relationship with the country boys.

Defense Secretary McNamara's daughter Kathy was in my same anthropology program, but she dropped out, so we took over her apartment lease because we had been living in a dump in a dangerous neighborhood on West Columbia. I earned my masters in anthropology that year. Yes, I was interested in anthro (who wouldn't be?), but to be honest I was in grad school to avoid the draft—or rather the dark day when Selective Service would remember I was already drafted and I would have to report to an induction center. But I didn't feel quite like other students in my program. I remember having a beer one day after class with one such student. She confided to me her ultimate fantasy: she would be funded to take a year off, and she would lock herself in her apartment and "just read all the anthropology journals, nonstop, I mean, complete freedom to just *read*!"

Hmmm... that was not exactly my ultimate fantasy. Did I belong in grad school with such eager beavers?

I left Chicago just short of graduation ceremonies to serve as best man at my friend Steve's wedding at Ft. Detrick, Maryland. I therefore missed the infamous Democratic National Convention to nominate Hubert Humphrey, when a crowd of police unleashed by hippie-hating Mayor Richard Daley savagely clubbed the young, the old, and the middle aged who might be supporters of Sen. Eugene McCarthy, who was running against Humphrey. Steve was marrying an officer's daughter, and I got to talking to two of the waiters at the wedding. They turned out to be COs, conscientious objectors and they were performing alternative service by being, in their own words, human guinea pigs for highly classified experiments in CBW, that is, chemical and biological warfare. Ft. Detrick is where the US government placed German scientists who developed the chemicals used in Nazi concentration camps (see Annie Jacobsen, *Operation Paper Clip.*)

I thought, God, COs might end up there?

The CO Meets the Lord of the Draft

Soon after I returned to DC, my draft board basically told me I could expect no more education deferments. I had benefited greatly from the advice of the National Interreligious Service Board for Contentious Objectors (NISBCO), a group representing multiple pacifist churches such as Mennonites, Church of the Brethren, and Amish—in fact, pretty much all of them, minus the Quakers, who had their own similar CO organization in Philadelphia. So I wrote back immediately and applied to register as a CO.

I had to return to Ft. Holabird to take another pre-induction physical, as 2.5 years had elapsed since the earlier one. I tried several maneuvers to fail the tests. One was the old moral turpitude trick, to get rejected as too immoral to kill for my country. We all had to fill out a checklist, and one question asked whether I had a history of arrest. I could say yes! My switchblade incident from when I was 12. But wait. What if I needed that juvie record as proof? Alas, it was probably expunged. At some point during that busy day at the induction and testing center, a young, prematurely balding John Malcovitch-look-alike army shrink called me into his office to discuss my moral turpitude. He seemed to have little time for malingerers, and just wanted to know if I had been "rehabilitated."

"No," I replied, perhaps too eagerly.

The shrink frowned and observed, "But it states here in your record that you earned a master's degree from Northwestern University."

How to explain away that little aberration, my detour among the law-abiding? I couldn't, and it was clear to this shrink that I was simply not enthusiastic about joining the army and getting shipped to Vietnam. In any case, by mid-1968 the military machine didn't care much about a little moral turpitude from the past. I was found fit to kill.

I prepared for an in-person hearing at my draft board. My super-helpful draft counseling group NISBCO had told me I was lucky that when I moved from Berkeley to Washington, I registered in the latter city. The California state Selective Service Board Director made it a point of personal pride to *never* grant CO status to "any of those goddamn hippie-commie-draft dodgers from Berkeley." He was acting against the law, but I suppose he didn't care.

I studied the entire Selective Service system, especially CO regulations, and prepared myself to make the case that I had a deep moral revulsion to ALL forms of war, even though I reached this conclusion without benefit of an organized religious community. I was even ready to answer trick questions popular with draft boards, like: "So, kid, what would you do if a madman were poised with a hand grenade, about to lob it into a class full of innocent schoolchildren? You happen to have a .38 revolver in your hand. Your only option to prevent a massacre of children is to shoot the madman. What would you do?"

I no longer remember my carefully crafted answer to this question, but in any event, I was classified as a CO without even having to appear for a hearing. My experience was most unusual, I later learned. NISBCO advised that I would almost certainly be called up for alternative service, and they guided me toward readings on the procedures, rules, and legal precedents. To keep alternative service from seeming too attractive, COs had to suffer "relocation" challenges roughly comparable to soldiers leaving their homes to basic training—not to mention thousands of miles away to Vietnam.

With the advice of my draft counsellor, I managed to find a job on my own, intentionally making the whole CO-alternative service process easier for the Selective Service system—for The Man, as we used to say. I managed to find a professional-level position (its minimum requirement being a master's in a behavioral or social science) in a psychiatric ward of DC General Hospital, a vast, cinnamon-colored building founded in 1806 and only closed—controversially—in 2001, as the city faced bankruptcy. I was the sole Caucasian male on the ward staff of Area B Psychiatric Ward, where I worked as a vocational rehabilitation counselor. This position allowed me to gain intimate knowledge about Afro-Americans, the term in use then, from psychotics, manic-depressives (as they were called then), alcoholics, addicts, and veterans with PTSD, as well as about my doctor and nurse colleagues. Our catchment area was southeast DC, which by the late 1960s was almost all Afro-American, although some poor Appalachian Whites still lived in the Anacostia neighborhood. The poor Whites I counseled were invariably affable alkies, happy to learn of my interest and guitar-pickin' skills in country music.

I grew to admire the Black doctors I worked with, and even more so the under-trained, under-paid Black LPNs—licensed practical nurses—who were hard-working, good-hearted, and efficient, making a difficult, underfunded system work probably as well as it could. In fact, I had a basis of comparison: Chestnut Lodge, a private, psychoanalytic, expensive mental hospital built on then-rural five acres of pleasant meadows in 1886, in Rockville, MD. I had no fewer than three unrelated friends who were patients there in the 1960s, and I would visit them. My observation is that poor Black patients at DC General were treated almost as well, at least as compassionately, as those at super expensive Chestnut Lodge. DC General nurses even tried some of the latest types of therapy, such as group and music therapy, although they lacked formal training.

Among the doctors, one larger-than-life character was wise old Dr. Henderson, born in Mississippi around 1900, or even earlier. He was tall and distinguished looking. His low, quiet, but authoritative voice carried great weight, and his deep Mississippi accent was captivating. I never saw him smile, but I couldn't help but be drawn to him. He trained Black doctors from Howard University during their probably brief exposure to psychiatry, taking them along on his rounds with patients. He was always very dignified and formal with them and me, and I still remember a comment he made about increasing medical and academic specialization: "We are learning more and more about less and less, until eventually we'll know everything about nothing."

And there was laid-back Dr. Bushulte from the sunny Caribbean, with his lilting accent. He was far less formal with me and other professionals, probably because he had not suffered the same indignities as Dr. Henderson had growing up in Mississippi. Sometimes he invited me to sit in on his patient interviews. During these, he leaned back with his knees against his desk in an odd manner. I once asked him why. He said, "If any patient lunges at me, I will push my desk out to block their attack, and then run for the door. We are often dealing with dangerous psychotics here. You never know what they'll do."

I still remember White cops bringing in Black men of all ages who were under the influence of drugs or booze, and the cops sometimes apologizing for not dumping these dregs of society in prison. Recidivism rates among the jailed were extremely high, as you might imagine, but then they reclassified addiction as a disease, one deserving a stay at a psych ward. A four- or five-day detox with us at DC General helped slow their downward trajectory, and let the hospital cure STDs and treat vitamin deficiencies. My job was to counsel men (women were in a parallel ward) on ways to change their lives through training in skills, landing jobs, and generally finding and using community resources. During my few weeks of on-the-job training myself, I don't recall ever hearing about Alcoholics Anonymous or other peer support groups where we might direct our "clients."

Fascinating as this job was, and as surprisingly decent as DC General was, our vocational rehabilitation system was flawed at a most fundamental level, yet it was not the fault of the hospital. The system rewarded counselors for moving our clients from the hospital (called something like Status 101) to a job or job training program or a halfway house (Status 102). There were no incentives for follow-up. If I moved Mr. X from Status 101 to 102, even if 102 fell apart the next day, I myself was rewarded with some notation moving me one step closer to a salary hike or a promotion. Much as I liked absorbing African American life and culture in my job, I began to feel uncomfortable around the whole system of moving patients forward as quickly as possible, even if it was less to benefit them than us.

Midway through my alternative service, NISBCO offered me a job as a draft counselor. Since counseling COs about their legal rights took burden off the Selective Service, it was actually an approved alternative service job for this peace organization—who would have ever thought? Now, COs were not supposed to change jobs during the required two-year period of service. But I did. In fact, my new office was a mere three blocks from the White House. And this job, like the earlier one, proved to be very educational, and it put me at the epicenter of the anti-war movement. It also taught me much about the history and practice of pacifism, the Anabaptist religious traditions and, of course, the laws and regulations pertaining to the Selective Service system.

With my recently obtained United Church press pass, I got front-row seats in major anti-war events. Once I found myself squeezed right next to celebrity peace activists Jane Fonda and Shirley MacLaine.

And then there was Gen. Lewis B. Hershey, whom I met and interviewed for a church publication. He was the feared and often loathed

Director of the National Selective Service system. The underground press called him "General Mars Bars" (Mars was Hershey Chocolate's rival, get it?). Men of my age might remember him as the author of a Selective Service directive that changed the rules so that if anyone "mutilated" or burned his draft card, he would at once be reclassified 1A, meaning "available for service" in Vietnam—he'd jump to the head of the line for mortal combat. Outrage followed this provocative move, including an increase in public draft card burnings. A federal court of appeals later overthrew Hershey's directive. But we draftables never forgot: Hershey was the embodiment of the hated military-industrial complex.

On December 1, 1969, I stood not far from Gen. Hershey at the first nationally televised draft lottery, which the government had set up to determine the order of call to military service. There was a public exercise in which Gen. Hershey explained how names would be randomly pulled out of a large, translucent rotating drum containing plastic capsules, each containing a birth date on a slip of paper. Life-or-Death bingo.

I wore a coat and tie, and my hair was short. No one would have suspected that an anti-war activist had slipped into this live TV event, watched by millions of draft-age men and their families. I had the impulse to take one of the 365 plastic capsules, jump in front of the live TV cameras, break open a capsule and swallow a slip of paper—which would have invalidated the whole grim lottery enterprise. I might have gotten myself on the cover of *Time, Newsweek,* and *Rolling Stone,* no matter that I'd have been fired from my job.

Public Draft card burning in front of Selective Service Headquarters

Why didn't I? I suppose because I was entrusted with a press pass that NISBCO had provided me, showing how much trust they had in me. My stunt would have ruined the good working relations between my place of work—in fact, my oasis from the war—and National Selective Service Headquarters, relations that took many years to develop and that had helped perhaps thousands of legitimate COs have their status recognized when they appealed to the national level. And I admit I was afraid of the consequences of committing such an outrageous act.

Hershey was actually sympathetic to genuine religious objection to all wars; in fact, he (like Richard Nixon) came from a peace church background himself. I myself was something of a fraud, inasmuch as I didn't have the conventional peace church background documentation that is usually required to be in one's Selective Service file.

Gen. Hershey indicating his birthday at the Selective Service Headquarters, 1969.

In fact, Gen. Mars Bars in person wasn't such a bad guy—and I don't just mean in the banality-of-evil sense. Despite the multi-generational difference in our ages, he seemed affable and down-to-earth in our interview, more like a favorite uncle than the Grim Reaper. At one point he mentioned that one of his all-time favorite gospel songs was *Will There Be Any Stars in My Crown*? I had actually performed this song as a duet on stage, at school, and told him this. So we had a bond! As it happened, I was walking beside the general and talking with him as we both left the building after the national lottery. Mass protests were going on right outside the Headquarters. As soon as we stepped into the open air, there in the crowd before us were Yippie leaders Jerry Rubin and Abbie Hoffman, brandishing a large birthday cake, poised to launch it in the face of Gen. Mars Bars. I instinctively stepped in front of the frail, old general and in that brief moment of hesitation, the cops grabbed the two Yippies. The cake was not thrown.

By the time I was a draft counselor and had viewed the national and local DC statistics regarding draft deferments and exemptions, I realized just how unfair the whole system was. It was skewed in favor of wealthier, educated males and their families, and against poorer, non-White men and families. One day, I looked up which neighborhoods in DC had the most the 3-A draft deferments for financial "hardship to dependents." I found that most came from wealthy Northwest neighborhoods, and few came from where they should have: in the poor, African American neighborhoods of Southeast DC. Who did draft counseling there? Not one of the young men I counseled was Black or Latino, although I had some poor, rural Whites. I read later that few Blacks served on draft boards, yet at least one board in Louisiana boasted of having a Grand Wizard of the Ku Klux Klan.

Of course, consider the war in Vietnam itself: Black soldiers were more likely to be sent into combat, assigned menial duties, denied promotion, targeted for punishment, and end up with a dishonorable discharge.

Yet compare my own experience to others' of my Sixties generation: I benefited from: 1) 2.5 years of induction postponements; 2) classification as a CO without the ordeal of a personal appearance at my draft board, and without the documented credentials the Selective Service law usually required; 3) an enviable, professional-level position at a mental hospital which only later got approved as alternative service by my benign board (not the normal procedure); 4) remaining in DC, despite SS regulations that a CO should endure relocation difficulties and disruptions; 5) switching jobs for my second year of alternative service, despite the rules discouraging this; 6) working only 30 hours a week, the SS minimum (thanks to NISBCO), so I could return to grad school part-time at Catholic University; and 7) finding and using an obscure clause in Selective Service law to end my alternative service a month or two early, so I could start a fulltime PhD program, based on when my academic year began. Any one of these would have been considered unusual good luck, but to have *all of them* fall my way suggests something was wrong with the whole Selective Service system. It was unfairly administered, benefitting young men with backgrounds and neighborhoods like mine. Being in college *and* "progressing normally" toward a degree was a large part of this.

Chapter 4
Adopted by a Runaway Slave Society
in the Amazon Forest

On my way to lunch one day in 1970 when I was working at NISBCO, I happened to pass the office of Caribbean Airlines, now defunct. In the window display, I saw a book opened to a picture of a "Bush Negro," as they were called in bygone days, and he looked exotic in his toga and loincloth. I read that these people were descendants of African slaves who burned down the plantations where they were enslaved, and ran away into the rain forest where they established free and independent societies. And this airline had fares to Suriname (formerly Dutch Guiana) only slightly higher than the those to Puerto Rico. It happens that Shannon and I were planning a spring vacation in Puerto Rico, since it was so cheap, and we were looking forward to relaxing in the sun. But suddenly we could reach the Amazon rain forest for only $50 more per ticket.

I was still working as a draft counselor in downtown DC. Shannon was pregnant at the time, but didn't show yet. With some persuasion, she was willing to change our plan. I mentioned the new trip plan to an occasional friend from college, Lee, who had just married a woman named Remington, and he asked if they could come along. Suriname was a place I had never heard of a week earlier, a colony that wouldn't achieve independence until 1975. Lee saw this adventure as his honeymoon, and he managed to persuade his new in-laws to fund the trip.

Before long, we landed late at night in a jungle airport, with no electric lights or signs of human habitation visible in any direction. The tropical heat and humidity gave off a somewhat rotting odor, which increased as we were driven the 30 miles from the airport to Paramaribo, the capital city—make that "town." Paramaribo had cream-colored, red-roofed Dutch colonial buildings, spread out along the Suriname River. Despite the country's population of less than a half million, it was hard to find one more ethnically diverse. There were Indians ("Hindustanis," both Hindu and Muslim), Creoles of African descent, including Maroons (about whom much more), Javanese, Dutch, Portuguese, Brazilians, Amerindians (notably, Arawak and Caribs), Chinese, Lebanese, and West Indians. Yet virtually all these groups shared a *lingua franca*, called Sranan Tongo, an English-based Creole language, with Dutch- and Portuguese-based words added over successive generations.

Lee began fancying himself the Great White Hunter, and dressed and acted like a colorful character from an old Tarzan movie. He had purchased and brought along all kinds of gear to survive in the rain forest. I believe he even had matches that were supposed to light under water, but this memory fragment might well be a trick of time.

Now, I am not especially assertive or brimming over with self-confidence. Nor am I particularly mendacious or manipulative. But Lee? He looked up the National Museum director and audaciously told him he had come to Suriname with the support of the Smithsonian Museum and the National Zoological Society to "make contact" with the least accessible Maroon tribe extant. I later saw his CV, where I found these outrageous claims and other equally spurious ones, such as "made contact with lost tribe in the Amazon, killed sacred boa constrictor."

On our second night in Paramaribo, the museum director Piet Bolwerk and his wife invited us to dinner. He was a mixed-race Surinamer, perhaps mostly Hindustani, and she was pure Dutch and proud of this fact, as it became clear. I was introduced as an anthropology grad student, which might have been the only honest remark out of Lee's mouth all night. Perhaps they saw me as Lee's junior assistant.

Director Bolwerk was happy to talk about anthropology since he felt isolated from the academic world of ideas there in Suriname. He showed us specimens of "primitive art" he had collected, and excellent slides of his travels among the Amerindians and "Bush Negroes." He was truly an old jungle hand. One series of slides of the Trio Indians showed the initiation rites boys had to undergo in becoming men. The youths were tied to a tree and their chests slathered with honey. Then the older men brought out stinging bees of some hideous variety, which they had kept trapped in a woven basket and shaken up to make them angry as... hornets. Perhaps they *were* hornets. They pressed these buzzing insects onto the chests of the hapless young men. As I recall, they were supposed to remain silent through the pain, to prove they were worthy of manhood.

Given the time available and our desire to visit a lesser-known people, Bolwerk suggested we visit the Matawai, one of the smallest of the six Maroon tribes, and one that had not been studied. To paraphrase an early article of mine: The Matawais are descendants of runaway slaves who have lived in tribes in the interior rain forest of Suriname for nearly three centuries. They numbered only about 2,000 in 1970, although about half of them lived or worked temporarily in coastal Suriname, especially Paramaribo. The pattern of wage laboring and emigration to the coast had emerged recently, by the early 1970s. Rural Matawais subsisted through slash-and-burn agriculture, along with hunting, fishing, and gathering. Matawai society had no real chiefs with any real power. It was egalitarian, and based on kin-group organization, in this case matrilineal clans, and lineages. Although they strongly valued tradition and political autonomy, Matawais were quick to take advantage of economic opportunities. By the time I started my nearly two years of residential fieldwork in 1971, they had come to regard certain imported, manufactured articles as essential, they had become somewhat dependent on mission-sponsored medical clinics, and they valued Western education, locally available in four government-supported missionary schools.

By Dugout Canoe into the Rain Forest

The rural Matawais lived along the Saramaka River. To reach them, one had to take a train to the tiny railhead town of Kwakoegron, just at the periphery of tribal territory. One proceeded upriver by dugout canoe, deep into the rain forest. Bolwerk told us what we might expect on this journey, and he had arranged a boatman and a dugout with an outboard motor. The Matawai lived in the heart of the jungle's malaria zone, so we'd have to start the prophylaxis (chloroquine) that had been prescribed to us, right away. We went over all the supplies we would need: kerosene lantern and stove, hammocks, water purifying pills, insect repellent, shotgun and shells (optional), food that wouldn't spoil (like salami.) Mrs. Bolwerk told us that by bringing wives along we would serve notice that we were family men, and thus not ill-inclined. We left the Bolwerks at midnight, by which time they were nearly as excited about our trip as we were.

We reached the railhead and motored by dugout up the Saramaka, a calm, winding, piranha-filled river whose smooth surface reflected the bulbous cumulus clouds. We heard the coos and screeches of birds as well as rustles from the lush, tightly packed trees, as from animals moving away from the river and the noise we made. It was, indeed, wild country.

Late on the first the day, a heavy tropical storm erupted suddenly. We had to find a village where we could wait it out. Fortunately, we were not far from one. So we pulled up unannounced, and people directed us to a hut where we could dry off. They said the *kapiten*, the village chief, would see us presently.

Now, I had read enough about how in slavery times White plantation owners hired mercenary soldiers to find runaway slaves. Those captured would be drawn and quartered, or skinned alive. And now here we were, showing up in the chief's village. I mean, *my* ancestors—some of whom were, indeed, Dutch— might have tortured and murdered *his* ancestors. They brought us before the chief, who went into a passionate harangue in Matawai. It seemed to go on for an uncomfortably long time. I felt we were in trouble.

Our boatman translated.

The chief said he had consulted the ancestor spirits and learned that the people downriver (that is, the wider world) had the wrong idea about Maroons. "They think we still hate the White people. But we don't. It is good that one of you visitors has been sent by the ancestor spirits to live among us for enough time to tell the Whites that we are good, peaceful people who just want to be free." He went on to reveal more about what the spirits had told him and, of course, this response was not at all what I had expected. I found his worldview appealing. I wondered if I lived with the Matawai for a couple years, my own materialist, logical-positivist worldview would become enriched, expanded, and cross-fertilized with ability to communicate with unseen spirits in a magical dimension.

And yes! I must be that very person recognized by the ancestors. At that moment, I felt certain I was destined to fulfil that role. Forget my then-current plan to do fieldwork in Southeast Asia. The war in Vietnam was only getting worse, and the professor who would presumably guide my work was mentioned in an exposé about possible collaboration with the CIA to find ways to "win the hearts and minds" of villages in Indochina.

Any tension on our part immediately dissipated. A case of beer appeared, young men with drums began to warm up, and soon we were all dancing.

By the second or third day, Lee's Great White Hunter behavior had become more and more embarrassing to all three of us. My wife and I decided to split up from Lee and Remington on the third day. Remington looked like she also wanted to split up from Lee. She told us years later that she did. Moral of this story: never marry anyone you have not spent a week with in a jungle, because until you do, you don't *really* know a person. And yet I confess, without Lee's chutzpah, I am not sure what Shannon and I would have done. Perhaps taken a guided tour to the Interior. And then? This trip might have been only a vacation. And I'm not certain I would have returned to do fieldwork.

Soon after returning to DC and Catholic University, I changed my fieldwork plans from Thailand to Suriname. I was proud that almost no one— even anthropologists—had heard of the country where I would do my PhD required fieldwork. A year later I was "in the field."

Off to a Bad Start

My first field note of my extended stay with the Matawai (1971-1973) reads:

This has to be the worst day in the history of ethnography. Everything I needed to get started is lost. My father drove us to the airport (Dulles, Washington, D.C.) and we had so much stuff in the trunk that I guess the trunk was not fully shut. My briefcase fell out. In it were all my key reading notes, my two letters of introduction from my professors ("Dago Dazzlers," as they are arrogantly called at elite British universities like Oxford), a letter from the Suriname Minister of Education whom I had chanced to meet on my preliminary trip, most of my cash and all my traveler's checks, essential medications to keep us alive until we could access proper medical care, and the list goes on. So I called my parents en route to Suriname, from an airport in Curaçao. My stuff had been found! A vigilant D.C. transit bus driver found my briefcase and managed to track me down to my parents' house. This was not as easy as it might seem. A couple of addresses he found were from my old Chicago apartment. But he managed to track me down, thank God.

It was tongue-in-cheek, or just cheeky, that I wrote about the worst day in the history of ethnography—as if I would ever be part of that great history.

Once I reached Suriname, I faced a new setback. Before anyone thought up obstacles like Institutional or Ethics Review Boards, there was still something called getting formal permission from the host country to do research. I made my first contacts with the folks who would become "my tribe" at Njoecombe, a low wooden building in the middle of Paramaribo, where "tribal" people from the interior could sling their hammocks, sleep, and cook during their short trips to town. On my first visit there, I met an American woman, a PhD linguist whose research focused on learning the language of the Maroon tribe neighboring mine, the Saramaka. She had been sitting around waiting for government approval for *two years*.

Yikes! I had two years for my entire research, at most. I wasn't sure how to avoid such paralysis. But I took steps, anyway.

A worker at the hotel where Shannon, one-year-old Timmy, and our big dog Karl stayed for the first week or two told me about a guy from the Matawai tribe who was, or had been, a member of Parliament. So I found Jarien Gadden (Shannon nicknamed him Gadfly") and informed him of my plans to do a study of Matawai rural-urban migration. Gadden was happy to have a *Bakaa* (White) guy want to get to know him and his tribe. He would find me a language teacher: his uncle. But then, Gadden said he himself would be my teacher, every day for one hour. Toward the end of lesson 1, I broached the subject of payment. Gadfly was embarrassed, and indicated that he didn't expect anything... "Maybe when you have a cigarette, you give me one." I persisted, and he protested. When I suggested that we could talk about it later, he seemed greatly relieved. I decided that a gift would be more appropriate than money. As it turned out, Gadden lived some two kilometers from his office and had no car. Our lessons took place around 6 or 7 p.m., so I could drive him home after his day's work and converse in an easy, casual way

I had lessons in both Matawai and Taki-Taki, the informal name for Sranan Tongo, the English-Dutch-based Creole. It was the lingua franca for Suriname and all the diverse ethnic groups could speak it. Months later, I would visit a Carib Amerindian village, and it was most gratifying to be able to speak with the village chief in Sranan Tongo. After about two months, I felt I knew enough Matawai, and Taki-Taki to fall back on if needed.

So one fine day we all simply showed up in the Matawai village of Niewkonde, courtesy of a small, medical missionary plane. We set down on a landing strip at the edge of the village, which consisted of thatched huts clustered around a semi-secret shrine to ancestor spirits, the *faaka pau*. This was not the village of the *gaanman,* the Paramount Chief, but our plan was to move upriver to his village, as courtesy dictated. When we did, he cordially assigned us one of the huts, that of his maternal nephew, who was away. I began doing fieldwork, and waited to hear from the government about permission to do what I was already doing.

Among the Matawai

Once in Posugrunu, Shannon and I lived in an ordinary thatch hut, dressed like others in the village—at least on some occasions—and took part in the rounds of daily life. In Posugrunu, with the help of my matrilineal kinsmen, I cut down bush and cultivated my own garden for rice and maize, fished with a net, and paddled my own dugout canoe (which I bought from neighbors) for travel away from the village. In some ways it was a simple existence, before the extraordinary changes the Matawai would see over the coming decades.

Village life was communal. Everything could be heard through thin walls, and huts stood close to each other. If a man and his wife were not carrying on sexual relations as usual, neighbors would miss the telltale sounds and inquire if there were perhaps a problem in the marriage.

Beyond the clustered huts was the jungle, and the boundary between civilization and bush began abruptly. One day I was poised with my machete to strike the last branch of a small tree when I happened to notice a snake coiled up and ready to strike back. I looked at it, and it looked at me as I slowly and gradually backed away. I think it was a fer-de-lance, a highly venomous pit viper. I later read in the *Encyclopedia Britannica* that it is "so energetic when it strikes that it lifts itself off the ground," and its bite "causes many deaths." I was alone so I am not sure what I would have done if bitten.

The border was porous. There was always a fear that a snake or a jaguar could enter the village and swallow or, in the case of a jaguar, carry off a child. If a Matawai found a boa constrictor in a rice storage hut, which sometimes happened, there was a careful procedure for gently coaxing the reptile out, because a spirit was believed to inhabit boas. It was a sin to kill a boa.

Deliberately kept hungry and vigilant, there were semi-wild hunting dogs that slept just outside villages, and they served as an early warning system against beasts of the forest entering the village. Our faithful Karl never saw or interacted with his wild cousins.

Matawais swept the villages daily, and kept them admirably clean. And they took personal hygiene seriously. People were expected to be seen bathing twice a day, in the morning and at sunset. If Shannon or I missed a bathe, they would ask if one of us were ill, just as later in my fieldwork, they would express concern about the state of our marriage. There was no hiding anything from our friends and neighbors. I felt secure and cared for in our adopted society.

I still remember those morning baths. The Matawai language is musical, mellifluous, full of pleasing vowels—in fact it is classified as one of the few tonal Creole languages in the world. Women would cry out morning greetings ("Awake!" "How did you awaken?" "I woke up strong, you hear!" "I woke up healthy, you hear!"); and if someone were going by on a boat, the lilting, sing-song greetings would rise in volume and pitch and echo from the shore, down the river, through the morning mist. It was such a nice way to start the day.

One day near the end of my fieldwork, a Dutch tourist woman, one of the few tourists we ever saw, an alternative lifestyle hippie from Amsterdam where her father was an ex-mayor, decided to spend the night and the next morning, she rose early and strolled through the village stark naked, en route to the river to join the other woman. People talked about that for weeks to come. She was clearly not a missionary.

But we were so readily accepted, in spite of the barbaric history of slavery, of White-on-Black violence. As my anthropologist colleague John Lenoir, who was living with the Paramaka Maroons, would sometimes muse, "I try to imagine the reaction of folks in the small Oklahoma town where I grew up if a foreign Black stranger appeared one day, and declared that he was here to study the town and learn its secrets. 'And where can I stay? Any spare houses?'" The Paramaka welcomed John, just as our adopted tribe did us.

I was later to read how Margaret Mead had the governor of Hawaii meet her boat in Honolulu, and enjoyed a research fellowship with the Bishop Museum at her disposal, a house with Japanese servants scurrying back and forth with every variety of delicacy, free Samoan lessons, and a complete grammar book lent to her. Then upon arriving in American Samoa, she had the US Naval commander and the chief medical officer of the American base taking care of her. More free Samoan lessons, with a nurse who spoke "perfect English" (see Derek Freeman, *The Fateful Hoaxing of Margaret Mead: A Historical Analysis of Her Samoan Research*, 1999). Plus, she had the acknowledged father of anthropology, Franz Boas, as her advisor, as well as a decent grant for her fieldwork.

I had begun with nothing, no leads, only the tiniest of grants, no idea how to learn the Matawai language, no real contacts. And wife who didn't want to be there, a child who had just learned to walk, and a German shepherd/St. Bernard mix whose long hair was meant for snow and ice. The only thing I had in common with anthropology Mother Goddess Margaret, as she was later known, was a lack of training in field methods. For that matter, almost any research methods. Not even statistics (my own fault). My adventure would be sink-or-swim.

In our early months in Posugrunu, we had a few lessons in the Matawai language arranged by the gaanman, but we gradually learned to speak by simply using the language. We ate canned meat bought from a rural dry goods store just outside Matawai territory. It looked like dogfood. One day Timmy announced that he would not eat *anything* from a can in the future. I need to mention monkey meat here. I still remember the time during early fieldwork when we had a monkey carcass in a boiling pot of water. Shannon and I realized the little carcass looked too much like Timmy. We never again cooked or accepted monkey meat. We eventually entered into reciprocal trade relationships with hunters for occasional wild, non-simian meat. I soon learned to fish with a net and fish became our staple.

The Curious One

The first day we arrived at the village of the Paramount Chief, people laughingly called me *Womi Mii*, the word for "son," which is how I introduced Timmy. When folks saw that we meant to stick around for a while, they asked the elder, Naatan, to choose proper names for me, Shannon, and Tim. After some thought, they bestowed *Afibiti*—"The Curious One"—on me because of my continual questions. Afibiti is also the name of a little fish that swims to the head of creeks, to see what his origins are. "When there is no more water, afibiti jumps out of the creek" to survey his surroundings, and satisfy his indefatigable curiosity. I, of course, felt honored, and in the first long sentence I spoke in Matawai, I explained my name and its meaning. Timmy and Shannon received names of little fishes that swam along with afibiti upriver, or were the diminutive form of afibiti. Thus, Piki Dungidungi for Timmy. Nearly a half-century later, the Matawai children or grandchildren of my friends might not recall my name, but still remembered Piki Dungidungi, such a great name to speak aloud. It just rolls off the tongue. Some descendants of my generation of Matawais would even remember the name of our large, hairy dog Karl, which they pronounced "Ka-lu." Kalu knew a couple of tricks, like sitting at my command, and then shaking hands. People were delighted and amazed that he would respond to orders in Matawai.

About my role as a participant-observer: people came to accept us quickly and were surprisingly friendly. At first they thought we were a missionary family pretending to be otherwise, for some reason. Once that illusion dropped away, they felt they could resume singing bawdy songs and telling tales with sexual content without fear that I'd judge them as sinners. Men now felt free to ask questions that had long intrigued them, a favorite being, "Afibiti, how many times can a White man make love in one night?" No matter what answer I gave: 2, 5, 12, it was met with gales of laughter, and when I reversed that question to inquire about Matawai stamina, I got only more laughter.

By 1971 most Matawais had been converted to Christianity, but they still liked their sexually suggestive songs. The message of God's forgiveness appealed to a people who lived in fear of avenging spirits, launched originally by a sin committed by someone in one's own lineage. I wrote an early article on this subject. (The idiots at the journal *Ethnohistory* published my name as Edwin C. Green. It took decades for me to straighten out their mistake.)

We participated in the kinship system as well. Our adoption into the Lafantie and Asafu lineages might have begun as a joke. But it also solved the real problem that once one was more than a visitor, one was supposed to be addressed by kin terms. As the months rolled by, our adoption became more real. For example, a Matawai male is supposed to be available as free labor for his in-laws, to fulfill kinship obligations. My grandmother-in-law, Mama Alontu, became demanding that I help her with chores. Since one must marry outside one's own lineage (a practice called "exogamy"), Shannon and I belonged to different lineages. And since any true kinsman is the center of a complex web of obligations, avoidances, and prescribed behaviors, and since the system's subtleties probably would not have emerged from more objective methods, I threw myself into the role of a model kinsman. Seeing this, villagers constantly taught me general rules of behavior and ways to address particular situations.

About six months after our arrival, government officials came to the village of the Paramount Chief for a formal meeting. (Paramount Chief is a title that the Dutch colonial government bestowed on the top chiefs of each "tribe" of Maroons.) There I was, sitting with the council of elders (I was considered an honorary elder, despite my youth), and I guess the sight of this strange White guy set off alarm bells for the government men. Before they left that day, they asked the Paramount Chief what I was doing in his village. The chief said, "No problem, this is Afibiti whom we've adopted, and who is currently laboring in the planting fields of his (adopted) mother-in-law, just as a good Matawai should." In other words, I had been adopted by the Matawai, and I was behaving in an appropriate proper manner. Because Maroon tribes possessed a certain autonomy in those pre-independence days, that did the trick. No government permission needed.

Matawai men, some in traditional dress, 1971.

It became a pet project of numerous Matawais to see how native they could make me go. Eventually, I was participating in virtually all aspects of tribal life, from ritually purifying a corpse, to helping out in lineage council meetings, to receiving a share of inheritance when a "kinsman" died, to being elected as a spokesman to negotiate with lineage elders on behalf of a bride-seeking "brother." My wife and I even went through a wedding ceremony to legitimize our merely "legal-by-White-law" marriage with our respective adopted lineages.

I was lineage brother to Naatan, and months into my fieldwork he was getting married and I was supposed to join our other brothers and teach Naatan about "adult matters" (*gaan sombe sondi*)—that is, the birds and the bees. And so I did, even though Naatan had been married before. We brothers played our roles as human reproduction advisors, with reasonably straight faces. What stands out at this wedding—and it was typical of that era—was the insistence by the woman's lineage members that the groom promise not to move to town, that the new couple stay put in the wife's village and raise children there, as per kinship norms. And Naatan promised, just as all men do in weddings I witnessed. But inexorably the lure of making money in town or in coastal Suriname would overcome well-meant vows, and more and more Matawais would emigrate to town.

The Game of Secret Knowledge

"The Curious One" with boatman Lonati, 1972.

Although Matawais did not know what an anthropologist was, they seemed to readily understand the game of "outsider trying to go native." One or two elders had an idea what a professor was. Once, a year or so into my fieldwork, I was visiting a Kwinti village and a Matawai happened to be there as part of an anti-malaria campaign. The Kwinti are the smallest Maroon tribe, and they actually came under the authority of the Matawai Paramount Chief. This Matawai fellow told the Kwintis that I was an adopted Matawai, and that I was learning Matawai wisdom (*koni*) so that when I went back to my country, I would become... a professor! People were suitably impressed. But then my kinsman asked the group if they actually know what a professor was.

No one did. The Matawai anti-malaria guy explained, "A professor is someone who can look at you and *know exactly what you are thinking!*"

The assembled group began to look around as if they hoped they had not been having any bad thoughts.

One possible drawback of exploiting the going-native game was that a 27-year-old adopted kinsman did not go around asking questions about the abstruse and sacred "things of the elders." To overcome this limitation, I added a new dimension to my role. I became a no-doubt comical tribal pedant, a White-skinned super-elder who was always ready to surprise people with his arcane tribal wisdom. Eventually, knowledgeable elders taught me clan histories specifically to show me off to visitors from other villages. For example, they would have me recite the order of former (abandoned) villages of the clan of the visitor—all to the astonishment of Matawais who didn't know me so well.

I enjoyed my role as show-off, especially since it allowed me to ask a lot of nosey questions. And if I went too far, someone could simply say, "Afibiti, they sure gave you the right name. You know too much already!" This, of course, was preferable to their taking offense or becoming unduly suspicious.

I remember thinking at the time: In my adopted society, I can be a totally different person. For starters, I don't have to feel insecure. I mean, it wasn't my adopted matrilineage that told me I was doomed to failure, right? I could be a self-confident elder.

The show-off elder role also paid unexpected dividends. I learned some well-guarded secrets from competitive types who needed to show me, or others, that they knew important things that I still didn't. I was never sure that I had won in an information-eliciting game unless I was later able to corroborate the facts from other sources.

Of course, my ever-patient Matawai hosts were fully aware that they and I were participating in a game, the goal of which for me was gaining privileged, secret information. They themselves have always been skilled at the game of keeping information *away* from intrusive outsiders. Matawais and other Maroon societies presented what has been called a "layer of spurious culture" to the outsider, to mislead him and preserve their cultural integrity. Anthropologists all call this the art of "institutionalized prevarication." I know from the sparse literature that it appears possible to live with Maroons for years, and return with a highly distorted picture of their life. I met missionaries, for example, who were greatly misinformed about the nature and extent of "heathen activities" going on right in their own villages.

There was exactly one Matawai in our first village who never came to accept this nosey White man going around asking questions: *kapiten* Pompeia. He was the chief of the village of the gaanman, and perhaps in his late 70s. He would sometimes gently, but emphatically and publicly, scold others in our village for revealing so many secrets to a White outsider. Nonetheless, he was unfailingly decent and courteous toward me. And I completely understood his position. I might have taken it myself had I been in his shoes, and at his stage of life. But it was amazing that he was just about the only Matawai who displayed suspicion in public.

One thing that especially impressed me about the Matawai was the broad fund of skills each one could draw upon. They were generalists not specialists. Each man or woman could do pretty much what every other man or woman could. For men, that meant slash-and-burn farming, hunting, fishing, boat-building, carpentry for house-building, cutting and drying thatch for roofing, making beautiful woodcarvings as part of the traditional courtship process, singing traditional songs with more or less equal talent... but wait! How can artistic talent be evenly distributed in any population? Yet in my day, before the pace of cultural change accelerated, all men seemed to be at least adequate in whittling attractive woodcarvings, some exceptionally intricate and beautiful.

I will leave women's roles for Shannon to write about someday, but they seemed to parallel and complement those of men. There was a division of labor that seemed to work.

My new friends naturally assumed that White people were also generalists in their artificial world of technology. They figured White people were truly smart to be able to manufacture airplanes, automobiles, outboard motors, wristwatches, and other marvels they were familiar with. This led to some hilarious requests such as, "Afibiti, my watch stopped working, please repair it." When I replied that I couldn't really do that, they were a bit a disappointed in me, concerned that I lacked the basic skills a White man ought to have. I could imagine them thinking, "Why did they send us *this* guy?" My Matawai hosts had seen at once that I was poor at the many things the Matawai could do, but now it was becoming apparent that I was also inept at White man's skills. So what exactly *could* I do?

Of course, this is a question I have always asked myself, and it touches upon on the deeper problem of self-confidence I have had all my life. But they needed an answer here and now! So I said, "Well, if I have knowledge (*koni*) it was to learn and understand the ways of different people, such as the Matawai." There was a polite little clearing of throats. Let's see: I could play the guitar I had brought with me... what else? Finally, someone pointed out that fishing nets were made by White folk. Could I at least *mend* them? I didn't have to actually *make* them. I jumped at the opportunity to teach myself how to tie little knots to mend fishnets that had perhaps been torn by flesh-eating piranha (whose true "deep" name was *akwadjikedgehundge-bassiaoebassawata*, the last part meaning "lord of the lower river," This was also the longest Matawai word I knew to date, and of course I would occasionally steer conversations toward piranhas, to show off.)

So—net mending! Why not? It had the added advantage of giving me an excuse not to go trudging off to hunt for scarce animals with the menfolk, but instead to sit in the middle of the village and mend nets while listening to, eventually participating in, village gossip. I would periodically duck into my hut and write up field notes. My dissertation advisor had emphasized the importance of producing different types of field notes, whether they were descriptive, analytic, linguistic, or notes about my own role—whatever, just so I produced some notes every day. I followed his advice, and at the end of the whole fieldwork enterprise, I had hundreds of notes to draw upon to write my dissertation. Note-taking is also a habit I brought with me when I turned to applied anthropology in future countries.

A Day in the Jungle

About a year into my fieldwork, I had become conversant in the Matawai language. I knew that I had lucked out in finding this group for my initiation to fieldwork. The Matawai are some of the nicest, kindest, most generous people I have met anywhere. And I have visited or lived in 100 countries or overseas territories, so I have a solid base for comparison.

Here is a fieldnote that provides a flavor of my life in 1971–73, and gives a feel for how participant observation works, even if by a relative beginner:

My 'biological clock' woke me at 2:30 a.m. for my penicillin pill. I have infection in two fingers accompanied by mild fever from lacerations while cutting undergrowth two days ago for the horticultural plot (*pandasi*). Went right back to sleep again... Never any trouble sleeping in my hammock. It supports my limbs in a way a bed never could.

Up at 6:10, take my knife, machete, plate, paddle and go to the riverside. I have a feeling that bringing the implements for cleaning fish demonstrates hubris and so the spirits will reward me with an empty net. I paddle to the mouth of the creek and pull my net. No fish. Next time I'll just come with my paddle and I'll probably catch some fish.

After breakfast I take Timmy to my field to examine the work bassia (assistant matrilineage chief) Alexi and I did yesterday. I linger because Timmy is learning to swing from branches and the jungle is unusually pleasant: dry and cool. I take a picture of Timmy swinging from a vine. Then I go to the river to wash and shampoo and think of a way to get out of helping the Tivrede people chop down trees today. I got my thorn lacerations two days ago and I feel a bit of a sissy using this as an excuse, but *damn it*, two of my fingers can't close and I know my infection will reignite if I don't take it easy today. Also I don't have the necessary boots. I decide to go to the Tivrede fields late, and shoeless.

So I get to return to work mending my net. This is strung up between two trees in the middle of the gaanman's compound and I can absorb village life while I work. A couple of other people have fishing nets, but no one is able to mend them, so I'm trying to become an expert in this.

While Tanta is teaching Timmy a traditional dance, I have the opportunity to test a class of what I call 'adverbs of intensification' (like: '*gbilin gbilin gbilin,*' or 'Absolutely!') on the gaanman. He asked me what I thought of the dancing. I replied with several of these adverbs, which I apparently used correctly. No startled looks.

The gaanman is pleased with himself because he has just finished making the door of the store he is building for himself. I chat with him for a bit.

At 11 am I strip down to my loincloth and go over to Tivrede. This is Shannon's adopted father's matrilineage village, and I've developed a trading relationship of food and labor with these people. Arriving there, Ana calls me over to tell me she has some plantain for me and to urge me to take her machete with me into the bush. She is my favorite old lady. I speak with Adolphina and Estella before heading down the long jungle path to the planting fields. I walk slowly, enjoying myself and remembering how torturous the path seemed last week carrying great loads of rice on my head.

I finally come upon Emil and Alexi and we go over to where Chiefs Feedi and Koneesi are sharpening their axes with Tata Bene. As I had hoped, they told me I couldn't possibly work without protective boots. I had come during a rest period so I stayed and chatted. They concurred that they should all come over and help me chop trees in my field Saturday morning, since I had carried rice for them (did they know that the women had paid me for the rice?).

We talked about America. They wanted me to wait for them in the rest camp, but I wanted to return to my net and to listen to village gossip.

I worked on my net for a couple of hours, mostly alone on the periphery of conversations. Shannon peeled peanuts and pounded rice and socialized with Tanta quite a bit. Timmy played with his usual gang of village kids. I looked forward to the batch of (natural, organic) peanut butter that Seena was to make for us that afternoon. When it came (three good jars for 1 guilder, and it's 'half that price' in Boslanti), we polished off half a jar, eating it warm and crunchy with forks.

My son "Piki Dungidungi" was quickly accepted by Matawai children.

At 4 pm I took Timmy to Tivrede in my boat. I chatted with the women for a while before taking some plantain and eggs and heading back. I met a man on the river I chose to be my honorary father-in-law, and we exchanged pleasantries. He's introverted.

Walking back from the river I encountered the *obzichte*r (visiting government functionary), Mr. Waterfall, with a towel around his waist. I stared at this visitor and he stared back at my loincloth. Then he told me that while traveling here with a certain Matawai named Afibiti (not the *real* one, of course) and Luti, their boat tipped over at Weti Sitonu and all their gear was either lost, damaged, or wet. As he told the story the two boatmen appeared from the guesthouse and added to it. Soon a group of villagers came to help dry the remaining baggage in the sun. We decided to donate food to the unfortunate travelers (I gave some canned hamburgers and beans because the two boatmen are friends of mine and because I knew they'd only get great quantities of rice and plantain from others).

I then finished my net and began on the gaanman's net (he provided the string for mine). Countless hours of work are ahead of me.

On the way to the creek to set my net at sundown, I heard a saxophone on the opposite bank! I paddled over to the Forestry Service camp because I can't resist music. There were Ndjukas and Amerindians staying temporarily at this camp. They were surprised to see me because I never deigned to socialize with them, since they're not part of the village life at all. I spoke first to the saxophone player and discovered another musician among their ranks, an Arawak Indian who played mandolin, American country music style, no less!

After dinner, I begin writing this note up when three adolescents come in and sit down, Malena and her male friends. Malena must like me because she finds occasion to touch or lean on me. We talk about some strangers who were in the village four months ago, and then somehow they ended up getting me to write down the names of all the types of fishes and birds they can think of, with them filling in the many gaps. I just manage to modify this so as to further my village census when Luti comes over for a visit. He tells me about Waterfall's census work and I decide to ask the latter for a look at it tomorrow. After he leaves, the kids tell me the stories of two bush spirits. They want to start a 'spider story,' but I postpone this until tomorrow because I want to write the stories up before forgetting the details. (I give them some candy.)

I wrote that down, and more of these notes until 11 p.m.

An Unearthly Sound and the Three Names

Let me share another paranormal, or anomalous, story. Strange things do happen when one lives with a tribal society in a rain forest, even if anthropologists virtually never attempt to publish these stories for fear their reputations would suffer. They tend to restrict their telling to parties held during professional conferences, and then only after several drinks.

Early in my fieldwork, before I spoke much Matawai, we chanced to stay one night in a nearly depopulated village, in a scary looking, deserted home of a Dutch Moravian missionary who had died a mysterious, sudden death around 1910, after he had deliberately broken up sacred shrines of the indigenous religion. He had intended to show the heathen Matawai that their old gods and spirits had no power against Jesus Christ.

I was with Shannon, Timmy, and Karl. We were sleeping in hammocks when odd things began to happen. I woke up in the middle of the night with a feeling of dread. My hammock had subtly begun to rock by itself, back and forth. Then came the most blood-chilling, inhuman, unearthly, distant sound I'd ever heard, and it seemed to advance toward me from out of the rain forest, from all directions at once.

The sound came closer and closer. I was petrified with fear. But what could I do?

Finally the sound came right *into* the windowless room where our hammocks were tied. Whereupon it suddenly vanished.

Abandoned house of deceased missionary.

I jumped out of my hammock and woke Shannon. Had she not heard the terrible noise? No? Timmy hadn't either. Well, Karl had, and he was agitated and whining, scurrying around in circles. Shannon said, "Go back to sleep. You've been dreaming." Her reaction reminded me of three years earlier when I woke her up in our apartment in Chicago and informed her that Bobby Kennedy had just been assassinated in LA. I remembered her saying, "Why do you always say these crazy things in the middle of the night? Go back to sleep."

Always??

I climbed back into my hammock, still very frightened. I eventually relaxed... until my hammock began to rock again, ever so slightly. Well, I supposed that it was okay to be rocked. Why not? Maybe this area was a gentle earthquake zone... zone... zone... I was so tired... .

But then my hammock rocking seemed to accelerate, gradually swinging wider and wider. I climbed out and hugged a trembling Karl until the sun arose.

The next time we were downriver, in the railhead town of Kwakoegroen, I eagerly sought out the shopkeeper Watkins, a Guyanese mystical healer. He had quickly become my friend and confidant; we were both native English speakers, and interested in occult matters. I lacked enough fluency in Matawai to describe to anyone in my adopted society what had happened to me, but I could tell Watkins. I tried to describe the frightening sound. What had happened and what did it all mean? Watkins assured me that he'd heard that very same sound when he was a young man, while hunting in the same part of the forest. He might have mentioned that this sound had something to do with the spirit of the howler monkey. I have since googled the howler monkey's howl, and it is, indeed, unearthly. But the sound I heard was different. Plus I only heard the unique sound once more in my life, though if howler monkeys had made it, I probably would have encountered it again.

Watkins disappeared for a bit into a back room, and when he returned, he told me he had three names that would protect me from this spirit. He said that the ungodly sound would definitely come back to scare me again, but when that happened, I could banish it forever by uttering these three protective names.

I commented that the names didn't sound Matawai, or African, to my ear. Watkins said, "No, no, Mon, they're Hebrew. From my secret book. You see, I'm a Rosicrucian. I am a keeper of Secret Knowledge. Only initiated people can know these things."

About three months later, I was staying upriver, deeper back in the jungle, by now living in the village of the gaanman, the Paramount Chief. On this occasion, I awoke in the darkest hours of the morning, somehow already with a sense of foreboding. I could do nothing but wait for whatever was to come. Presently and inevitably, the same macabre, bone-chilling, inhuman sound I had heard downriver began to come toward me from the forest, seemingly from all sides at once. It rushed at me faster than the first time. But where were the three Hebrew names? They were written in my notebook... but where the hell was the notebook? Plus I need a flashlight to read in the dark... panic arose.

Just as it seemed like the ungodly sounds were entering the hut, I remembered the three Hebrew names, and I was about to speak them aloud. That was all it took. The moment I *thought* the names, the sound or spirit vanished. I never heard it again, even though I spent nearly two years in Matawai-Land, and have been back several times since the early 1970s.

I related this story to a number of people, and evidently it reached the ears of a certain American Evangelical pastor. Some American missionaries were fundamentalist, and they seemed to differ from the better educated PhD missionaries I'd met from the Summer Institute of Linguistics (SIL). One day in Paramaribo, months after the event, this man confronted me on a busy street during rush hour and told me he knew I had been messing around with occult forces. He commanded, "Get down on your knees, and I will drive out the demon that you have let yourself become a vehicle for!"

Now this was totally unexpected. Ending a sentence with a preposition? He had a Saramaka Maroon, a Christian convert, with him, so I addressed this guy in his language (a close cousin to Matawai), saying essentially, "This man you are with is a bit crazy, don't you agree?" My comment only served to frighten the Saramaka. He might have thought he was witnessing speaking in tongues, something diabolical.

But I declined the offer to have demons driven out of me. As I walked away, the pastor shouted after me that I would never again be allowed to enter a house of the Lord, because I carried a demon within. He said I probably *thought* I was merely doing anthropology fieldwork, and just keeping an open mind... but that is exactly how Satan works! He just loved to enter the heads of so-called "open-minded" people like me.

Shannon and I were on good terms with SIL Bible translators, the lead group among foreign missionaries. A few months later, around Christmas time, they invited us to church in Paramaribo for a special Christmas Eve service. The head missionary greeted us at the door—he knew me quite well because I had taken his course on Sranan Tongo during my first month in Suriname. And there was the demon-chasing pastor, lurking near the entrance, apparently just waiting to see what would happen if I tried to cross the hallowed threshold.

We entered the sacred place and no devils had to struggle with God, as far as I could tell. Later, a missionary wife sang a beautiful, haunting soprano solo of "Oh, Holy Night." It gave me shivers. Perhaps it tamed my demon, if it was there.

Many years after this experience, I discovered that anthropologists had started to publish "Paranthropology: Journal of Anthropological Approaches to the Paranormal." This was reassuring. My experiences were considered valid by those in my own profession.

Lost Child and Divination

Although Matawais had largely become Christians by the early 1970s, pre-conversion beliefs remained, as in fact we find throughout Africa. In both Africa and the circum-Caribbean region, people convert to Christianity (or Islam in Africa), but magic, witchcraft, and ancestor veneration underlie the new religions. Examples from the New World include Rastafarianism, *vodun* ("voodoo"), and *santeria*. In Suriname, people's formal allegiance to Jesus rested on a foundation of indigenous beliefs and practices. A decade later, I would meet Swazi spirit mediums who found no contradiction between being vehicles for spirit possessions during the week, and good, churchgoing Christians on Sundays.

So it was among the Matawai.

One night around 9 p.m., women banged on my door to tell me that a child, Gelenti, had been missing since sundown. I got my flashlight and went with them. Half the village was searching. They thought Gelenti had probably fallen asleep under a house or inside an unused one. Most of the men were out of the village, and a couple of others were reluctant to get out of their hammocks.

The women said they would spank the boy soundly when they found him. After two hours the number of searchers had grown. People had been sent to the two adjacent villages, and some of those villagers came here.

By 11:15 p.m., there was nowhere left to search except the surrounding jungle, and the group sat down to wait until dawn. The electric generator, which normally shut at 10 p.m., was left on. Shannon and I went to sleep, but many or most villagers stayed up.

Voices roused me at around 6 a.m. Gelenti had been found sleeping in the jungle, only about 20 meters from the village. Now he stood naked and whimpering in undergrowth he had cleared amid a thicket. A large group was before him, and he was afraid to come out and face his punishment. The adults wondered how he could have slept naked in the jungle without being cold, bitten by insects or snakes, or carried off by a *hogi mbeti* (jaguar.)

The group of searchers had grown to include people from five other villages, and individuals from more distant Boslanti had been alerted and were on their way to Posugrunu.

Women were thanking the (pre-Christian) spirits for delivering the child, and they entreated him to come out of his hiding spot. They had decided not to punish him, and told him so. Finally, they cut a path to him with a machete, and the oldest woman in the village, the spirit medium Mama Aluntu (my grandmother-in-law), performed a purifying ritual. She lay the boy down on a clean piece of cloth and anointed his head with *keeti*, a chalky white clay used ritually. Then she shook a small bark rattle, and continued while two people carried him in the cloth back to the medicine woman's hut.

For the rest of the day Gelenti, who was previously naked except for a tiny loincloth, wore clothes and his head was tied in cloth. Under the cloth was keeti and feathers.

As far as I know, Gelenti's behavior was never explained. Note that in times of crisis, Matawais returned to familiar, pre-conversion beliefs and practices. No one seemed to pray to Jesus, at least visibly.

Oscar Lafantie explained to me that Mama Aluntu had performed the cleansing ritual because "perhaps an evil spirit might have carried the kid off." Later, Oscar told Alexander that when the boy's mother returned from town, she would have to pay the medicine woman eight bottles of rum for her services. Alex told me the mother wouldn't mind paying.

Oscar related this news with some contempt, telling Alex, "You know how these people are here." He may have been commenting on the "superstitions," rather than the amount demanded. Oscar was the most Westernized of Matawais. He was a big fan of Marvin Gaye, whom he listened to faithfully on his radio. Some years after I left Suriname, he became Paramount Chief, but only because rules of matrilineal succession demanded it.

In 1977 I brought Timmy back to Matawai Land. Gelenti became his special buddy and minder on that trip. Gelenti was about four years older than Tim, but they were the same height. Gelenti had somewhat bowed legs, from rickets I supposed. No other Matawai seemed to have signs of malnutrition. I was proud to see Tim go off into the bush with Gelenti for a few hours of unsupervised fun, somehow communicating in mysterious kid language. Yet, to my surprise, he had told me before this trip that he remembered nothing of his earlier life in Suriname. He was just under three when we left, but still, you'd think he'd remember *something*.

The Mini-Terror

Here's another incident that went unrecorded in my formal field notes.

I had noticed that Matawai kids did not seem to go through "Terrible Twos," or for that matter any other special phase of naughty, I-am-the-center-of-the-universe behavior. Kids were almost always well behaved, at whatever age. Dr. Spock's advice seemed unneeded in this tribe. At the same time, a Matawai village is a place where matrilineal family members live together. Everyone is addressed by a kin term, like uncle, auntie, brother, sister, or grandmother. If a child misbehaves, any adult has a right—even an obligation—to discipline the child. Usually it's just a verbal corrective, though the adult might pull a branch off the nearest tree and threaten or deliver a light whipping. There was one exception to this rule, our son, Piki Dungidungi. No one could bring themselves to even raise their voices at him. Why? Because he was just "so... cute, so White, so *blond*!" Hence by degrees Timmy grew naughtier and naughtier. He was gradually learning that he could get away with any type of behavior, including antics he saw other kids get whipped for. He was growing more willful by the day. Finally, the gaanman felt he should raise the issue with me.

I responded, "No, you're right, and I totally agree! Yes, you certainly have my permission to discipline Piki Dungidungi. He needs to be raised right, and not turn into a slithery snake (an expression I had heard Matawais use)."

We didn't have to wait long for the next episode of naughty behavior. One afternoon, Timmy was throwing sand in the faces of his playmates, and some of them were following his lead. Anarchy was erupting; a Lilliputian revolution against Matawai norms was underway, with my son leading even the older children. The gaanman looked my way and I signaled back that yes, the time had finally arrived. Now, the gaanman was a large man with a booming voice, or at least he could make it boom, even though he was mellow and soft-spoken by disposition.

He shouted (in Matawai), "Piki Dungidungi! Bad boy!" And stripping a branch off a tree, he said, "I'm going to *whip* you!" A small crowd was gathering.

Piki Dungidungi looked defiantly into the face of the Paramount Chief for a few seconds, then... threw a handful of sand right smack in his face!

We were all shocked. No one said a word, or even moved. The background sounds of the forest seemed to pause. We all looked to see how the gaanman would react. His anger quickly dissipated, then his face crumpled into a crooked smile and he whispered to me, "I just can't make myself do it. He's just too... cute!"

Piki Dungidungi only grew worse.

A couple of months later, we had moved to the downriver village of Balen, and soon people there were observing that Piki Dungidungi was getting away with behavior totally unacceptable for Matawai kids. We had the same conversation there as with the Chief upriver, including with a tough, youngish widow called Akotikumatjalo ("She Cuts with Machete"). As with the Paramount Chief, I gave her my full permission to treat my son like any other kid in the village. Almost immediately, as if she had been just counting the days, the widow found reason to strip a branch off a tree and chase Piki Dungidungi around the village, whipping his legs as he fled in terror. He came running to me and panting, stumbling over the syllables, cried out, "I *don't like* Akotikuma... ma...!"

And so it was, on that day in 1972, Timmy attempted his longest word ever in any language (how did he even know this woman's name?), and he began to act like any other boy in the tribe. His Terrible Twos melted away into history.

Broken Bones and Illusion Walls

The history of slavery is awful everywhere, whether the colonial masters were Dutch, Portuguese, British, French, Belgian... you name it. More than a century after emancipation in Suriname, the Matawai used the dreaded White man the way some parents used the Boogey man when I was a kid. The local variant was "You better behave, or the White man (*Bakaa*) will come to take you away!" Early in our fieldwork, we might arrive in a village for the first time and a young child might see a White person for the first time. Sometimes the kid would take one look and start wailing, while the mother or auntie would try to calm the child: "This is just Afibiti. He's a *good* White man."

On the other hand, when kids saw Timmy, they immediately accepted him and he became part of their group. This happened without fail. On the same day we arrived by the missionary supply plane, two three-year-olds took Timmy (age 14 months) by either hand and led him off to the village. I have a slightly fuzzy photo that captured this unique moment. Racism has to be *learned*; it's not natural, I am convinced.

I used to listen to stories from slave time (*saafu ten*), from life on the plantation (*pandaasi*). Here is one, and I'm translating more or less directly.

Matawai's enslaved ancestors used both good and bad magic every day on the plantations. Magic was the only weapon slaves had. There was no other way to counter the total power of the slaveowners.

On one occasion, the ancestor spirits decided it was time to cure a boss (*dikitor*) of his chronic whipping of slaves. So they "magically" prepared a man, and he went and courted a whipping from the Boss. The latter ordered his assistant to start whipping this slave. The victim urged the assistant to whip him harder, harder, until the Boss yelled, "Stop' it's killing *me*!" Because he himself could physically feel each and every whip stroke.

"Most of the dikitors were Portuguese Jews," the elders say. This is historically accurate. In the colonial era, a substantial number of Portuguese Jews (mostly Sephardic) had been expelled from Brazil, where they had run plantations. We remember 1492 more for a certain exploration and discovery than for the Alhambra Decree, an edict ordering the expulsion from Spain of all Jews who refused to convert to Catholicism. Four years later, King Manuel I of Portugal, who began the Portuguese colonization of the Americas, issued a similar decree. After a massacre of Jews in Lisbon, some left Portugal for the Ottoman Empire, while a smaller number went west, to places like Suriname and, temporarily, Brazil. Jews expelled from Brazil owned and ran many 17th century plantations in Suriname, and the ancestors of the Saramakas and Matawais had especially fled these.

I was told that Matawai ancestors had escaped from a plantation called Hamborgu. Slaves were worked so hard and so incessantly, and whipped (or worse) for the slightest infraction or human failing, to the point they could no longer stand it.

I was told of the hierarchy on the plantation during slavery: dikitors at the top, *kapitens* under them, and *bassias* under them. Bassias were the most numerous, and they did the whipping. Kapitens were fewer, and told the bassias whom to whip. Slaves filled both these positions. The dikitors were the European overseers of the whole plantation. After Emancipation (*maspasi, fili*), the Dutch colonial government established formal offices for gaanman and kapitens. The present political structure among Maroons of kapitens and bassias replicates that of the plantation. Before freedom, there were no roles like kapitens and bassias among the arriving slaves; Whites imposed the positions.

Here is a story about a dikitor and his son, an apprentice dikitor:

The son lusted after a particular slave girl. One day, the son sent the slave girl on an errand that compelled her to pass through a remote part of the woods. He went seeking her there with his single-barreled shotgun. Presently they met. Now, if you are a slave and a dikitor approaches you, you must throw your machete on the ground, submissively. So the girl did this. The son approached and grabbed her, and they tussled. The girl managed to push him into a ditch and flee. The son shot at her, but missed.

She ran right to the plantation center, where the senior dikitor was seated in church. The girl dashed up to him with his son right behind her and begged for protection, but just then the son caught up with her, and he crushed her arm with the butt of his shotgun. The girl howled in pain. The dikitor was enraged at his son for treating a slave so. He instructed the girl to summon the other slaves. When they all arrived, the dikitor asked if there was a cure for the girl's crushed arm. The slaves acted pessimistic at first because they wanted the dikitor to pay dearly for his son's cruelty.

Finally, the assembled slaves said they knew of a medicine man at another plantation. The dikitor told them to take the girl there and have her fixed up. In reality, the medicine man was right on the same plantation, already preparing the medicine.

So a slave delegation went off, and later returned. They told the dikitor that the medicine man was unable to come himself, but he said he could fully restore the girl's broken arm in 7 days—for 1,500 guilders. The dikitor agreed.

The girl lay secluded in a hut for the seven days. When she reemerged, her arm was "better than new."

Now, it happened that a week later came Emancipation—the end of slavery. Everyone dispersed. The dikitor and his son moved to town. So did the slave girl, along with her father and brother. In those days Paramaribo's population was tiny. While the girl was walking one day, she saw the young dikitor. She said nothing, but went and told her brother. He asked where the young dikitor lived, and then they went there. He cut himself a long stick, and retired to the shadows to await the White man. When the abuser emerged to go wash, the brother crushed his arm with the stick, then fled.

Later the dikitor recognized some of his former slaves on the street, and he told them that someone had broken his son's arm. Could they please take him to the same medicine man who cured the slave girl? The ex-slaves said they thought something could be arranged for, say, 1,500 guilders. And so the dikitor paid twice. "Those early slaves were no fools!"

In fact, Maroons today have a reputation for traditional medicines and techniques that are particularly effective for repairing broken bones. It's sad to think how they developed this expertise. And it's most interesting that none of the stories I was told about conditions during slavery times were as bad so those described in the accounts in, for example, the 1779 journal of mercenary Captain John Stedman, who recounted that escaped slaves, when caught, were sometimes skinned alive, or were drawn and quartered, and their body parts hung on trees as examples for slaves dreaming of freedom. It's as if, over the generations of elders sitting around a fire, some of them toned down the tales, because, after all, White masters certainly could not actually slowly strip the skin off of living people. That would be totally inhuman, right?

The Matawais, and indeed, all Maroons had devised clever strategies to guard their secrets from outsiders. Obviously they had more than enough reasons to mistrust Whites. They presented the aforementioned "layer of spurious culture" for outsiders who asked too many intrusive questions. That is, one might inquire about traditional culture and a Matawai could provide a nice, tidy answer consistent with information previously disclosed, so it all fit together—but it could all be untrue! In the Matawai language, there was an everyday vernacular form and then there was "deep language," which was less similar to Sranan Tongo and more African-sounding.

Add to this, various forms of elliptical speech (*bila tongo*). Informants, once I had gained enough trust, told me this type of speaking goes back to slavery when the slaves could keep their secrets, and even mock the slave-master to his face by inverting and disguising their language. In the early 1970s there was still a type of Pig Latin slang that teenagers would use within earshot of elders so the latter could not understand them. (It was hard to *not* be within earshot of others anywhere in a Matawai village.) Every new generation invented a secret language (*koopina,* bila tongo) so that the elders wouldn't know what was being said. I learned that young people added nonsense syllables as superfluous suffixes and infixes to ordinary Matawai words. After I first caught on, my friend Lonati told me that words ending in "i" or "e" get the suffix "*eperepe;*" or in "o," *oporopo*; and in a, "*aparapa.*"

As I usually hung out with elders, one of them asked what I had been discussing with Lonati and other young guys. So I told him I was learning the latest secret teen slang. He asked for an example, and he quickly translated it into standard Matawai. "These kids! It's so easy to figure out what they are saying. Now when my friends and I were their age, we had a great bila tongo." He gave me a few examples, and, indeed, they seemed opaque.

But I got to thinking: I had been hanging out with elders almost exclusively. I decided to try socializing with guys my own age, the mid-20s. The late-teen and early-20s-age cohort was a distinguishable group, different from the elders in interests, outlook, attitudes, and as mentioned, even in language. Until this time, boys/men in this age group had ambiguous feelings about me: I appeared friendly, but aloof. But I had focused on the elders because I saw obvious signs of rapid culture change. I felt I needed to immerse myself in traditional culture before it changed irreversibly, and, of course, the elders are the guardians of traditional culture. Also, elders were starting to take pride in what their comical White adoptee could remember about, for example, the names of former villages associated with different clans. We might be at an all-night wake, and some elders would ask me to recite names of long-dead villages, or maybe proverbs I had been taught. Then they would ask twenty-somethings to do the same, and they could not. The elders would then chastise the young guys in public, "You don't even know what this proverb means. But Afibiti, a White man—he knows!"

Such digs of course did not endear me to guys my own age. So I sought closer ties. Here is a partial field note about my attempt, dated 11/9/72:

Young Matawais are often town- and outside-world oriented. They look to such outsiders as Creoles working on this river as partial adult role models, whereas elders are reserved and mistrustful of these same Creoles. (Creole in this sense of an ethnic group refers to Surinamers of African background whose ancestors did not win their freedom by fight and flight with and from the early plantations.) The young men seem to feel the town pull acutely. Many mates of their age are working in town, and those in the villages probably feel left behind (they'd feel less so if they could make more money here in the bush). Their town cousins are buying modern desiderata, going to movies, eating and boozing comparatively well, learning about marijuana, dressing in the cool styles, meeting girls at dances, etc.

I don't think many Matawai youth are avoiding town for ideological reasons—for loyalty to traditional Matawai values. They'd probably go if they had the opportunity. Obviously, understanding village youth is essential to understanding tribal future. One could get a mistaken impression of cultural continuity and the viability of the status quo by hanging around only with the elders.

So I started courting the friendship of young guys like Lonati and Ludwig. Since my first attempt, a group of them have dropped in on me every evening. I think they always felt I should have been in the younger age-group all along. I try to be entertaining about the pleasures and problems of the outside world. Two evenings ago, they began to teach me their koopina (coded) teenager language—a good sign! They are good informants in certain areas that definitely constitute "a layer of spurious culture" for many adults.

That night when I was feeling a little sad, the visiting guys had an important question for me, now that we were speaking more freely. They asked for the meaning of: "If loving you is wrong, I don't wanna be right." They had heard it on the radio, and so had memorized it. I tried to translate and interpret the words of this popular song. They seemed disappointed. A rumor had been circulating that if you spoke those words to a beautiful woman, she wouldn't be able to resist you.

Typhoid Lurks

We knew the Saramaka River contained numerous pathogens. Our plan from the start was to drink no river water without treating it. We had brought chlorine tablets, and used them for a while. But it made the water taste like a swimming pool. Some villagers had corrugated tin roofs and used them to collect rainwater in barrels. We were able to drink rainwater and, believing it to be purer than river water, we used less chlorine to kill any organisms the water picked up as it slid down the roofs. But we could not always follow our own rules.

One day, Shannon and I, with Piki Dungidungi in tow, went to help women carry large baskets of watermelons from their patch downriver to canoes for hauling to our village. Matawai women could balance three large, heavy watermelons on their heads while they walked a couple hundred meters from the patch to the waiting boats, sometimes with a baby on their backs. The women saucily wondered out loud how many melons Afibiti could carry. I was determined to carry at least the equivalent of these women's load. Accordingly, I tried to carry a similar load and, well, the path to the boats in the heat and humidity seemed winding and never-ending. I must have I briefly lost consciousness, because the next thing I know, I was on the ground and had skinned my nose as my load fell from my head, and my nose was bleeding. Great merriment all around. White folks are weak! But not said in an unkind way.

I was probably dehydrated. That day was so hot that we had run out of potable water sooner than we had expected. In retrospect, we should have split a watermelon and eased our thirst that way. I guess we didn't think of it. We just wanted water, desperately. Finally, Shannon felt she had to drink untreated river water, but just a little. How much difference could that make? Enough to cause—we were to discover—typhoid fever.

Shannon became extremely sick with fever. We had to interrupt fieldwork temporarily, and we all returned to Washington. At the time, all three of us were running high fevers, and I didn't know what else to do. Soon after we returned to seek medical help in Washington, Timmy and I got better, but Shannon continued to get even worse. It took many days and consultations with several doctors who fancied themselves qualified—if not experts—in tropical medicine, because they had served on Pacific islands during WWII. Finally we accessed the State Department doctor at the time and he recognized typhoid fever. Young doctors in residence and medical students were so excited to be able to observe a typhoid case up close. Shannon had been running dangerously high fevers for days, before finally getting a correct diagnosis. Dr.

Marty Wolfe at first put Shannon on a less recommended drug, according to the Merk Manual, which all anthropology fieldworkers carried with them to distant lands where few or no doctors ventured. After a couple of days, he switched to the preferred prescribed drug, and she finally started to get better. I wanted to ask him why he didn't put her on the preferred drug for typhoid in the first damned place? (I would see Dr. Wolfe twenty-odd years later when I picked up Mycoplasm pneumonia in Mozambique, and no one else could diagnose it.)

I soon returned to Matawai Land, and after weeks of recuperation and phone calls from me begging her to return, Shannon followed, but I have to say, most unenthusiastically. I wonder if I would still be married to her if I had not prevailed upon her to return to Suriname.

Mr. Detroit Comes to Matawai-Land

By the 1980s, it was recognized that ethnography was less than objective in several ways, and one was that anthropologists tended to omit any references to contemporary civilization. The anthropologist gains intellectual authority from being on intimate terms with the Primitive world, with the aboriginal, autochthonous other, leaving students and readers of our ethnographies in awe. (Gosh, Dr. Green, did you really live in the jungle with a never-before-studied tribe?) Thus it seemed necessary for me to leave out anything that would compromise the image of the exotic aboriginal. In the words of Sidney Mintz, writing in the 1990s, the ethnographer plays down or omits intrusive, Western elements in all their guises, "leaving behind an allegedly pristine primitivity, coolly observed by the anthropologist-as-hero."

I left out stories that today's postmodernist anthropologist would not only include, but analyze to the fullest. Here is one, which I wrote up only about forty years after the experience:

One day an American tourist showed up in a motorized dugout canoe, with some men from my adopted tribe. An American entrepreneur in Paramaribo, George Girdler, was trying to get tourists to venture into the tribal territory, and he hoped that I, the intrepid anthropologist, would serve as an occasional guide and culture broker. I'd get a cut of whatever the tourist paid. An anthropologist at Yale, who was advising me on fieldwork at this time, warned that I must never enter into such commercial relationships. They are shameful and they compromise science and I would be left with no reputation in professional circles. But I needed the money, I told myself, plus the prospect of being paid as a guide in the Amazon forest seemed an opportunity that would never come my way again. And, who knows, I might actually want this on my CV someday. So I played the role only once or twice, not often enough to corrupt myself or compromise science, I assured myself.

The tourist this time was a middle-aged, blue-collar worker from Detroit. Around the Coleman lantern that first night, he told me how he saved his money from working at his factory job and could thus take a fishing expedition to an exotic part of the world every few years. In preparation for a trip, he visited libraries and studied up on local fish species and the best lures for catching them. He had everything figured out scientifically: he felt he knew exactly which lures to use (he made them himself) and even claimed to know where to find the fish. He already knew the English or scientific names for the larger fish in the local river, and I only knew these names in the local language. I taught him some of these names when I recognized pictures of certain fish in his guidebook.

But I remember feeling superior to this guy. After all, I had lived with my tribe for nearly a year and I spoke the language quite well by then. And here this American pops up out of nowhere, thinking he was going to catch large and elusive fish like the ones we called *kumalu, anumaa,* and *tukunai*! I tried to explain politely (but it was probably smugly) that there were certain ways of doing things around here, including fishing. We think of these ways broadly as IK, or indigenous knowledge. If there was a better way to catch fish, didn't he see that my tribesmen would have figured it out long ago and would already be doing it? I described the exotic and elaborate fish traps the men made of wood and bamboo to catch anumaa.

My brother-in-law Akukupaia making fish trap, 1972.

But Mr. Detroit was undeterred. Bright and early the next morning, off we went downriver, with me as translator. He suggested we turn into little tributaries where, I was assured, the most prized fish would be waiting for us. (Hey, who was guiding whom here?) Irritatingly, my own Matawai guys, my adopted tribesmen, seemed to believe everything this intruder told them—even though all communication went through me, the translator. Couldn't they pick up on my increasingly sarcastic tone?

Mr. Detroit cast his line and almost immediately he began pulling in one fish after another. Dozens of them, scores of them after a couple of hours— kumalu or anumaa—only the best fish, and more than I had managed to catch in my net for a whole year! American technology and this man's ichthyological studies had trumped Indigenous Genius! I felt somehow betrayed. What good was anthropology if a paleface could show up with all his preconceived notions, with his cultural baggage, with his technological fixes to all the world's problems—only to be proven right!

What happened next was even more unusual. I had taken my tourist on a guided walk through a couple of villages the previous evening, explaining the finer points of the local culture I had learned, as no other White man before me. The fisherman said little. But now, in the canoe weighted down with fish, he asked if he had been right in noticing that some of the elderly ladies we saw in doorways appeared to be living alone. I said he was right, most of them were, indeed, widows. He then asked if it would be culturally appropriate for him to make a gift of these fish to the widows, since he and I and our boatmen could only eat a limited number of fish, and we couldn't preserve them. And those elderly ladies were probably needy, without husbands to hunt or fish for them. Here I was able at least to supply an apt proverb: *"ei mujee na'a manu, a ta njanmee kaaboe,"* meaning "If a woman has no husband, she must eat fresh water crabs."

I also said that was a wonderful idea. Let's go feed the widows!

So that night, the widows of the villages of Balen and Njoekonde feasted on the best succulent fresh fish, roasted on open fires. After the feast, observed by all, the village elders commented to me that America was certainly a wonderful place. They said, "Look, America has given the world great men like Muhammad Ali and Smokey Robinson & the Miracles. And now the generous fisherman has come from your country and provided fish for the weak ones among us. America is truly great!" Not the Great Satan. In retrospect, America's reputation around the world had probably peaked some years prior, and it only went down with the war in Vietnam and the Watergate scandal. But that night, all seemed well in the world.

When I finished my fieldwork (and how does one know when one has gathered enough information?), I left with a feeling that I—Shannon and I— had accomplished a feat that was not easy. We had paid in a certain suffering from illness. For instance, Shannon had suffered typhoid. Looking back, Tim was put in danger from wild animals and parasites, true, but otherwise he had a great time, a rich experience—and he developed multicultural social coping skills that served him well in later life.

I never knew in grad school if I was really cut out for the life of an anthropologist. When I wrote my dissertation proposal, I kept my options open by saying I would study rural-urban migration patterns of the Matawai Maroons, and it was impossible to say how much time would be spent in town versus jungle village. But in the end, I wrote a fairly standard ethnography of a "previously unstudied tribe," exactly what anthropologists had been trained to do, for generations of fieldworkers.

A month or two after I had completed my fieldwork, and Shannon had recovered from typhoid, I met a woman at an anthropology conference where we were both looking for jobs. She too had just completed her own fieldwork—on Martha's Vineyard, Massachusetts, where there had been no typhoid fever and none was anticipated. No snakes or scorpions or vampire bats or jaguars or spirit possession. For her work, she was awarded a PhD from Harvard. But I felt a newly won self-confidence. I had gone through immersion in a culture markedly different from my own, and come out alive, wiser, more tolerant and self-confident, thanks to the tolerant, welcoming Matawai.

I had come to think of Dutch anthropology and its practitioners as competitors. And when a married pair of them showed up in "my tribe" a year into my fieldwork, they were dismayed to discover me already there, having staked out my claim, as it were. After completion of my work, I took Suzie, my typist and later my second wife, with me to visit Amsterdam, mainly because it was where rebellious youth could smoke dope in Vondelpark, and jump on the Hippie Bus for Kathmandu. But I made a call to Prof. Andre Kobben and to one other anthropologist.

I had dinner with Kobben, near the end of my visit. What I remember best is how learned, cosmopolitan, and well-read this multi-lingual polymath was. He could speak on any topic, it seemed. There seemed no limit to his broad scholarship. He was definitely not showing off, but I felt so *unlearned* by comparison. At one point, Kobben was telling me how the position and title of professor was much more esteemed and respected in the European tradition than in America. I thought, if he was an example, the respect was well deserved.

Kobben also wondered why I waited until a couple of days before my departure from Amsterdam to contact him, yet he was pretty sure that even at this late moment, he could assemble Dutch scholars from diverse disciplines who had worked in Suriname. He could organize a special dinner in my honor, to celebrate the completion of my fieldwork and dissertation—and to welcome me into the esteemed Dutch and European society of scholars.

My immediate thought was Oh God! I am not good enough. I will be exposed as a fraud. I knew next to nothing, compared to this, this brilliant professor, in the time-honored, European sense of this word. I am definitely not who this kindly, celebrated scholar thinks I am. I declined the invitation, saying that the next day was my last day and I had a farewell dinner planned with the Dutch friends I was staying with. (They were in fact hippies illegally squatting in old buildings slated for demolition in the old Jewish Jordaan neighborhood of Amsterdam.) Professor Kobben seemed disappointed, and even tried to talk me out of passing up the great opportunity he was offering me.

My self-centered fears won out, to my lasting regret. I had just successfully completed 20-odd months of fieldwork, but here was my old lack of self-esteem rearing its ugly head once more.

A Home Next to the US Ambassador: The Matawai in 1997

Because of my growing connections in public health and related subfields, and perhaps my convenient base in Washington, DC, by the latter 1990s I had gotten consulting gigs all over the world. One opportunity even came my way to return to Suriname. In fact, it was an intriguing job related to ethnobotany, with Maroons helping to identify promising plant medicines for new drugs. The assignment came under the heading of conservation, a field in which I had no credentials. But a friend who worked in this field knew I could speak Saramaka, a close cousin to Matawai, and wouldn't it be useful to hear directly from the tribal Maroons who were the beneficiaries of this project? Here is the basic idea of the project I was to evaluate, from an article I published later that year:

The Suriname branch of Conservation International (CI/Suriname) took the lead in developing the broader proposal for that country. The pharmaceutical partner was Bristol-Myers Squibb. The benefit sharing project in Suriname allowed for two processes of drug discovery: the ethnobotanical route, in which discovery was assisted by information provided by traditional healers; and the random route, in which no such assistance was involved. CI/Suriname persuaded Bristol-Myers Squibb to provide "up-front" or "good-faith" funds (USD 50,000, later increased to USD 60,000) to local forest-dwelling groups, as an incentive to participate in joint drug discovery and develop a workable mechanism for benefit-sharing. After consultations within and between indigenous groups, CI/Suriname helped broker the establishment of the Forest Peoples Fund. It was agreed that the funds would be used for projects involving community development, biodiversity conservation, and health care.

So I returned to Suriname, on a consultant salary this time. In fact, I was team leader of a group of three evaluators. I remember our arrival at the airport, around midnight. After clearing customs, exchanging our currency, and the rest, we three team members got in a taxi for Paramaribo.

It turned out to be a decent project, and the traditional healers (*deesiman*, *obiaman*)—usually called shamans in the Western Hemisphere—were elevated in status and paid as consultants (not at the foreign team's rate, alas) to point out which herbal medicines they used for which illnesses.

We gave the effort good marks, as these things go. But it later turned out that it was actually more economically efficient to randomly scoop up several pounds of rain forest soil, then let machines search through the sample for antiviral properties here, and antibiotic or antifungal properties there. This finding is counter-intuitive and cuts out the need to tap into indigenous ethnobotanical knowledge and practices. It also eliminates the need for anthropologists like me, and, of course, traditional healers.

The Matawai seemed less politicized than the Saramaka or the Ndjuka Maroons. These latter suffered massacres from the post-independence military regime, whereas the Matawais have remained relatively unmolested, meaning not victims of slaughter. During the time of the anti-authoritarian Jungle Commandos (1986-1992) led by Ronnie Brunswijk, Matawais formed a defense group in Kwkoegroen called Mandela. I asked, "Defense against who or what? The government?" No, against the Jungle Commandos.

It was the old divide-and-rule strategy: Maroon pitted against Maroon. Once again, the Matawais seemed fairly innocent of the nasty things going on in other parts of the country. They seem relatively unaware of cataclysmic events in the Jungle Commando time, such as the massacre of Ndjukas, a slaughter of men, women, and children by the government in a place called Moiwana. The official government story was that soldiers were going by and villagers shot at them, so naturally the soldiers shot back, and it repeated the government story at the Interamerican Court of Human Rights in Costa Rica (see Richard Price's 2011 book *Rainforest Warriors: Human Rights on Trial*).

But now I had an opportunity to catch up with Matawais: My lineage brother Oscar Lafantie had become the gaanman, and he was now living in town most of the time. Suzie and I went down to the "hammock building" Njoecombe to see if any Matawais might be there. I wasn't sure this place for temporary visitors still existed, but there it was, still functioning.

As we arrived, large groups of Ndjuka Maroons were assembling for an all-night funeral ceremony. A Ndjuka told us that the Matawais occupied the last room down at the end. When I found the right place, I poked my head in and found three Matawais: a 30-ish woman named Shirley, a tall skinny young guy who seemed a bit sickly, and an elderly bassia who had his hammock in a separate inner room. They were surprised to see me. They seemed to remember me a little, though none came from either village where I once lived. I took them all over to a local bar and we had a drink. Then the sickly young man brought me over to Makaati, the compound where the Maroon gaanmans each have an official government-provided house when they come to town. When we showed up at gaanmans Lafantie's house, a group of elderly men were hanging out below it. I greeted them with the customary "*ataapau.*" It turned out most of them were from Posugrunu and environs. They all remembered me and were delighted to see me. But the Matawai Paramount Chief was not there, as he lived full-time in an expensive house downtown.

One man a little younger than myself, Cornelius Sedney, accompanied me to a place on Saramaka Straat where Hindustanis will let you make a phone call a few Suriname guilders. Cornelius phoned the gaanman's house and went into a slow, deliberate Dutch explanation that Afibiti was back in town. I found out later he was talking to the gaanman's granddaughter. He repeated "Afibiti" a couple of times, and then clarified, "Edward Green!" three or four times, with rising volume. As we walked back to Maakati, I asked Cornelius how he knew my name, since I had not mentioned it. Come to think of it' I don't remember *ever* using or telling my Matawai hosts my real name back in the 1970s, if only because my name would have sounded strange to them, and therefore would have been quickly forgotten. How did this man happen to know it?

Cornelius looked at me with mock surprise and said, "Didn't you live in Posugrunu? Didn't I know you then? Shouldn't I remember your name?" He then spoke in what I remembered as the bila tongo (pig-Latinized Matawai) of his age set. Though I didn't recollect him, he must have been one of the young guys who had come into my hut that night and decided it was time for me to stop hanging out exclusively with tradition-bound elders. That was my initiation into the bila tongo of the time, and here was this guy speaking early 1970s bila tongo to me as if I had just seen him last week! (I remembered *Mipiripi kekerepe chochoropo*: "I want to get laid!" I managed to dredge this example up, and got a broad, knowing smile from my age-mate in return.) And I assume that somehow I must have mentioned my American name to this group, probably in response to a direct question.

When we got back to Maakati, we sat around and drank beer and talked about who was living, who was dead, whatever happened to so-and-so, whatever happened to Mutulu (Shannon), what Piki Dungidungi (Tim) was up to these days, how long I had been with this new woman Suzie. We made a plan that I would meet the gaanman the next day at 9 a.m.

They asked me about Kelesi, that is, Chris de Beet, the Dutch anthropologist who arrived with his wife, Miriam Sterman, in Matawai territory some eight months after me for their PhD research. I said I hadn't seen them in 25 years. They informed me Chris had come back for a visit about a year ago, and that he and Miriam had split up. What must they think of us faithless White folks? The two couples who lived with them both got divorced. Their husband-wife bond in a matrilineal society was supposed to be weak, but a great many marriages of people I knew and was to visit later (up to 2016) remained strong, stronger than those of the visiting anthropologists. A moralistic amateur anthropologist wrote in 1900 that "the Bush-Negro knows nothing of love, and marriage means little to him." Yet he added, "We

Europeans are worse." As I write, both Dutch anthropologists have died, Miriam just recently.

The next day, we went back to Maakati, and there was Oscar Lafantie. I didn't recognize him at first since he had gained weight and his hair and beard had somewhat grayed. He had driven up in his yellow van, and was sitting there with a briefcase at his feet. I had brought along with me an ebony-inlaid, carved walking stick from Africa as a gift. I also had a couple of reprints of my articles on Matawai culture from a quarter century ago, and a stack of 8 x10 photographs of people from upriver. We went through the photos. Some of the same elder men were there from the previous evening. They were eager to see good, clear pictures of such notables as Kapiten Laban, Mama Alontu, and elders such as Mama Sei, Akukupaia, Tata Bene, Kapiten Emii, and Fediiki. Many of these people have since died. (But not Akukupaia, whom I would see again in 2016. He and his wife were special friends of ours.)

Oscar drove us to his house to greet his wife, who had been Shannon's special friend. As we got closer, I commented that he seemed to live in a posh neighborhood. He pointed out the US ambassador's residence, and said his grandchildren played with the ambassador's kids. Oscar was speaking in Suriname's lingua franca, Sranan Tongo interlaced with Dutch, just as he used to in the old days. I was glad I had not given him the article I wrote about rum in *Social and Economic Studies*. I had used him as an example of how traditional Matawais don't want their kids to behave. Of course, I didn't use anyone's real name, but now that Matawais are beginning to learn English, somebody might have pointed out that he was my example of non-Matawai behavior. Looked at another way, one could say he was pointing the way to the future.

Oscar's wife Eloise appeared and, except for being a bit heavier, she hadn't changed much. She was still shy, quiet, and sweet. We went through all the photographs again, and drank mango juice. Oscar and his wife were flying to Holland and a couple of neighboring countries on Monday afternoon. He seemed to be going there *soso koili* (just to travel), with no particular purpose. We exchanged business cards and I asked him to come visit me in America. This invitation led to the inevitable discussion about airfares. It seemed a flight to Holland cost the same as one to Washington, yet Holland is much further away. We agreed that the airline companies are thieves and cutthroats.

Oscar told me he had been to Edmonton, Canada, to go hunting with a guy he knew there. He still has the Canadian rifle he bought. He asked me to remind him of the name of the great animal that roamed about Canada. Moose? Yes, that was the name. It hadn't been moose hunting season because they were pregnant or giving birth, he said, so they went duck hunting instead.

Oscar's 28-year-old daughter showed up on a bicycle and sat down with us. She was too young to remember me, and was surprised to see a paleface speaking Matawai, especially since her parents no longer spoke it normally at home. She told me in Matawai that she hardly understood the language at all until she worked as a teacher in Kwakoegroen. She also spoke a little English, and used a bit with us. In my notes of this visit, I didn't mention Oscar's teenage son, Oswald, but he watched me carefully and would later come to visit me in Washington and Maine in 2009, and in Gainesville, Florida when I was a visiting professor at the University of Florida.

I talked to her father about the passing of Watkins, the Guyanese Rosicrucian who had given me the words to banish the terrifying spirit of the Howler Monkey, if that's what it was. After more talk, Oscar drove us over to Saramaka Straat to help me buy a hammock and two nets. He got us a good price. We ran into Cornelius and another guy from the previous night outside the store. He wanted me to greet a Matawai woman whom he had told about me, and who hadn't believed that there was a White guy who spoke Matawai.

I learned that Lonati from Posugrunu was crippled and got around in a bicycle wheelchair. He was married, but had no children. Lina, grand-daughter of Laban, was also now married and in Balen with her children. Akukupaia (or "Sandi") was still with his wife in Posugroenoe. But many elders in my photographs had died. Between death and urban migration, "the villages are breaking up and people are disappearing," as I heard several times from Matawais. One never heard songs like "*Denduwosu Konda*" anymore, "only town music." When I played my tape of old songs to some kapitens and elders at Makaati on Sunday night, many became quiet and reflective. One chief from Misalibi wanted to buy the cassette tape. I gave it to him so that others could copy it from him. I had a copy at home.

Poisoned Water and Satellite Dishes: The Matawai in 2016

In the early 1970s, the Matawai lived in huts surrounded by jungle, and used half-wild dogs to keep the jaguars at bay. When I returned to Suriname in 2016, the fish were more hazardous than the jaguars, due to pollution. Much else had also changed.

The Amazon Conservation Team (ACT) had contacted me early that year, and I got to thinking about my research days in Suriname. The ACT had a project focused on the Matawai, so I asked if my wife and I could tag along the next time Rudo Kemper, a young anthropologist, went back to Suriname. He said fine, and so in April 2016 we did just that.

We spent a few days in Posugrunu, where Shannon and I first lived. The village was largely depopulated, most people having emigrated to coastal and urban Suriname. A road from Paramaribo was under construction.

The President of Conservation International (CI), Russ Mittermeier, happened to arrive in Posugrunu the same day as we did. I had first met him at a briefing for the job I did for CI in Suriname in 1997. By 2016, CI had established a large conservation area smack in the middle of Suriname, extending from just a couple of kilometers west of the Upper Saramaka River and reaching pretty much to the border of Guyana. It was seeking to protect more land in or next to Matawai territory. Back in the early 1970s, people would have asked, "Protect it from what?"

But then gold fever broke out.

I heard about it from Oswald, the son of Gaanman Oscar. Among many other things, he was lead singer on at least one commercially-produced CD of Suriname Creole music—a true Renaissance man. I had interested him in accompanying Suzie and me to Niewkonde, in what I called the "Middle River" area of the Matawais. Shannon and I lived there for the latter part of my fieldwork. He had not visited it for years, and Oswald explained the impact of gold.

Its discovery in 2004 brought Brazilians and assorted town Creoles (*foto nenge*) to the Middle River area. The Amazon Conservation Team observed, "Deforestation caused by gold mining has been growing steadily since the turn of the century, and rapidly in the last five years." This rapid expansion of mining was and is harming the habitat of many unique species, not to mention poisoning the environment. Yet it provided work and the possibility of wealth.

Oswald's father, the late Matawai gaanman, had been able to assert some rights over the mining concession in Matawai territory. He taxed outsiders, and the money went into a fund for the betterment of the local Matawai people. This solution worked for some years, but after Oscar's death, the set-aside funds stopped, and by now the Matawais seemed to be just low-ranking workers in gold mines in their own territory.

Oswald told me that once anyone discovered a major gold deposit, the government moved in, started a concession, deployed gold mining machinery, and tried to move Matawais away. How did the Matawais feel about this? Again, they seem less politicized than the Saramaka or the Ndjuka Maroons. Indeed, as I write, Suriname's Vice-President is now a Saramaka. He is Ronnie Brunswijk, the former leader of the once anti-government Jungle Commandos.

Gold mining polluted the river with mercury and other heavy metals, and made many fish unsafe to eat. Students of a Ghanaian-born anthropologist from Oregon had their hair samples tested for mercury, and their bodies were, indeed, contaminated. Fish that eat other fish, such as the coveted anumaa, are no longer edible, though those that just consume fruit and berries seem okay. Oswald called a Matawai friend of his who seemed unconcerned about slow poisoning by mercury. I listened to the conversation in Sranan, and I heard Oswald say he believes in evidence. He told his friend about the tests on the students' hair, but the friend just shrugged off the warning. In any case, we were told we should bring in our own drinking water, and buy locally hunted bush meat from local Matawais, and avoid fish.

I wondered how aware people were of the contamination. Oswald said that since most of the active gold mining had by then stopped, people didn't believe the water was anything but clean, and the fish as well. They didn't understand that the ecosystem had suffered permanent damage. What a tragedy that a people who have relied on fish as their major complete protein source for three centuries could no longer safely eat them.

Once, Oswald said, he was bringing $10,000 worth of gold downriver from a mine, and he got robbed. He believes the likely thief was a man in his own musical band. He wasn't 100% sure, but everything pointed in that direction. The suspect knew that Oswald was carrying the gold, and he disappeared as a member of the band that same day, with no explanation to any other member. Oswald worried that his father would be furious. But he almost cried with relief when his dad, my old pal Oscar, said, "Well, son, I'm just glad you weren't hurt. That's the important thing. This gold was taxed on my authority as gaanman. It was intended to benefit the Matawai people, so it was a loss to all of us." This thief was not a Matawai himself.

As CI well understood, the Matawai are losing their land. Richard Price, in his book about the conflict between the Saramaka and the government of Suriname, observes that the state's strategy seems to be to simply wait until Maroon villages depopulate themselves, or flooding, gold mining concessions, or occasional outright massacres drive the people away. Once the Maroons have pretty much disappeared from rural areas, there can be no substantial resistance to land grabs by the government or its clients, grabs for timber, gold, or other mineral resources, as well as illegal cocaine processing operations by Colombian cartels.

My mentor Russ Bernard wrote me about this issue in the Americas, "Indigenous people everywhere have, since 1492, been prey to land-grabbers and worse. In the last 50 years, some indigenous people have acquired the ability to engage their predators in legal battles (not military ones) that will determine the extent to which the indigenous people can benefit from the natural resources on their lands. Supporting indigenous people to acquire the tools and skills to fight those legal battles is one way to help."

At the same time, the Maroon population has grown dramatically, even though most of them have moved to town or the coast. In a 2013 article Richard Price wrote for the *New West Indian Guide*, he noted that though the total number of Suriname Maroons had been about 40,000 in the late 1960s; by 2013, it was approaching a quarter million, including those dwelling in Paramaribo, French Guiana, and the Netherlands. The Matawais themselves had increased from about 1,300 living in the interior back in my day, to some 7,000 living mostly in Paramaribo. According to Price (2013),

"The 2012 Suriname census enumerates 117,000 Maroons and the Suriname newspaper *de Ware Tijd* writes of their 'explosive growth' and a 'baby boom' that has suddenly elevated Maroons to a position well ahead of Creoles as 'the second largest ethnic group' in the country (trailing only Hindustanis, who 'remain the largest group with 148,000 people')."

The interior was actually now somewhat globalized. A road ran to Niewkonde (official name Niew Jacobkondre), and another to Posugrunu was nearing completion. All-terrain vehicles, some of which could go 60 or 70 miles per hour, had apparently first made this track into a more or less regular road, though it still greatly benefited from 4-wheel drive. Some Matawai men here now own a car. At least we saw one or two, and one guy said that he would drive anyone to Paramaribo for 250 SRD, or nearly 50 US dollars. So Niewkonde is now reachable by road! Amazing to me.

The increased traffic brought downsides, as usual. One affected me personally: Oswald died tragically in 2020, in an auto accident.

It saddened me that the Matawai language was changing right in front of me. People were no longer using words like *saba* (week) and *sukumaoudu* (fermented sugar cane beer.) Matawai was becoming more like Dutch with every passing year, as more and more Dutch (and Sranan) terms were entering the vocabulary. Matawai was no longer a language of prestige and Matawais didn't seem to respect or appreciate it as they did before. Many young people believed the older language was more African and less like the White man's tongues. This loss was not an academic or sentimental matter. As Russ Bernard wrote to me, "When indigenous people abandon their language, their claims on territory are attenuated. This is one material reason for helping indigenous people revitalize their languages."

At the same time, Matawai society is now more exposed. Maroon languages like Matawai and Saramaka used to have a "deep" level of speaking that kept utterances secret from anyone except their Maroon society. Black people from town couldn't understand. Now more and more Maroons, apparently led by young people, are more interested in learning about the outside world than in keeping secrets to themselves.

We got to talking with a Matawai guy about changes in village life. Oswald said, "You probably don't even plant your own food anymore, do you?" The guy admitted that he did not. I asked what he did for a living. He said he fished, but he assured me that he only caught and sold non-carnivorous fish, which are presumably safe. I asked if he had a store because his home looked a bit like one. He said he didn't, but just sold a few fish here and there. I later asked Oswald how many people still plant their own fields. He said probably very few, and they rarely grow vegetables anymore. They bring things from town like *soporopo* (bitter melon, which I could never learn to like), if they even eat vegetables these days. They do eat plenty of fruit from local trees. It's hard to imagine that if a Matawai were hungry they wouldn't eat fish they catch. Oswald agreed since they probably think the end of gold mining means the end of danger from the fish.

I asked Oswald what Nieuwkonde might be like in 50 years. He said, well, there might be some tourism, but he couldn't really think of what else. He thought that Matawais should raise chickens, and in spite of cost of shipping them to coastal markets their feed would be locally grown and cheap, and therefore the overall cost could be competitive with chickens raised in town.

Numerous fascinating topics are still crying out to be researched in Suriname, even if most of the world has never heard of the country. Not just about new Creole languages developing in real time, but—just as one example—it has lately become clear that there were once great civilizations in the Amazon rain forest, and apparently even in Suriname, as an archeology professor at the University of Florida told me in 2011 (the reader is guided to the popular book 1491). Back when I lived in Suriname, such an idea would have seemed absurd: tall pyramids and roadways in this jungle? Pass me more *ayahuasca*!

Sadness Descends

After nearly two years in Suriname, living in the rainforest under difficult conditions, especially for a young wife and mother of a toddler, Shannon and I separated and later divorced. I am not sure what to say here about of the end of a 5-year marriage. I can console myself with observations that marriages often do not survive the rigors and stresses of challenges like Peace Corps overseas assignment or anthropological fieldwork, but still... we are talking about *my* marriage. I loved my wife and didn't want my marriage to fall apart. But I knew things were deteriorating.

One action I took to foil what appeared to be the inevitable was to visit a psychic at the urging of an enthusiastic nonagenarian I met at a healing ceremony in the Suriname bush, the Yale-educated engineer, inventor, and globe-trotting member of the Explorer's Club, Louis C. Whiton. He urged me to visit a psychic, Reverend Anne Gehman who was then living in Florida. She had put Lou in touch with his late fiancé from World War I—but that is another story. I visited Rev. Anne in January 1973, en route back to Suriname while Shannon was being treated for typhoid. Anne held up my wedding ring and, allegedly by using psychometry alone, proceeded to give me the bad news: Shannon and I wanted fundamentally different things out of life. Out of some 10 measures of relationship compatibility, we were discordant on 8 or 9 of these. I told Anne that Shannon and I could surely overcome whatever incompatibilities there might be and save our marriage. Rev. Anne just smiled sadly.

Shannon came back to Suriname with me, but it was against her wishes and those of my all-controlling mother. Months later, soon after we returned to Washington from Suriname, Shannon asked for a trial separation. On my first night alone, crashing on a mattress in a friend's group house (now known in elite B&B circles as The Mansion on O Street), I met Suzie. She had grown up on a farm in West Virginia, typed 140 words per minute and worked as a secretary for Mrs. Robert S. McNamara's Reading is Fundamental, a non-profit literacy group. I needed a typist. I was also broken hearted, so I had multiple needs. Suzie and I have been together since 1973, although we didn't formally marry until 1998 (in Vietnam, during a short assignment). She has proven to be happy to travel the world with me, and live overseas.

Chapter 5
Breaking and Entering Applied Anthropology

Back in the summer of 1975, I'd grown tired of working in the used bookstore Suzie and I had set up. For two years, I had been teaching anthropology at local colleges such as Federal City College (later, University of the District of Columbia), Towson State College, and historically Black Morgan State College. Once when I was in College Park, Maryland, to interview for teaching a course at the University of Maryland, Suzie happened to see a sign that a small store space was available for rent. She immediately saw possibilities: "Why don't we rent this space and start our own shop! We could sell second-hand things, like books, hats from the 1930s, mandolins and autoharps, flapper dresses... whatever we want! I will quit my job with Mrs. Mac, and you don't need to add another adjunct job to your CV!"

So that is what we did.

The Pyramid and the Ring

I want to relate another paranormal story, related to a visit to Mexico for a 1974 anthropology conference. I was a grad student at the Catholic University, in Washington, DC. One Saturday, my dissertation advisor Michael Kenny drove our small group of grad students to the great Pyramid of the Sun, in Teotihuacan, one of the largest such structures in Mesoamerica, and the 7th largest pyramid by volume in the world. The name is from Aztec and means "the place where the gods were created." It was built more than 2,000 years ago and was abandoned for unknown reasons around AD 700. That morning, I saw some tourists climbing the great step pyramid, and I wonder if they still allow ascents today. When I would visit the Egyptian pyramids of Giza in 1983, visitors were forbidden from even touching the more ancient structures. But of course, show me a pyramid and I have an impulse to begin climbing it. So I did. Soon, a local boy scampered after me, trying to sell me something. I couldn't shake him. I came to realize he would never leave me alone unless I bought an item from him. So I stopped climbing and looked at his offerings. My eye caught a silver-looking ring with an odd design. It was a little small for my ring finger and it felt odd, but I bought it anyway, to have the little guy leave me alone.

When I got back to Washington, I gave the ring to Suzie and she was pleased with it. But a month or so later, I missed seeing it, so I asked for it back. Suzie already had many rings. I can't remember any other occasion when I took back a ring from anyone.

Now, a few months later, I found myself at a Rosicrucian conference in Pittsburgh (yes, I too am a Seeker like Watkins, the Guyanese Rosicrucian I described earlier.) About 100 men and women gathered in a Pittsburgh auditorium that afternoon, and among other presentations, we heard one on psychometry, a psychic technique of intuiting information while holding a physical object. The presenter said this and other psychic talents were actually widespread, only most people don't develop them. As proof, she asked us to look around and find a complete stranger, then pair up and try this technique with one another. We were to select a metallic object from which to pick up vibrations. The object had to have been in close contact with our bodies.

So I paired off with a woman seated nearby, and gave her my Mexican ring from which to pick up my "energy." The presenter on the stage instructed us on how to empty our minds and then let any vibrations from the object cohere into thoughts to express to one's partner. Mine seemed reluctant to speak at first. But I encouraged her, and finally she said, "I know this will sound weird, but... I... I see a pyramid!" I urged her to go on.

"I am feeling that you gave this ring to a close friend, but then... you took it back. Does this make any sense at all?"

Of course, I was astonished, and I was thinking... and probably saying out loud, "What are the odds that this "reading" could be mere *coincidence*?"

She had nailed the two salient and improbable facts about this particular ring. Of course, I assured her she wasn't crazy and told her about the Pyramid of the Sun. She was an actual Rosicrucian, and I was by then thinking maybe I should be one too, in spite of Woody Allen's quip than he couldn't see himself joining any religion that advertises in *Popular Mechanics*.

This Pittsburgh experience called for an immediate epistemological recalculation. Yet I have told myself (and some others) the same thing every time I have had a metaphysical experience. But then the humdrum little forces of normal life (or "consensual reality") always nudge me back into deeply grooved, familiar patterns of knowing and behaving. And I walk around looking for all the world like a normal person.

How common is psychic ability, I wondered? National studies, such as a 2005 Gallup survey, found that about three in four Americans hold at least one paranormal belief, with ESP leading the list. Checking comparable French survey findings, they are less credulous. Yet Einstein himself once commented, "The ancients knew something, which we seem to have forgotten. The more I learn of physics, the more I am drawn to metaphysics." Freud said something similar near the end of his life, and William James, considered the father of American psychology, gave full attention to paranormal research. In 1996 I conducted what might be called a spontaneous focus group on the paranormal in northern Mozambique. I was the leader of an evaluation team which was assessing the impact of a US-funded health project. So there we were, a group of six, in an empty house provided through somebody's connections.

Now, I don't like to be the leader or boss of anyone, anywhere, ever. It causes me to fall back into lack of self-confidence and low self-esteem. And there is always the narrative playing in the back of my mind, "Everyone hates bosses. I myself *really* hate bosses. Therefore, in a leadership role, everyone hates me. They must surely see me as an illegitimate Nazi *obergruppenführer!*"

But sometimes greatness is thrust upon us. On this occasion, I tried to think of a team-building exercise. Some in this role have suggested that everyone go round-robin and share their most humiliating experience. This is supposed to remind us that we are all human, fallible, and vulnerable. I tried to be different. I suggested we go around the room, and each person share the most supernatural experience they had ever had. I said it was okay to simply pass.

Well, although I had was no random sample of any population, every single person had had a supernatural experience. The reader knows I've had a few, but one of our guys, while fully awake and conscious, and not under the influence of any mind-altering substances, saw his dead father materialize in his kitchen. Father and son proceeded to have a conversation through telepathy.

Relating that experience certainly broke down any interpersonal barriers, and soon we all felt good about one another, and we all got along and worked well together for the entire 3-week assignment.

I looked up out-of-body experiences (OOBE) and found that one in ten people report having had at least one OOBE during their lifetime. Pretty amazing percentage. There are two broad categories of possible explanations; 1) OOBEs are an epiphenomenon rooted in physiology; and 2) something like an etheric or astral body actually leaves the physical body. The first lies in the realm of medicine, the second in the paranormal, with parapsychology perhaps a bridge between the two. As this book was going for final editing, an update on James' classic *The Varieties of Religious Experience* has just appeared, called (what else?) *The Varieties of Spiritual Experiences.* The authors propose a typology of transpersonal experiences: numinous (communion with the divine); revelatory (visions or voices); synchronicity (events bearing hidden messages); unity (feeling one with all things); aesthetic awe or wonder (profound encounters with art or nature); and paranormal (perceiving entities such as ghosts or angels). So if we accept this, only my experiences with Monica and Wayne (Wayne story to follow) qualify as paranormal. But the transcendent experiences I have had most often are OOBEs, which don't seem to fit into this typology.

The Hundred Dollar Face-Off

Here is another team-building exercise at the beginning of an assignment. I was once a team member on a project evaluation in the Gaza Strip. We were sitting in an outdoor restaurant in Khan Yunis, a city at the southern end of the Strip, about to share plates of delicious Palestinian food, when our new team leader suggested that we each tell a story of a time when we were the most brave and noble. Another converse of sharing one's most humiliating experience.

I related the following:

I was a visiting assistant professor of anthropology at West Virginia University. I had been missing my girlfriend Suzie who was in DC (though she is a native of West Virginia) because my divorce had not yet come through, and we thought it prudent not to cohabit. I had recently asked her to come join me in Morgantown. I felt she should work and help pay the rent, so she cheerfully got a job at a smokey, low-class, subterranean dive near downtown. She didn't get off work until 1 a.m. And I would usually be asleep when she came home.

On one occasion, she called me at about midnight, when I was already asleep. She sounded very agitated. She explained that there were two half-drunk, rowdy truck drivers whom she had been serving for a couple of hours. She happened to have a $100 bill in her hand from some other customers, and she accidentally gave it to one of the rowdy guys as change for a $20. Then they refused to give it back, denying that she had ever given it to them. For a mistake like this, she would get fired or have to repay the bar with her own meager tips. She asked tearfully if I could come and help her.

Suzie knew how I hated to have my sleep interrupted, so I knew it was serious. Now, the very day I met Suzie—and that was August 16, 1973—I saw at once that she was sweet and naïve, trusting people far too much. I happened to be staying at his house on the first day of my trial separation from Shannon. I knew from the start that someone had to protect the waif-thin, unwary country girl from, well, the guy who picked her up and brought her to where I was crashing that night in 1973. This feeling was reinforced when I discovered she was raised on a West Virginia farm with no indoor plumbing, nor enough beds for seven kids. Listening to *Coat of Many Colors* would bring her to tears. And so for nearly a half-century. I have been protecting her from people who would take advantage of a guileless country girl.

What to do that night back in 1977? I couldn't just stalk into the bar looking like a mild-mannered assistant professor (not even on tenure track) and challenge two large, dangerous, possibly armed drunks, and demand they return the money... or... or *I will have to kick both yo' asses* (the phrase the macho cubic inch of my reptilian mid-brain suggested as my opening line).

Or could I?

With the possibility of violence in mind, but without a real plan, I dressed in my oldest, scruffiest Levi jacket and stepped into my tallest boots, to add inches to my height.

I soon descended into the noisy, smoky, subterranean bar and, to my relief, I saw three friends of mine playing country music, including a hefty, down-home looking guy named Stu Archer. As soon as I walked in, Stu said "Ted! Hey man, come on over and join the band!"

This comment made people notice me and so, stepping into my occasionally rehearsed Steve McQueen role, I replied that "I might do that, man, but first I got me some *bizness* to take care of."

Suzie pointed to the truck drivers, so I strolled menacingly over to the pair and gave them both the evil eye. After a cool pause, I said "I know you guys have this here lady's huner'd dollar bill so what y'all gonna do is give it back to her, *raaght now!*"

The truckers looked around uncertainly at the people at the bar and at the guys in the band. They said nothing, but quietly took the $100 bill from one guy's wallet and handed it to me, whereupon I handed it to Suzie. The tension in the room eased at once.

But what if they had said, "Fuck you and the tricycle you rode in on" (and you ain't even on tenure track)! There was no Plan B. But they didn't, and Suzie gave me a big smile and told me I was her hero! I did play a little fiddle with Stu and the boys, and I felt better about myself than I had in a long time.

You Don't Want to Be Tied to a Desk!

In the summer of 1977, I unexpectedly had a chance to visit five countries in the African Sahel region to help evaluate "population" programs (the preferred name for birth control). The Population Crisis Committee had provided this opportunity, and, yes, my dad was on its board of directors, and we carried out this evaluation together. So I don't count this job as my first consulting gig, but it was an excellent introduction to the continent of Africa and its various demographic, political, social, health, and related problems.

The more I spoke with the people in health and nutrition programs funded by large donor organizations, the more I felt convinced that anthropology was a largely missing element, if not the *central* element, in their efforts. How could foreign programs change the behavior of tribal and peasant peoples if they didn't understand that behavior, not to mention the beliefs, values, attitudes, and indigenous knowledge systems that underlie and to some degree determine it?

In a moment of illumination, I realized that anthropology could actually alleviate suffering and save lives! I remembered an insight I had in 1977, when I was visiting the African Sahel. An officer with the U. S. Agency for International Development had commented to me, "You know, we have a terrible malnutrition problem among pregnant women, meaning their babies are born underweight and vulnerable. We have one good local source of protein—chicken eggs—but there's a taboo against pregnant women eating eggs. Now, if we could just figure out how to get around that taboo."

I thought: I could be figuring that out! I could be an applied medical anthropologist. These two related fields had been around since at least WWII, but I had never taken a course in either one. (Both fields have grown substantially since 1977.)

Large donor organizations and international NGOs (non-government organizations) were on the scene, but the more I spoke with people in health and nutrition programs, the more I grew convinced that anthropology was a critical missing piece. At that point in my fledgling career, I had squeezed out a few scholarly papers on the mysteries of matrilineal kinship among the Suriname Maroons—a largely unknown people in a country virtually no one had heard of—yet trying to do some good in the world with my academic discipline had not fully occurred to me.

I met Mike Warren in Accra, Ghana in 1977. He was an anthropologist with tenure, and he applied anthropology in interesting ways. For example, he started a program in which Ghanaian health authorities worked with indigenous healers to prevent deaths from diarrhea and dehydration. I saw it clearly: instead of teaching introductory anthropology for the rest of my life, I could be saving lives by applying the useful things anthropology had to offer. When I expressed interest in Mike's project, he strongly encouraged me to be involved. I was not used to this kind of invitation. I thought established scholars jealously guarded their turf and regarded neophytes as gatecrashers. Life was a zero-sum game where my gain meant your directly proportional loss. Even outsiders see anthropologists this way. From *The Riddle of the Labyrinth*, by Margalit Fox, of the *New York Times*: "Under a time-honored anthropological tradition that owes much to the colonial imperative, the first investigator to set foot in a village or excavate a ruin retains an unspoken proprietary interest in the place. Future claimants enter at their peril."

Of course, I did go on to become an applied medical anthropologist and, in fact, used Mike's indigenous healer project as a model for similar programs in several African countries. Mike encouraged me enthusiastically every step of the way. Another established scholar of African healing and ethnomedicine was Prof. John Janzen, whom I met in Swaziland in 1982 when he was on a Fulbright grant. He too welcomed me to the field. How different the academic world can be when people are nice.

Among the more impactful of Mike's contributions was the way he used "indigenous knowledge systems," or IKS. The IKS strategy starts with recognition of the depth, empirical accuracy, and functionality of indigenous knowledge related to health, agriculture, and nutrition. Mike packaged these systems so USAID, the World Bank, and UN organizations could immediately understand them and, more importantly, incorporate them into their approaches to economic development in developing countries. The Center for Indigenous Knowledge for Agriculture and Rural Development (CIKARD) at Iowa State became the prototype for IKS centers in some 33 countries.

Unfortunately, Mike died suddenly of an embolism on December 28, 1997, just a day after he had returned to Ara, Nigeria, the site of much of his recent research and development work. He was buried there, in accordance with his wishes. His funeral attracted the largest crowd in the history of Ara, according to residents. Kings, chiefs, professors, and untitled folk whose lives Mike touched all had much to express at graveside. The comments of Professor Bola Ayeni of Ibadan were representative: "Mike, you were a bundle of blessings to humanity. Ara is proud of you. Nigeria is proud of you. The whole of the African race is proud that you came its way. You were a tireless apostle of helping the disadvantaged, the less privileged and the rural people all over the world."

Mike was a model, an ideal, of how I would like to be remembered.

But soon after meeting him, I began plotting my escape from West Virginia University. This didn't prove difficult, since I had been hired on a non-tenure track, "soft money" arrangement, and hundreds of over-qualified "academic gypsies" were migrating from job to job, ready to jump into my position, at any salary. I had been lucky. Not one but two temporary teaching jobs—in Kentucky and West Virginia—had been offered to me, out of the hundreds of CVs to choose from, simply because I mentioned that I played the fiddle and it happened that the professors I would be replacing were both in Appalachian string bands, and so their bands had vacancies too.

I next did what a lot of junior faculty seemed to be doing at the time: I got further education courtesy of a federally funded, post-doctoral fellowship. Vanderbilt University was offering a year of post-doc training in something called "mental health policy analysis." Vanderbilt, of course, was in Nashville, the mecca of country music. I grabbed the opportunity, seeing it as a way to break into international health work in—hopefully—Africa. I had a second post-doc opportunity at UCLA, in ethnomusicology, but I could envision no future in this field outside of teaching. Plus I would have to learn to read music, after years of playing by ear.

After a most satisfying year indulging in folk and country music on the side, I completed the program. I began looking for a job that would send me to Africa. I managed to wrangle an internship in the International Activities Branch of the Alcohol, Drug Abuse, and Mental Health Administration of the old Department of HEW. At the time, 1978-79, this office was helping plan a program of decentralized mental health services for Southern Africa. My "product" was a monograph, and I also published three journal articles on health policy analysis, two focused on Africa.

For the next year and a half, I picked up intermittent short-term assignments with private consulting firms in the Washington, DC area. Sometimes the work directly related to what I wanted to do professionally, such as designing a schistosomiasis control project in Sudan. Other times the work was different, such as assisting in the 1980 campaign in Houston, on behalf of Leonel Castillo, the first Hispanic to run for mayor. But I was usually unemployed. I even worked as a day laborer once, digging ditches no less. As with any job that's intrinsically interesting, competition was keen in international development, and it was hard to enter. The gatekeepers tended to treat newcomers with bemused condescension. I was smilingly told I lacked practical field experience in activities related to development— I was over-educated and under-experienced.

My PhD advisor Michael Kenny knew my desire to get into international work, and one of his former PhD students, Elliot Liebow, became something of a superstar from his published dissertation *Tally's Corner: A Study of Negro Streetcorner Men*. He based it on participant observation studies of people in a poor, downtown area of Washington, DC. (Hey, I could have done that! Why had no one suggested it? My wife would not have gotten typhoid fever.) This instant classic became a must-read for policymakers, bureaucrats, Black Studies professors, race relations sociologists, and those in several other disciplines.

This was the era of Malcolm X, Black Power, assassinations, urban riots, marches on Washington and state capitols for equality, in the midst of which comes along a very readable book that shed insights on the "Negro Problem." It was foundational in the debate over whether there existed a "culture of poverty," that is, a set of norms passed down through generations that kept poor, Black people on the lower rungs of society. The book sold almost a million copies by the time of Liebow's death in 1994. Secretary of DHEW Daniel Patrick Moynihan called the book brilliant. It got Liebow a comfortable job at the National Institute of Mental Health (NIMH), just outside of DC.

Given my experience with Suriname Afro-Americans, Dr. Kenny thought I should meet Liebow and maybe he could help me find government employment. I definitely needed a job, or I was the failure my mother foretold. So I forced myself to phone Liebow one afternoon. I hate to seek favors, but that is what I found myself doing. I was "cold calling" a fellow anthropologist, as if trying to sell him a life insurance policy.

Liebow immediately tried to put me at ease, brushing away my self-doubts, because not long before he had been on my end of many phone calls, looking for a job where he could use his training in anthropology. But I was unprepared for him to exclaim to me, "Whatever you do, *don't* do what I am doing! You may need financial security right now, but believe me when I tell you this is boring, soul-crushing work. If you get a position somewhere like mine, or in some other bureaucracy, you will look back and remember I warned you not to throw away your life!"

Soon after this odd, deflating phone call, I wrangled a formal job interview at USAID headquarters in Washington. As I approached the officer coordinating my interview process, I passed a conference room filled with serious looking USAID officers, checking their watches and perusing what appeared to be my CV. I said I had to duck into the john, where I took out my emergency Valium (consultant's little helper), just to ensure I didn't take this whole interview too seriously and really blow it, embarrassing everyone. I stealthily chewed up a little 2.5 mg pill, and 15 minutes later I was facing the small group and calmly explaining with self-assured, but detached, chemically enhanced equanimity why I wanted to work for USAID,

One of the participants came up to me afterwards and informally told me pretty much the same thing Elliot Liebow had: "An adventurous guy like you who has lived in the Amazon forest—you don't want to be tied to a desk! We who work here never get to the *field*. You should work for a USAID contractor or nonprofit, and they can send you all over the world, and you can have the adventures I am sure you really want."

In any case, there were no job openings at that time, and thank God. I eventually was able to break into consulting jobs, working for various USAID contractors, and so I got to do the field work that the candid USAID bureaucrat wanted for himself. I didn't find myself just organizing and doing the paperwork for funding various on-the-ground activities, I got to do the actual activities. I got sunburn, not carpal tunnel syndrome. I was adopted by at least two tribes on two continents. The advice Elliot Liebow and the USAID official gave me was good: It was far better to be where the action actually was.

The Interview Specter

A word about interviews. A few years after my USAID experience, I had gathered enough experience to be asked to write a chapter in a book called *Stalking Employment in the Nation's Capital*. I was to illuminate the ways an anthropologist could get into the USAID, World Bank, European Commission, and other such worlds. In fact, by this time I was doing pro bono counseling, giving advice to anthropologists like myself at an earlier, supplicant stage: people with degrees, but little or no practical project experience in the extramural world. They wanted—or were forced—to transition from academia to international health or development. Often enough, a regular-seeming man or woman would confess to me (but would never have let on during an actual interview) that they totally lacked self-confidence, and that they couldn't imagine themselves calling someone cold to ask for an interview—or enduring an interview where several people scrutinized their credentials at the same time. They couldn't even really manage public speaking.

And of course, I told them I knew exactly what they were talking about because I was just the same way—perhaps even worse! I might have shared an experience with them of a disastrous job interview to prove my point. But I'd assured them that with perseverance they would catch a lucky break. And take it from me, I would advise, there are genuine frauds in the development biz and, performance anxiety (full-blown panic attacks) or not, you will eventually do just fine. A few years into providing such informal counseling, I was able to relate stories of nervous, self-doubters like them (and myself) who went on to thrive in development and/or international health. I like to think I did some good by sharing my experience and imparting advice.

But once in the early 1990s, I was the lead speaker on a panel at a conference on HIV/AIDS. A woman speaker next to me seemed to be fidgeting, then abandoning all caution, she leaned over and warned me she might suddenly run for the exit door and I should not take it personally. She confided that she was experiencing an abrupt, kick-in-the-gut loss of self-confidence. *Hah!* I was actually experiencing something similar at the same moment, if not to the same degree. So I was in a position to empathize and help.

I said, "Look, whatever you say is going to be just fine. It's not as if someone is going to grab the audience microphone and cry out, 'I don't like your paper and you're a damned fool!' I mean, has that ever happened? Just read your paper. You can read, right? Okay, then, you'll be fine."

She relaxed visibly, and thanked me for calming her down. When her turn came, she was ten minutes into reading her paper when a woman in the audience took the microphone and cried out, "I don't like your paper!" The provocateuse was a New Age-y woman I knew who was on my side of the debate about whether to work with traditional healers. She was now attacking my colleague for not speaking about a role for healers in AIDS prevention. I mean *nobody* at that session spoke about a role for healers in AIDS prevention, probably even myself. But my hapless, low self-esteem colleague just happened to have the bad luck of being attacked. She was struck dumb for a few moments, and she looked at me as if I had been part of a plot to publicly humiliate her.

Chapter 6
Swaziland, the Switzerland of Africa:
1980s Until Present

Later that same year, 1980, I acted on a tip and helped write a proposal for Westinghouse Health Systems for a schistosomiasis and cholera project in Swaziland (this country's name was recently changed to Eswatini). I found that this organization, and many others since then, actually appreciated the holistic anthropological perspective I brought. In effect I showed the limits of the standard USAID "KAP" quantitative survey, and emphasized how such surveys typically missed the most basic dynamics, even if pre-tested. I remember being inspired by demographer John Caldwell. He completed a survey in Nigeria or Ghana, as I recall, and after he had collected and analyzed all the data, he took his completed book to a wise chief in the study area to get his opinion. How many big-name scientists would do this? This chief didn't want to appear rude, but he politely told Caldwell that the study was okay as far as it went, but the professor had missed the major issue! I don't today even remember what the major issue was, but I have never forgotten the takeaway: The Western researcher had overlooked what should have been the central focus of the study, according to the people of the area.

Beyond this critique I suggested a better approach: Add substantial *qualitative* research, especially open-ended, in-depth interviews with so-called key informants. That way we'd get the full, stereoscopic picture for those implementing the project because we would be mixing survey with more informal, anthropological methods.

As it happened, ours was the winning proposal. Now in those days, after some negotiations over costs of project components, a courier had to fly to the implementation country with a "best and final" offer. There was a strict deadline, the close of business on January 3, 1980. For some reason, the manager of Westinghouse thought now might be a good time to save a little money. Instead of using a tried-and-true courier service, she gave the task to a startup that promised to get the offer to USAID/Swaziland at a somewhat lower price. Alas, this guy made a wrong connection in Europe, and the offer arrived hours late. So USAID, by law, had to turn to the second best proposal, which was that of the Academy of Educational Development, in Washington. I learned through a friend that their anthropologist had dropped out, and so they suddenly needed one, right away. Such life-altering opportunities do arise, especially if you happen to be in Washington and can come for a job interview with no delay.

I arrived in Swaziland in 1981 on a two-year contract with the Academy for Educational Development (runner-up to the disqualified Westinghouse proposal) to serve as the social scientist for a USAID project to combat schistosomiasis and cholera. When I arrived in this beautiful, mountainous, landlocked country, our chief of party picked me up at the airport. He was a red-nosed boozer originally from Northern Ireland who was replaced a few months into the project.

The drive from the airport reminded me of California: beautiful rolling hills with higher mountains in the distance, and spring-like weather in the Southern Hemispheric fall. I was taken immediately to the Swaziland Theatre Club, a private club at the time, mostly for British expats. (Twenty years later, the majority of club members were Swazis.) There were drinks to salute my safe arrival. They introduced me to a voluptuous British woman who immediately tried to sign me up for the play the Club was producing: *One Flew Over the Cuckoo's Nest*. They were desperate for an actor with an authentic American accent. All of which is to say, I quickly felt at home in this curious kingdom, the last true monarchy in Africa. I was already drawn into complex social networks that included Swazis and expats from South Africa and various countries in Africa and the world.

Swaziland was known as the Switzerland of Africa, probably because of its mountains, but also because mail tended to land there by mistake. Like Switzerland, the mountainous kingdom also proclaimed its official neutrality in the sometimes-violent struggles between South Africa in the apartheid era and Marxist Mozambique, although evidence exists that the conservative Swazi monarchy leaned toward stability, predictability, and the status quo. It quietly cooperated with South Africa in various ways during the apartheid era.

Years later, Swaziland changed its name to Eswatini. To avoid mailing errors? No, it was actually because King Mswati III decided that the old name sounded colonial. Moreover, there are actually no z's in the Swazi language. The new name means "in Swatiland" in the *Swati* language (note the substitution of "t" for "z.") As I recall, Anglican missionaries called the country Swaziland because the neighboring Zulus—who do use z's—had provided them with the name that stuck for over a century.

Swaziland (allow me to use the old name, in use during my years in-country) lacks villages in the usual sense of the term. Yet there are clusters of dispersed extended-family homesteads that have a clear sense of belonging together, and come under the authority of a recognized leader, either a chief or a prince in the royal family.

The Zulus and the Basotho provide other local examples of traditional monarchies, though they operate within the borders of South Africa and Lesotho respectively. They feature centralized decision-making and general authoritarianism, and the development of certain structures of a parliamentary democracy had done little to change the essentially pyramidal political system. So it was hard to account for the strongly egalitarian ethic clearly evident among Swazis. Perhaps decades of struggle for basic rights by Swazis laboring for South African mining companies, and for foreign owned corporations in Swaziland, bred a questioning attitude toward authority, as well as a keen sense of equity and fairness, at least among Swazi men. Yes, Swaziland was and is patriarchal and patrilineal, like most of the rest of Africa. In theory, the King (*Ngwenyama*, or Lion) rules jointly with his mother (*Ndloviukati*, the She-Elephant), but except perhaps for rain-making, almost all power resides in the King.

Interestingly, the Matawai Paramount Chief in Suriname once told me that he believed patrilineal kinship systems are the proper, traditional African way of arranging society through kinship, yet Matawais were matrilineal, tracing descent through the female line. Why? The gaanman went on to explain the advantages of matrilineal descent for societies eking out a living in rainforests, where cooperation between large groups of kinsmen is necessary to survive. Although this Paramount Chief had little schooling, he spoke like an anthropologist who had pondered this very question.

One day not long after I arrived in Swaziland, I happened to be with some Swazis who worked for the Red Cross. We stopped by a cluster of rural homesteads—little thatched-roof huts in compounds that together made up a named community, under authority of a subchief called an *nduna*. Toward the end of this visit to a "cadre" called Rural Health Motivators, I was bold enough to ask the nduna if my wife Suzie and I might occasionally stay in one of the huts, perhaps on weekends or for particular celebrations. As in Suriname, the question seemed reasonable to local people. The nduna replied that we could use a hut normally occupied by his grandson who was away at school, staying with kinsman who lived closer to town and where the schools were better. So basically, yeah, take the hut over there for the next few years! This provided a great opportunity to work on the Swazi language and get a real feel for rural life, which was the life of most Swazis in the early 1980s. Outside of Peace Corps volunteers, precious few Whites spent time in a rural hut.

This experience was our entrée into rural society. In addition to my government advisory job at the health education unit of the Ministry of Health, I distinguished myself from my fellow project team members by having a hut of my own, a foothold in rural life. Before long, we were attending weddings, funerals, and other such village events.

It happened that the nduna's son, Petros, spoke good English and helped me get oriented and communicate with Swazis from the start. I was so naïve about the part of Africa I landed in that, for example, I had never heard of Robben Island. Petros couldn't understand how anyone could not have known of the place where the apartheid regime in South Africa imprisoned Nelson Mandela.

During a wedding early on, we heard that there was a woman who was in the same "regiment" (called an "age grade" by anthropologists) as the oldest of old King Sobhuza II's advisers. We walked over to her hut to find that members of the wedding had lined up to greet her, if only to simply touch her leathery hand and then tell others they had greeted her. Later that day I did an interview with *Gogo* (Granny) Maziya. She didn't know her exact age but we figured out from historical events she was witness to that she must have been at least 103. She could recount stories from before the coming of the Whites, back when the Swazis and Zulus were at war.

When Zulu warriors came marauding, a woman would grab a child and head for a hidden cave in the mountains. Women practiced spacing of births—one every three years or more—so that when running from an enemy, she only had to carry one kid. I would later pass this recollection on to various Western donor organizations, who often seemed obsessed with African fertility rates. They could then argue that family planning had historical legitimacy in Swaziland.

I had to ask how she had managed to live so long. She began, "Well, I always smoked a lot of pot." Petros, who was translating for me, interrupted to explain that she was referring to the ritual use of cannabis, *dagga*, when people communicated with their ancestor spirits. Gogo was basically telling me she and her ancestors were living in harmony, and they were rewarding her with a long life. I published my first interview with her in *The Times of Swaziland*, and it was later picked up by *Bona* (*Look*) magazine in South Africa, which was published four languages spoken there.

When I was not working, my extracurricular activities soon exploded: I was in two bands (folk and jazz). I performed with a folk quartet at the British High Commission on the occasion of the royal wedding of Prince Charles and Lady Di. I acted in a play. I was elected Social Director of the Mbabane Theatre Club (in the twilight of British colonialism, when almost identical clubs existed in Harare and Lusaka, and doubtless elsewhere). I wrote for (and contributed photographs to) *The Times of Swaziland*, and twice for a popular South African magazine that published in Zulu, Tswana, Sotho, Afrikaans, and English. I sang in a choral group, even performing at King Sobhuza's funeral in 1982. And the list could go on.

We ended up staying in Swaziland for four years, the last of them consulting directly for the USAID mission there, which proved open to my anthropological ideas. When it was time for me to leave, an article appeared in *The Times of Swaziland* about the "White man who learned wisdom from Gogo Maziya." I was proud of this. Most *belungu* (White folks) came there and elsewhere in Africa to teach their specific technical skills. Communication tended to be one-way. I heard that Black audiences in South Africa loved the photo of me sitting at the knee of Gogo Maziya, so to speak, learning from her. This extraordinary woman seemed to choose her time of death later in 1981. In fact, she sent for me to be at her village, Maphalaleni, for her funeral with the request that I write it up for *The Times*. I heard that word had reached her that some young relatives felt that by not joining the realm of the ancestors with others of her age-grade, Gogo was holding up certain inheritances. So she decided to die and have me on hand for the funeral ceremony.

She Pulled Up Her Sweater to Cover Her Face

Back to my official reason for being in Swaziland. The project called for a KAP (knowledge, attitudes, and practices) study relating to water and sanitation in Swaziland. Its primary purpose was to provide baseline data for designing a national health education strategy to reduce the cases of water-borne diseases. We were budgeted for a conducting a random sample survey. Yet I had doubts about how well such an approach would work, as already mentioned. In addition to the general problem of obtaining *valid* data through survey methods in rural Africa, data you could believe as true, I was after certain sensitive information related to areas such as personal hygiene, excretory behavior (*yikes!*), and health beliefs. The impersonal, pre-coded questionnaire typical of survey research is notoriously poor in eliciting this kind of information, even if it has value in measuring patterns that are already reasonably well established.

So I proposed that we first do an informal study of health beliefs and behavior, and that we rely on local-level health workers, traditional healers, and their patients as key informants. I hoped that such an informal approach would give us a fund of qualitative information that would be valuable in the design and interpretation of surveys, and might well reveal key facts surveys could never discover. In short, I approached the problem as an anthropologist would, not a sociologist. I planned to rely on traditional anthropological methods of key-informant interviewing and participant observation, at least at the outset. It was during my study relying on local-level health workers that I first attempted to come up with a quantitative national estimate from qualitative research—explained below. The health workers were called rural health motivators (RHMs, *bagcugcuteli*), more commonly called village health workers.

RHMs are women chosen by their communities to receive about eight weeks of training in preventive health care at a regional clinic. They then work among their neighbors, promoting homestead sanitation, the purification of drinking water, proper infant nutrition, and other practices that curb disease. I felt that RHMs would make good key informants—even culture brokers—since they were insiders in their communities yet they understood and promoted public health measures. I expected they would be likelier than their neighbors to give candid and truthful replies to sensitive and even embarrassing questions about what their neighbors thought and did. Furthermore, I could use a flexible, open-ended questionnaire, one we could modify.

From my reading, I had discovered that in many parts of the world the RHMs and other community-level health workers know almost everything about the health-related beliefs, attitudes, and behavior of the people they work with, especially if they come from the same community. Therefore, if we systematically interviewed them as key informants, we could quickly, effectively, easily, and inexpensively discover people's health-related beliefs and behavior. There was even the advantage that health workers were more likely than the general public to speak frankly about beliefs and behaviors that are unapproved by, or in conflict with, formal health education, or that are considered superstitious or backward. And then there are those embarrassing questions about... er, toilet questions (nothing sacred for nosey White folks). I remember one RHM reacting to such a question about outdoor defecation by pulling her sweater up over her face—it was winter in the highlands—to hide from the intrusive foreigner and blush. I found myself blushing as well.

RHMs might even volunteer important health information not specifically asked for by interviewers. I recalled Dr. John Caldwell and his wise old chief: I was designing a survey questionnaire (with Swazi input, to be sure) which might be okay as far as it went, but which rested on pre-existing assumptions and might miss critical issues.

Over the next eight weeks or so, and using an interpreter, I began my qualitative research by interviewing a convenience sample of 42 RHMs in eight regional clinics. The sample was non-random, yet I attempted to interview RHMs in roughly equal proportions from each of Swaziland's four major topographic zones to achieve rough geographic balance. I located RHMs at regional clinics where they came periodically to collect their modest salaries. The nurses holding the paychecks asked the RHMs to cooperate with me, which helped. The whole process was swift and simple. No RHM declined to be interviewed. Truthfully, I did not know how many RHMs I would interview when the process began. Time was less of a factor here than my lack of faith in my informal methods. They seemed improvised, and far less scientific than the planned and formal sample survey.

Since each RHM visited approximately 40 homesteads, the interviews provided information about nearly 1,680 homesteads, representing some 3% of the estimated 50,000 homesteads in Swaziland. It seemed possible to regard our RHM-visited homesteads as reasonably representative of Swaziland as a whole. It occurred to me that I might even try to obtain some *quantitative* data about the number of pit latrines already built or under construction at homesteads, since we needed baseline data on this factor and I would be asking about it in the sample survey to follow. It turned out that RHMs had no trouble providing the numbers since they were required to report monthly on latrine construction progress.

In 1981 I estimated the percentage of Swazi homesteads with a pit latrine in a simple way. The 42 RHMs reported 412 pit latrines out of the 1,680 they had covered. So I divided the 412 latrines by 1,680 homesteads, and got the result that 24.7% of homesteads in the RHM-covered areas had a latrine. I saw no reason why 24.7% should not approximate the *national* figure.

Wonder of wonders, months later, when we conducted the relatively expensive and time-consuming national random sample survey, we found that about 22.9% of homesteads sampled had a pit latrine. But another 3.9% had one under construction, and 0.2% had two or more latrines. Hence the total proportion with some kind of latrine was 27%. The RHM interviews had counted latrines under construction, and in fact, its 24.7% was within the margin of statistical error of our sample survey, meaning the two figures were essentially the same. My quick study using RHM key informants cost about $300, the money for gas, while the later survey cost tens of thousands of dollars. (Of course, I would not have advocated scaling up the program nationally (at a cost of millions of dollars) without the corroboration of the sample survey.)

The latrine estimate was the only finding in which I attempted quantification in 1981–82, but I began to wonder if I had stumbled on an important unrealized (or undiscussed?) potential of qualitative research. To quote Russ Bernard, qualitative data is crucial at the inductive end of research (to find out what questions to ask and how to ask them), and at the deductive end (to interpret the findings of quantitative data.)

A few years after the Swazi research, in 1985, I was asked to conduct a qualitative *study* of diarrheal disease KAP in Bangladesh, as in *the whole country*, using a purposive or convenience sample of 240 Bangladeshis. The national population, by comparison, was then about 100 million. Our quantifiable findings proved to be within 4 to 16% of key findings from the National Oral Rehydration Program random sample survey that came out around the same time. Good enough for a rough estimate.

The other opportunity that I stumbled upon was the value of research with traditional healers, who were already the de facto primary health care providers in both rural and urban Swaziland. There happened to be a sister project funded by USAID to find out more about healers, and I was asked if I could devote part of my time to investigating the role of indigenous healers. This research would be a side-project to my KAP survey.

I jumped in eagerly, because I already had thought long and hard about this question when I was at Vanderbilt, and had published an article urging African governments and donors that we should find ways to collaborate.

So, how to begin? It also happened that an American anthropologist who was teaching at the University of Swaziland, Fred Prinz, was leaving the country, and he introduced me to his key informant and mentor in matters supernatural, a man he had cultivated for a couple of years. (What a nice world it can be when anthropologists cooperate instead of compete!) Fred's guy was a short, rotund man in his late 60s, a church-going Roman Catholic who was nominally an herbalist. His name was Nyoni, meaning The Bird, but also implying the Lightning Bird, believed by Swazis and Zulus to be a servant or "witch's familiar" that sorcerers can send to attack a homestead or a person. His name might imply that he could thwart supernatural assaults of this sort.

Nyoni came originally from Malawai so he brought an outsider's perspective to his work. He and I were both outsiders. I would come to learn that in Sub-Saharan Africa, people tended to believe it is an advantage for a healer or spirit medium to come from elsewhere. They assume you not only know what is going on locally, but you bring additional wisdom from afar.

Nyoni was supposed to be an herbalist (*lugedla*), a respectable line of work in Swaziland. But beneath this veneer of phytomedicinal (plant-based) knowledge, Nyoni also knew how to work with spells and spirits, more like a *sangoma*, the regional name for a spirit medium. One night, he was asked to rid a homestead of zombie attacks, and what follows draws upon an early field note.

Nyoni was summoned to Zombodze. We drove to a homestead believed to be under supernatural attack in my project vehicle, with "Ministry of Health" emblazoned on it. Members of the homestead were impressed that this particular spirit doctor had a White chauffeur and assistant, from none other than the Ministry of Health. Nyoni presented me as his apprentice and explained that I would add power to the protective magic that was commissioned. When I said the prayer, in English, I was asked to add, "I have come all the way from America to say these words, so it must be thus."

The zombie invocation went something like: "Oh (presumed zombie kin-term address), stay away and bother us no more! Return to your grave and be at peace. Let no evil pass this place. Let any harm be sent back to the sender. May no sorcerer find this protective medicine and try to overcome it."

The evil spirits sent in the form of animals—snakes, moles, and other subterranean "spirit-familiars"—are called *tilwane* and they are invisible unless one has medicine to make oneself clairvoyant. If you do see one, don't show fear. We drove special medicinally treated pegs into the ground to keep zombies and tilwane from entering the homestead. The nails attached to the pegs attract lightning "sent" by sorcerers, activate the medicine tied to them, and beam the bolt back to the sender.

Our client had a fancy house on a homestead of otherwise traditional huts. His house was built at a cost of E5,000, a little over $5,000 at the time. I asked if envy was at the root of the sorcerer's attack on our client and his whole compound. Nyoni said it was, and it was not just because of the house. Did I notice that all of his children and cattle were healthy? One or more neighbors must have been jealous of the homestead head, and then sought his undoing. Nyoni observed, "Jealousy is a terrible thing in Swaziland; about 70 percent of Swazis are jealous." Good to know. I wondered about comparable rates in the US.

My notes that day, supplemented by ethnographic literature, concluded that fear of sorcery and also of sorcery-accusation, act as a disincentive to achievement among Swazi commoners. Sorcery and witchcraft seemed to be as much a "levelling mechanism" here as elsewhere in Africa. Swazi aristocrats appeared exempt from this egalitarian imperative. Chiefs and princes of the royal Dlamini clan could have five wives and a Mercedes without apparent fear of witchcraft accusation. It was their birthright. But for the Swazi masses—it was as if a few royal clans had been superimposed on an essentially tribal society characterized by strong egalitarian values and a "limited good" ideology (there are only so many good things to go around). I later changed my view about aristocrats after finding out that they in fact spent a lot of money on medicines to ward off jealousy and sorcery. I began to notice all the lightning rods at kraals of wealthier aristocrats, to ward off sorcery attacks.

This was all part of my qualitative research. I developed more systematic methods later, including surveys of healers, so that before the year was out, we were able to conclude that over 90% of healers favored collaborating with government health officials. We, that is, the Swazi Ministry of Health, began to hold workshops for healers with a view toward cooperating in public health goals.

The government of Mozambique would recruit me a few years later to start similar programs there. Likewise, when AIDS struck southern Africa with more force than anywhere else, there was sudden interest in convincing indigenous healers to help distribute condoms, and I became involved in a large, HIV prevention project in South Africa. I would become increasingly skeptical about the role of condoms in AIDS prevention, but I certainly felt we should bring healers together with government and private sector health workers, and then see what develops.

For example, an unknown number of healers in the region noted a relationship between male circumcision and HIV and other STIs (sexually transmitted infections, formerly called "diseases" as in STDs) many years before scientists could prove this. By 1991, when I was involved in workshops for healers from South Africa and Swaziland, it emerged that a healer from Soweto was routinely advising circumcision for his male clients to help prevent STIs. Once this topic had arisen, several other healers—particularly women, it seemed—strongly agreed, and reported that they too recommended that their clients become circumcised. In fact, healers in this workshop advised clients from non-circumcising societies, such as the Zulu and Swazi, to be circumcised, and there was anecdotal evidence that such clients were complying by visiting hospitals or traditional healers.

I was later shown a pamphlet mass-produced by the healer association TRADAP (Traditional Doctors AIDS Project) that advised: "TO CIRCUMCISE IS THE BEST REMEDY TO REDUCE SEXUALLY TRANSMITTED DISEASES." I learned that TRADAP had been advising circumcision as a way to prevent STIs since September 1991. As I was unaware of any African or international AIDS education or intervention program that promoted male circumcision, I asked how TRADAP came to learn about the relationship. TRADAP's President claimed that healers in her organization discovered it by themselves, through their experience with patients. They noticed that male patients repeatedly infected with STIs tended to be uncircumcised. They were said to have rashes, "dirt," or infections under their foreskins. Some healers claim they have convinced parents from non-circumcising societies to have their children circumcised to "protect them in later life." When I asked about potential cultural resistance, the TRADAP president observed, "When tradition and the health of our people are in conflict, it is tradition we must sacrifice."

I was so excited with this finding—and the previous quote, which was picked up by a few colleagues. By the late 1980s an anthropologist friend of mine, Priscilla Reining, had noticed a relationship between male circumcision (MC) and lower HIV infection rates. She and a colleague superimposed a map showing the groups in Africa practicing MC over another map of infection rates, and voila! The pattern jumped out. That was in 1989, and I had already noticed a relationship myself. In studies from the 1980s intended to identify possible risk factors, "lack of circumcision" kept popping up.

I did a quick survey and found that a fairly high percent of healers in South Africa believed in the MC factor. Armed with the amazing finding and Priscilla's 1989 article, I asked for a meeting with the head of USAID's AIDS program, in Washington. I pitched the idea that I be authorized to follow up in an investigation of knowledge and practices of the MC factor in South Africa and Swaziland.

The guy was appalled. He became suddenly nervous and told me this was a terrible, even dangerous idea. Foreskins equals explosive controversy! And USAID is very risk-averse. I told him it was not my idea. Awareness of the MC factor was bubbling up in the vox populi; it appeared to have entered the culture. This director, a gay activist from San Francisco, was adamant: He, and therefore USAID, would not "touch this thing with a ten-foot pole." Yet some traditional healers were already working on it. We might have learned a lot if I had received the go-ahead. That was in 1991. Starting in 2005, three randomized controlled trials (RCTs), the gold standard in medical research, would confirm that MC lowers risk of HIV infection by about two-thirds. Nowadays there are voluntary MC programs in many parts of Africa. Think of the countless thousands of lives that could have been saved had we promoted MC years before we actually did; if we had followed what indigenous healers were doing, both in societies that practiced MC and in those that did not—especially the latter.

Chapter 7
Bangladesh: The Five-Star Hotel
and the Poorest Village in Asia

Bangladesh was and is one of the world's poorest countries, and while I was still in Swaziland I was offered a gig there. I knew little about it aside from a couple of AID/Bangladesh telexes that were photocopied for me in Washington. They specifically sought a medical anthropologist—an uncommon request in 1985, though not today—to evaluate beliefs, behavior, and attitudes relating to childhood diarrhea and use of oral rehydration salts (ORS). USAID was planning to add ORS as a product line in its Bangladesh Social Marketing Project, which had been successfully marketing contraceptives for over a decade. Social marketing uses Madison Avenue techniques to achieve socially desirable goals, such as reducing infant mortality through adoption of ORS. At that time, I had recently done a study of child diarrhea in Swaziland, and we had asked questions about the acceptability of ORS packets—or alternatively about mixing the correct proportions of sugar and salt in a liter bottle of water to achieve essentially the same result of avoiding dehydration.

I was becoming a diarrhea expert! I would become that mysterious man standing aloof at cocktail parties, and svelte women in clinging dresses would ask, "Do you think that's *really* him... the Diarrhea Man?"

I had attended a social marketing conference in Washington the previous month. So I felt reasonably *au courant* on the latest approaches, as I had not five years earlier in Sudan.

I took a taxi down to the USAID office where I learned that I was expected to assess the feasibility of social marketing packets of oral rehydration salts (ORS), and to design qualitative research to guide an ORS education and communication program. There was a curious poster on the USAID office walls: IF YOU CATCH FIRE, FALL AND ROLL! Maybe this job was more dangerous than they were letting on.

My hotel in sprawling Dhaka had just opened a few years earlier. It was in the middle of one of the city's worst slums, a good part of which they had bulldozed and concreted over to make room for the hotel. But some of the old shantytown remained. From my window on the fourth floor I had an excellent view of the hotel's 40-meter swimming pool, health club, snack bar, and outdoor bar. Blocked from the guests' view by a high wall (but visible to me on the fourth floor) were little shacks propped on stilts and poised precariously over mud flats. Each shack seemed to have multiple residents. I wondered if such extremes of wealth and poverty could be found so close together anywhere else.

Talk about nonobtrusive research methods: I could imagine myself observing most aspects of life in this shantytown from my vantage point, including cooking, washing, and toilet behavior. An anthropologist who doesn't like roughing it could sit down by this window with a pair of binoculars, like Jimmy Stewart in *Rear Window*, and within a few months have enough data for a thesis. Not really, but I was reflecting for some moments about the hardships of my research in the Suriname rain forest, and the break-up of my marriage.

USAID was considering importing a new brand of condom. I saw a guy at the USAID office blow one of these condoms up like a balloon, and try to pop it with his fist. And I always thought those things were tested electronically, you know, with a machine that simulated copulation!

Thursday nights in Dhaka are like Friday nights in the Christian world. There was a Thank-God-It's-Thursday bash at the American Club in Dhaka on my first Islamic sabbath evening, featuring a Texas barbecue and square dance. The square dance band had actually never performed together before, and they were delighted to learn that I played fiddle, after a fashion. (Maybe the real reason I was hired for this gig: I reported to Jack Thomas, the USAID assistant population officer, who happened to be the back-up guitar and square dance organizer.)

Our band also had two banjo pickers, a mandolin player, and another fiddler, a sociologist. As the evening progressed, there was a great deal of pseudo-redneckery, of letting it all hang out in the company of fellow Americans. I myself became a Good Ole Boy for the evening and reveled in it all. After all, anthropologists ought to have a culture too. My project partner, a Sri Lankan with decades of Asian experience in family planning, somehow knew how to do Appalachian clogging. Unfortunately he couldn't make it to the dance, but I took him at his word.

On another night, a Bangladeshi filmmaker, who also created family planning ads for local TV and movies, invited the Sri Lankan and me to dinner at his home. Three beautiful Bengali actresses from Calcutta were there. They had roles in ads then being produced. It turned out to be quite a party: fine scotch, lively conversation, and excellent Bengali cuisine. I was the only non-native to the subcontinent. One guy from the locally staffed Social Marketing Project confessed after a few scotches that he couldn't understand how an American was going to come and illuminate Bangladeshis about the intricacies of their own culture. "We're keeping an open mind," he assured me. "Maybe we aren't looking at our culture in enough depth."

Good God, how to respond to that? I tried to justify my role as best I could: "Um, somebody needed to pull things together, perhaps with an objectivity that a Bangladeshi—even a Bangladeshi anthropologist—might lack. And someone with in-depth experience in other cultures might discern patterns and connections that others missed."

It didn't sound too convincing, even to me. I concluded that maybe much of the value of a person like me was simply that I could talk to both poor villagers and development planners and policymakers. But the reality was that an anthropologist arriving in a new land is in a shaky position, expected to be—or to quickly become—a country expert. And countries are complex, especially large ones.

With an annual income per capita of just over $100, Bangladesh was listed as the second poorest country in the world, after Chad. Life expectancy at birth was 48 years. Over 70% of the population was said to survive on less than 1,800 calories a day. Most women were anemic even before they were pregnant, and their babies were born weak and undersized, especially when births weren't properly spaced. To make matters worse, people typically discarded the colostrum—the first breast milk produced after childbirth, containing large amounts of protein and immunizing agents—as impure or dirty milk. Traditional birth practices themselves leave much to be desired. Neonatal tetanus abounded.

Still, the average woman produced 6.2 kids during her childbearing years. Bangladesh had a population density of about 1,620 per square mile in the early 1980s. The continental United States would only have that density if everyone on earth lived in it. India, which, of course, had its own population problem, had announced plans to build a fence along its border with Bangladesh to staunch the flow of illegal immigrants into India. Bangladesh, its pride wounded, then announced plans to build watchtowers at intervals along the same border to keep Indians from sneaking into Bangladesh.

Development assistance groups working in Bangladesh seemed to regard population control (no euphemisms here) as the number-one development priority. Some people felt that Bangladesh might need draconian measures, such as China's, to curb population growth. Many felt AID's Social Marketing Project exemplified the best approach a noncoercive or capitalist society could take, since it used entrepreneurship and the profit motive to spread contraceptive technology as widely as possible.

We went around Dhaka getting briefings from all the agencies that work in diarrheal disease control, especially those that promote ORS. I was especially eager to talk to sociological-type researchers who had looked into health beliefs, behavior and attitudes. It takes a certain art and diplomacy to get researchers to share their hard-earned and still-unpublished findings with short-term consultants who zip in and out of a country, and who then get credit for putting such findings in their own consultant reports. Since I had been the "local expert" in two other countries, I knew what it was like to have visiting consultants pick my brains. As the picker, I tried to be completely upfront with the pickees, and promised to give them due credit in my consultant report.

In Dhaka's Old Section

One afternoon, two colleagues and I went by bicycle rickshaw through Dhaka's lethal traffic to the old section of town. Much of the urban Hindu population who had remained after Independence—mostly from the Untouchable caste—seemed to live here. The streets were too narrow to permit passage of a rickshaw, but not the throngs of people that seemed to be pressing in all directions at once. There were rancid open sewers, stagnant now because of the dry season. Beggars of all ages, but mostly children, followed us and even tugged at our clothes. There was a Mother Teresa orphanage in the neighborhood, but demand appeared to outstrip supply, and many kids seemed to live in piles of rubble covered with cardboard, visible in tiny alleyways off the streets we walked along.

One little girl with large, soulful eyes followed me for the entire walk around Old Dhaka. Remembering how I was mobbed by scores of beggar kids some years earlier in Delhi, I waited until we had climbed back into rickshaws before slipping this girl a sizable banknote. She stuffed it in her torn dress and proceeded to run alongside my rickshaw, which quickly picked up speed as we maneuvered into heavy traffic. I tried to shoo her away because she was now clinging to the back of the rickshaw, and her thin legs were running faster than they could have run on their own power. I was terrified she'd be run over when she finally had to let go. Just when I was trying to get my driver to pull over, her strength seemed to give out and she somehow stumbled back to the sidewalk unharmed. Her eyes were still on mine as she was swallowed up by the crowd.

A Roadless Village

I was lucky to go on a field visit with a Bangladeshi anthropologist who was also looking into health beliefs and behavior. She had received her PhD from UCLA. I wondered if she knew Carlos Castaneda, whose UCLA dissertation in anthropology became the first of several bestselling books, and if she were tired of hearing this question. She was pleasant and we found we knew several people in common. It took two hours to reach the villages in Tangail District where she had been working, so we had plenty of time to talk. Four of her research assistants were with us, and they proved rich sources of information about topics like home remedies for diarrhea, and perceptions of qualities attributed to foods and medicines. In fact, people view as *nirog* (disease-free) and "cooling" many foods scientifically known to be nutritious, alkaline, and low in fat. Hats off to folk wisdom once again.

Before walking around the villages, we decided to cook up some lunch from strictly nirog foods purchased at a local market. I insisted on paying since everyone was devoting so much time to my nonstop questions. The research assistants did the bargaining; they knew prices would go up several hundred percent at the very sight of me. We eventually feasted on fried fish, rice, salad, and four cooked and elaborately spiced vegetables. Seventy taka (less than $3) fed seven people and we had food left over. The meager continental breakfast at my hotel costs 100 taka.

Activity on the Khulna River, Bangladesh, 1985.

After lunch we drove as far as the roads could take us, then walked the last stretch to reach one of the villages where my hosts had been doing research. The villagers we met were used to hearing questions so mine didn't seem to disturb them. There was some occupational specialty by village section. In one section, for example, an extended family owned no land, but managed to make a living by weaving cloth for the *lungi* skirt that men traditionally wear. They were proud of their craft, but complained that earnings were not keeping up with rising costs of all they needed to buy. Only the cash remittances from a brother now working in Libya seemed to be saving the family business from collapse. In a second section, people lived by farming and seemed slightly better off. We spoke with one man who was having an early dinner of rice garnished with a few peppers; he said he couldn't afford meat or other vegetables. Unlike the areas of Latin America and Africa I'm familiar with, villages in Bangladesh could have been essentially the same for centuries or even millennia. It boggles my mind.

By the end of a long afternoon, I felt I had absorbed a bit of the ethos of village life in Bangladesh. People were undernourished, but things didn't appear as bad as I had expected. The quality of rural life certainly seemed superior to that in the urban slums and shantytowns, and I was told most Bangladeshis realize this. Only the most dire circumstances, and then mostly among the landless, force people to take their chances in the slums. One got the feeling that if only fertility rates would drop quickly and decisively, life here could be better. My anthropologist colleague and I had plenty of time to talk shop during the long drive back. We covered such topics as whether there are incentives to write and publish among the non-academically employed, and why anthropologists tend to be apolitical. She told me she didn't see many fellow anthropologists in her line of work. I told her neither did I.

Cholera

The International Center for Diarrheal Disease Control, Bangladesh (ICDDR,B) operates a field cholera hospital and research station in Matlab, in the Comilla District, about 35 miles southeast of Dhaka. The best way to reach Matlab from Dhaka involves an hourlong speedboat trip down the Meghna River. ICDDR,B got a lot of support from USAID, so my partner and I, as USAID consultants, received a tour of the Matlab operation. Life on the Meghna, a tributary of the Ganges, seemed relatively unaltered by the passage of centuries. Fishermen in crude sailboats searched up and down the river for places to drop their nets. Some ventured as far as the Bay of Bengal, leaving their families for months at a time.

We visited a couple of riverine villages near the cholera hospital. Even though people enjoyed greater health and educational interventions in Matlab than anywhere else in the country, the villages seemed poorer than the ones in Tangail District. And few if any of the kids appeared to be attending school. Residents told us that school fees were high and, anyway, the kids were needed to help out at home.

An Indian woman in our group overheard a comment—apparently the villagers didn't think she understood Bangla—and drew its speaker into a conversation. He had grown suspicious of the oral cholera vaccine trials underway in Matlab. Since women, but not men, in the 5–20 age group were getting the vaccine, weren't these vaccines really a way to make unsuspecting women infertile? Our ICDDR,B guide explained to him that scientists couldn't use men in that age group for trials and follow-ups because too many were absent for too long from the villages.

We got a tour of the cholera hospital, including a children's ward where dehydrated kids were receiving ORS (oral rehydration salts) from their mothers. The children lay on army cots with a hole cut in the centers so buckets below would catch their diarrhea. Having seen this kind of ward in African clinics, I was impressed by the absence of bad odors.

Not everyone in our group felt the same. A tall, middle-aged German woman—silent until now—whispered to me, "We must see what they do with the dead bodies." I didn't know how to respond to this. A few minutes later, having gleaned some information somewhere, she leaned toward me and confided, "As I suspected! They allow the families to take the dead bodies home! This spreads cholera. We might as well cut off the money for the hospital and let them all die!"

On the boat trip back, a doctor in our group had to stop to deliver supplies to another children's cholera ward in a little out-station. There we saw a child so dehydrated that it refused to swallow any of the ORS its mother held to its lips. The sight was eerie: the mother was young and beautiful, and seemingly resigned to losing her child. She appeared passive and fatalistic as we tried to show her gentle force-feeding techniques. Some of the mothers I know back in the United States, like my own, would be hysterical and demanding to speak to the person in charge. Get the Surgeon General here at once!

Meanwhile, my hotel was becoming an armed fort. The Islamic Development Bank was gearing up for a big conference, and for the last couple of days, foreign ministers and heavies from all over the Islamic world had been arriving. Security was getting tighter every day. A metal detector and an X-ray machine stood at the door that had become the hotel's sole point of entry, soldiers with machine guns roamed even at poolside, and personal bodyguards of sheikhs lurked menacingly in the upstairs corridors. Anyone who knew of the view from my window understood how easily a have-not in the shantytown could lob a bomb over the hotel wall. I hoped I would get out of this consultancy alive.

Well, USAID and Population Services International appreciated my report, and PSI felt confident that indigenous theories of child diarrhea would not be a significant obstacle, and that promoting ORS packets ("sachets") via social marketing would work.

1985: Deeper into Bangladesh

A few months later in 1985, I was asked to return to Bangladesh to supervise a two-month study of knowledge, attitudes, and practices related to child diarrhea and ORS packets... really, just a more systematic, and presumably scientific, repeat of what I did on my preliminary trip to Bangladesh.

Now, I know a lot of "experts" in my position would pretty much stay in their 5-star hotel for two months, and guide the study from that comfortable perch while lounging by the pool drinking margaritas. I would soon meet someone just like this in Lagos. But as an anthropologist, I was interested in validity, not just reliability, and in any case the time and resources available made a population-based random sample survey impossible. So the USAID/Bangladesh Health Officer Jack Thomas, the guitar picker, suggested we do a national qualitative study within two months. I objected that there was no such thing as a "national qualitative study," but Jack replied, "Fine, you can invent one and forever take credit when they catch on."

So, with Suzie as my helper, and with a group of Bangladeshi interviewers led by my English-speaking assistant who was trained in economic geography, we drove to several provinces, and on the way to Khulna we took a paddlewheel steamboat right out of a Mark Twain story. I was too busy and exhausted to keep fieldnotes on the 2-month job. But the experience was... well, very different from rural Africa, and equally fascinating. My assistant, who I will call Muhammed, was perfect in every way—I should write a booklet just about him—and we saw one of the world's poorest countries in a way no tourist ever would or could—not that tourists flocked to Bangladesh.

Since we were not working with villages or households preselected by a randomized process, I was deliberate in ensuring that we captured the opinions both of rural and urban, young and old, male and female, poor and relatively middle class, more educated versus less educated. One incident stands out: Muhammed told me we were in the poorest province, and near what might well be the absolute poorest village in the country. He said he didn't want to take us there, and especially not my lovely wife, because the shacks would be such a terrible spectacle. Of course, this warning only made me—and Suzie—eager. She had grown up in rural poverty in West Virginia (but in a single generation, her family has all done much better and poverty seems a thing of the past).

Now, to get people to participate in about 90 minutes of questioning, we offered a slip of paper they could redeem for about 15 cents. In Bangladesh in 1985, that was not nothing. People took them without laughing in our faces. So on the day in question, we entered the poorest village armed with our 15-cent certificates and people took us to the village head, a skinny man with a white goatee. We sat under a palm tree in mid-village with a single coconut dangling from on high. After explaining our presence and introductions, the elder sent a boy up the tree to cut down the lone coconut, and then he sliced it open and offered us the juice and "meat." I thought, "Oh my God, this might the only food standing between these people and death from starvation." I didn't want to take it, but Muhammed whispered in my ear that protocol demanded that I accept this gift. In another twist, the proud elder told me he could not possibly accept the 15-cent certificate because I had travelled all the way from America to talk with him, so he was honored and could not accept anything from me. He after all was my host, and we were his guests. This was one of those moments when I was so glad I had gone into applied anthropology—meaning, I left university life and went on assignments wherever the current client chose to send me.

In another very poor village, the subject of desired family size arose. This informant told me if he tried to have nine kids, the chances were that at least one would be able to find work in an oil-rich Gulf state and send back remittances. I knew from the literature that remittances from countries like the UAE kept many Bangladeshis from starvation, but hearing it said aloud was so much more meaningful. By the way, I always liked to do a few interviews myself, using Muhammed for translation. Unexpected things have a way of popping up during interviewing and leading to new lines of inquiry, such as this comment about family size.

Village head in "poorest village," with post office credit.

The Single-Author Illusion

This assignment was one of those occasions that when I published an article in an international peer-reviewed journal on our study findings, I should have included the name of my wonderful field assistant Muhammed. I was used to reading and writing single-author articles in anthropology, but it dawned on me that in medicine and public health, one usually saw multiple authors. That made perfect sense: an outsider, with funding and permissions in hand for a study, shows up and works with local people essential to the research: translators, interviewers, fieldwork coordinator, perhaps statisticians, and others. Long before the time I speak of, research committees in medical fields had worked out formal protocols for the proper order in which author names appear. Yet anthropological articles and book chapters continued to appear often with single authors.

Finally, I had a conversation with a USAID health officer in Santo Domingo who said it was great that I was putting the Dominican Republic and our project on the map by publishing in international journals, but he hinted that it would be nice if I included as co-authors the names of one or more Dominicans who helped me carry out surveys.

Well, of course! I am ashamed to say this simply didn't occur to me until the mid-1980s, when I received the hint from that USAID officer. Later I discovered that my public health colleagues whom I helped in some capacity (such as Anne Outwater and Allison Ruark) would be especially generous in adding my name to a list of five or six other coauthors. Anyway, I adopted this practice starting, I believe, by including the name of my excellent assistant and field director Aldo Conde in the Dominican Republic. And soon I would head the list of several authors who helped in my studies. But I am ashamed I didn't start this practice earlier, and certainly in Bangladesh. Everyone I worked with there, including the social marketing research company that helped with statistical analysis was so eager to help, and so companionable and just fun to work with. I would sometimes smoke legal cannabis late into the night with the young guys who ran the social marketing research company, discussing the cosmos and the meaning of life. I felt like a graduate student again, when anything in the future was possible—yet so at home in an exotic part of the world.

Chapter 8
Nigeria: Spirit Mediums, Birth Control, and the Voice in the Gourd

I'd be flying into Lagos, the biggest city in Africa, a vast, humming sprawl. And I wondered what it would be like. In 1985, Nigeria had a reputation for being a difficult, dangerous country to work in, even for short-term consultants. I was venturing into a land led by strongman Ibrahim Babangida, nicknamed "The Evil Genius," who ruled as never-elected President from 1985 to 1993. The Babangida Era is one of the most controversial in the military history of that country of successive coups. It was characterized by a burgeoning political culture, with Babangida and his cronies earning themselves at least an estimated 12 billion USD ($23.9 billion today). This put Babangida in that elite club of kleptocrats that included the likes of former Zaire President Mobuto Sese Seko, who looted that benighted country to the tune of perhaps $15 billion. As part of his legacy, Babangida managed to stoke Christian-Muslim sectarian conflict during his years in power.

When criminals mugged Paul McCartney at knifepoint in Lagos in 1973, and stole the demo tapes for "Band on the Run," they cemented its reputation as one of the most hazardous cities in Africa—and that was saying something. Nigerians themselves used to get mugged while they watched public executions held on the beach by the Holiday Inn in Ikeja, a suburb of Lagos. A few years before my own first visit, an angry mob had surrounded and almost overturned a car containing an anthropologist colleague of mine. What was I going to find now?

I also faced a professional mystery. A Columbia University behavioral scientist had overseen a survey of Yoruba traditional birth attendants, or TBAs, which found to everyone's surprise that this cadre of health workers had disappeared. But then how could a substantial percentage of births be occurring at home? Well, as far as the Columbia team could determine, family members were attending the births, cutting the umbilical cord, burying it in the yard, and doing whatever else the TBAs used to do. I thought: How strange that a tradition which had lasted countless generations could end abruptly, just like that. Could this be right?

I made a pitch one day to the Population Crisis Committee (PCC, renamed Population Action International in 1992) arguing that traditional healers might well be happy to partner in promoting "modern" family planning, and certainly over-the-counter contraceptives such as condoms. I had worked with traditional healers in Swaziland, and had found them most eager to collaborate with Western doctors and public health officials in general. PCC liked the idea and we discussed trying a couple of pilot projects in Nigeria.

My adventure began at the Nigeria Airways counter at Kennedy International. Pandemonium reigned at the check-in counter as African passengers tried to load immense cartons containing color TVs, stereo systems, and probably kitchen sinks onto the baggage scales, then acted surprised and indignant when told they were overweight by hundreds of dollars. Before I pushed and climbed my way to the front, no fewer than three women asked me to count one of their pieces of luggage as one of my own, since I was only carrying one bag. I accommodated a woman wearing a dress of large, yellow polka dots. This meant me hefting her handle-less, leaden carton onto the scales, and almost throwing my back out.

Later, at 29,000 feet, two cockroaches rendezvoused on the empty seat beside me. It was the first time I'd ever seen cockroaches on a plane. It was also the first time I'd seen a plane run out of beer before the flight attendants reached row 19, my row. I think an entrepreneur sitting up front bought up all the bottles to sell them at a profit to people in the back rows.

I preferred flying a non-US airline, not because my chance of being blown from my seat by a bomb were perhaps 30% less, but because I couldn't bear one more American stewardess—ah, flight attendant—intercom voice saying, "The captain *has* turned off the seatbelt sign, but we *do* ask you... ." Of all the possible words to stress in this context, the auxiliary verb makes the least sense. I have never heard an American flight attendant *not* stress the auxiliary verb. They probably teach foreign-born ones to speak the same way. It bothers me.

I arrived in Lagos. The expediter that the US Embassy offered me via telex didn't show up, so it took about two hours to retrieve my bag and clear customs. All those giant cartons appeared on the baggage carousel before my anemic-looking, half-full bag emerged. I knew my bag would be bursting at the seams with Nigerian arts and crafts when I left.

Taxi drivers pounced on me when I emerged from customs, and I let instinct guide me in selecting one. On the ride into town my "car-hire" man told me I was wise to have avoided the yellow taxis. "They will stop the car not far from the airport, then they will harm you and rob your money and throw you by the roadside!" He pointed to several yellow cabs stopped by the road as if to show robberies were in progress. I could see the need to buy a protective amulet while I was here.

Before reaching the Kurama Lodge Hotel, a rifle-toting soldier stopped our car and inspected the contents of my suitcase. After he let us continue, my driver explained that the soldier had been looking for dash, that is, a tip or bribe.

Explaining the Mission

The following day, I found myself meeting the Minister of Health. On my first evening there! I had forced myself to remain awake at least until 7 p.m. after being up all night on the plane, to align my sleeping schedule with Nigerian time. By phoning the USAID Administrator at her home at one-hour intervals, and getting no answer, I managed to stay just this side of mental blackout. Just before 7, when I was sinking irretrievably into a dark abyss, I tried one last phone call and, of course, got through. The Administrator, Keys McManus asked if I could be ready to go in ten minutes, dressed in coat and tie. She said this might be the only time I could talk to her or to Dr. Sulaiman, the Ministry of Health's head of planning, since they were both about to leave the country.

Ten minutes later, Keys picked me up and we were off to the airport to meet a visiting delegation of Zambian family planning officials. Although Dr. Sulaiman wasn't at the airport, I met the Minister of Health and had an opportunity to explain the pilot project I was in Nigeria to design. It involved training traditional healers, indigenous health practitioners, in child spacing (the African euphemism for family planning, itself a euphemism for birth control) and other aspects of maternal and child health. We also hoped we could hold awareness seminars for chiefs and other local leaders. Actually, I only mentioned traditional birth attendants (TBAs) and chiefs, not traditional healers, since the latter were a sensitive and controversial topic among African physicians, and I didn't know how the Minister stood on the subject. I explained that the Population Crisis Committee was funding my trip, but that two USAID-funded organizations were interested in supporting my proposed pilot project, in theory.

From Lagos I was driven up to Ibadan, where I had talks with Pathfinder, the Planned Parenthood Federation of Nigeria, and the University of Ibadan. All went well. I thought the Pathfinder representative in particular was excited by the prospect of taking part in perhaps Africa's first systematic attempt to train traditional healers in family planning. My argument from the start rested on three points:

1) *Demand for contraceptives was weak.* Family planning programs were ineffective in Africa more because of pro-natalist attitudes than lack of family planning services.

2) *We knew who most shaped opinions about health.* Traditional healers and TBAs were the most respected health service providers for the majority of Africans, so they were the best positioned to influence attitudes toward family planning and provide contraceptives.

3) *These healers would join forces with us.* Elsewhere in Africa they had proven willing and capable of adopting certain "modern" or "Western" primary health care practices after participating in training workshops.

Additionally, in my plan healers and TBAs would make a 25 percent commission on contraceptive sales.

It all sounded logical and straightforward, but would it work?

I had learned that very recently the two top representatives of the National Traditional Healers Association dropped dead suddenly, one while waiting to meet the Minister of Health, the other while returning from a meeting with the same Minister. What kind of omen was this? I wondered how these deaths would affect the healers' interest in cooperating with government health services.

I also heard on the BBC news that Reagan ordered air strikes against Libya. Bombers blew up Qaddafi's own house and killed his adopted daughter. They also destroyed the French Embassy. It looked to me as if Reagan had fallen into Qaddafi's trap: There would be a worldwide outpouring of sympathy for poor little Libya, and outrage against US neocolonialism, imperialism, "state terrorism," and worse.

Before dinner that night I sat with three Americans who like me were staying at the Ibadan University Guesthouse. All were from American universities; two were Fulbright scholars. One of the Fulbrighters taught history at Gallaudet College, an institution for the deaf in Washington. He recounted a familiar saga of interviewing for academic jobs during the annual meetings of his professional association during the early 1970s. His fresh PhD from UCLA and his dissertation research in Nigeria seemed to make him no more employable than hundreds of other bright young scholars at the time. A job at Gallaudet came along, and even though it meant learning sign language, he supposed the alternative was driving a taxi. He said he never regretted his decision.

I had breakfast with him the next day. He told me his wife hoped they could move to Los Angeles after the Fulbright was up because she wanted to graduate from amateur acting to more professional work, something in Hollywood. His wife was a late riser, he said, but would probably join us for breakfast. She finally appeared and, as her husband had said, she did look like an actress: thin, girlish, green-eyed, mischievous. No words were spoken after she sat down, and I assumed she was still trying to wake up and face the day. Then her husband began communicating with her in sign language.

One of my meetings that day was with the head of the ob/gyn section of the University of Ibadan's teaching hospital. The hospital complex was too extensive for the main university campus—itself the largest campus I'd ever seen—so it had its own campus several miles away. Professor L seemed uncertain about me at first. The message I sent him yesterday hadn't arrived, so here I was, appearing with no advance notice, not affiliated with any local organization, and with a calling card that identified me as only an independent consultant. The professor seemed to suspect I was here to do self-advancing academic investigation because he told me how difficult it was to get permission to do research in Nigeria.

I fully explained my mission and Prof. L warmed up, but he warned me of the complexities of trying to bring traditional healers into the modern health system. I said that wasn't my aim; I simply wanted to see if healers could incorporate some public health and family planning measures into their existing practices. Prof. L seemed to relax further. He confided that the community-based family planning program that he now supervises had really opened his mind to the value of working through community people. But he warned me that some doctors and bureaucrats would oppose the idea of working with traditional healers. I had already faced this problem in Swaziland, where I developed the same kind of program. But yes, it seems always better to talk about "working through community people" than seeming to set up competition between trained doctors and traditional healers.

Prof. L said the Minister of Health had challenged Nigeria's traditional healers to submit their medicines and healing methods to scientific verification. The professor himself believed that some indigenous healing methods might be effective, such as a local treatment for sickle-cell anemia.

Back in Lagos, students were demonstrating for another day in front of the American Embassy, protesting the attacks on Libya and expressing solidarity with Col. Qaddafi. About half of Nigerians are Muslims. A petition was circulating with the names of students said to be willing to go to Libya to fight by Qaddafi's side. The Embassy closed after bomb threats.

A photo in the paper that morning showed a placard in front of the Embassy: FIRST IT WAS GRENADA, NOW IT IS LIBYA. NIGERIA TOMORROW?

Boarding Pass Blues

I had planned to have two pilot project sites, one around Lagos and one in Benue state, much further to the west and inland. The next morning, I was to fly to Makurdi, Benue's capital, and I made sure to reach the Lagos domestic flight airport a couple of hours early to get a seat. The airport was already mobbed. As I walked toward the rear of a long line—actually three or four lines in front of a single window where boarding passes were issued— I was repeatedly accosted by tough-looking young men who told me they could get me a boarding pass, no problem. Always suspicious of hustlers, I shook them off and joined the crowd waiting to get to the ticket window. After 20 minutes the lines hadn't moved. If anything, I'd been jostled back a few feet. Up by the window I could see burly men of the sort who had just offered me their services, struggling to push in front of each other, and probably negotiating bribes with the people who dispensed the scarce boarding passes.

I asked a perplexed looking, well-dressed Nigerian woman what our chances were of getting on the flight. She sighed and said she hoped her 30-naira dash would get her a seat. The airport wasn't always so packed, she told me, but this was the last day of school holidays and a lot of kids were returning from visits to Lagos.

Finally, after three hours the plane was full and I still didn't have a boarding pass, even though I had hired a menacing, muscle-bound, dash-man to fight his way to the front of the line and wave my ticket in the faces of airline officials. The heat was sweltering and I was drenched with sweat. I finally gave up.

I left the airport in frustration, and there was the driver who had brought me—Alhaji! He had guessed I might miss my flight. So he took me back to town, and he became my driver whenever I was in Lagos.

EDWARD C. GREEN 151

It was good fortune meeting Alhaji. He was one of those natural culture-brokers who could clearly explain his world to foreigners. He had an inquiring mind, even a philosophic bent. His answers to some of my questions clearly show that he'd thought about some of the interesting differences between his Yoruba customs and the strange ways of the pale-skins.

Alhaji was a Muslim Yoruba, which meant he was part of a religious minority in Southern Nigeria. As his name attests, he made his *Hajj* pilgrimage to Mecca a few years earlier, enabled by his earnings as a car-hire driver. He regarded himself as religious, but not strictly orthodox like the Saudis and others he met during his pilgrimage. For example, he eschewed alcohol in principle, but he drank palm wine because "we Yoruba believe it is not strong, and it is good for the stomach."

I once asked his feelings about *purdah*, or enforced female seclusion. "I don't agree with the strict Muslims," he said. "I have studied the holy Qu'ran, and I know that purdah was not meant to be put on a wife without cause. It is more like a punishment for a wife that strays from her home and looks for other men. If this is not what the wife is doing, she should not be in purdah. My wife is not."

There is something very practical and reasonable about Africans like Alhaji, I reflected. They are flexible; they're open-minded; they lean away from absolutism and fanaticism. Or so I thought before the rise of Boko Haram in the north some ten years later.

I returned to the Kuramo Lodge Hotel and they smugly informed me they were booked solid. Likewise at the Eko Lodge. I thought I'd better look for Tim B., the project director of a community-based family planning project funded by the Population Crisis Committee. I ended up at the Yacht Club, an expatriate social club on the harbor in Ikoyi, the most affluent neighborhood of Lagos, located on an island a bridge span from the coast. Tim was out sailing in a race, but someone said they'd get a message to him.

I idled around the club for the next few hours talking to some Brits. One woman who had lived with her husband in Nigeria for many years lamented that the largely British expatriate population was visibly dwindling. The best schools were "getting Blacker every year," she said, as White students become fewer. I asked if Lagos' reputation as a crime capital was justified. I might have guessed her answer. "It used to be that some boy would just break into your house when you were away. We expect that. But nowadays it's rape and beating and murder, and they're all on drugs so they're not even in control of themselves."

Before long, Tim appeared and introduced me to the alluring woman he had been sailing with. She was a Turkish Cypriot, she said, and she certainly had the dark, mysterious beauty found in the Eastern Mediterranean. We fell into conversation about life in Nigeria, and she asked me a bit about myself. She certainly seemed to be flirting. Why else would she be touching my arm playfully when she laughed? It occurred to me how easily I could fall into a "honey trap." A beautiful spy would simply have to cuddle up to me and tell me I was wonderful, and I'd probably spill the beans.

We were interrupted by a deeply tanned man who sat down with us, and introduced himself as my companion's husband. The beautiful Cypriot looked a bit sheepish. I tried to keep the conversation from flagging. Then the woman got the hiccups. Now it happens that a bout of hiccups is my cue to demonstrate some magic I learned in Suriname in 1971, so I announced that I could drive away the Spirit of Hiccups if someone lent me a wooden match. Drinkers from the next table provided one and took interest. The husband looked dubious. I lit the match, blew it out, and placed the match stick halfway into the wife's hair, just at the hairline, the burnt end sticking out. Using tribal invocations, I commanded the Spirit—of Hiccups— whose name I called out—to be gone at once! The hiccups stopped immediately, to the woman's amazement and delight. It never fails. I don't know if my little ritual somehow surprises people into forgetting about their hiccups long enough to overcome them, or if hiccups are in fact a mischievous spirit who vanishes when a person calls out its secret name.

Tim put me up at his comfortable house for the night. He had a club dinner to attend, but he instructed his steward to make me dinner and he invited me to watch movies on his video. We discovered we had attended the same boarding school, Fay, and that the experience left us both rather traumatized. We traded stories.

Traditional Doctor

Then it was Saturday, and I had nothing planned. In fact, I'd planned to be in Benue. Alhaji had told me the previous day that he could take me to a powerful traditional doctor he knew, one who specialized in delivering babies. I decided to give it a try.

We drove out to the slummy, but interesting-looking neighborhood of Mushin. The "doctor" had a maternity clinic consisting of an outside reception area full of clients in different stages of pregnancy, an inside reception room staffed by a woman in a nurse's uniform, a consultation room, a dispensary full of traditional medicines, a delivery room, and several patient recovery rooms.

I met the head of this enterprise in his consultation room. He presented his card:

With the compliments of Dr. (TR) A. Ejiwunmi, Member, Board of Traditional Medicine

The "Dr. (TR)" stood for traditional doctor. With Alhaji translating from Yoruba, I asked about the Board of Traditional Medicine. The government of Lagos State, I learned, actually recognized traditional healers through its Ministry of Health. It even registered and certified them via its Board of Traditional Medicine, made up of various types of healers as well as some state officials who were doctors or pharmacists. If true, Lagos might have been the only state in Nigeria that officially recognized traditional healers.

Dr. Ejiwunmi described himself as an *onisegun*, or herbalist, who specialized in delivering babies. He told me he had trained a number of other ob/gyn herbalists, many of whom practiced in greater Lagos and ran traditional maternity clinics similar to his own. His brother operated his own herbal clinic and medicinal herb wholesale business; a 1986 calendar advertising his business hung on the wall.

I explained to Dr. Ejiwunmi that I was in Nigeria to explore helping traditional and modern doctors work together. I hoped to start by organizing workshops where people could discuss modern and traditional methods and medicines openly. The doctor said this opportunity was precisely what he and his healer colleagues had always wanted, so when should we begin?

When, indeed? I asked him if he got requests for birth control. He said yes, many women come to him for "protection against pregnancy." One of his best methods was a special ring "cooked" with birth control herbs for six days. If the woman wore it during intercourse, she'd never get pregnant. He also used an herbal decoction that the woman drank one time only. Thereafter, she could never get pregnant unless she returned to Dr. Ejiwunmi and took a special antidote.

One of his apprentices interrupted us. He had just delivered a baby in the adjacent room. Dr. Ejiwunmi ducked out, then returned. No problems, a safe delivery. This prompted him to show me his recordkeeping system which included nicely printed prenatal care attendance records, appointment cards, admitting forms, records of medicines used, birth certificates, and patient release forms. The back of the attendance records listed dos and don'ts for pregnant women in Yoruba and English. The advice mostly involved diet and exercise and it seemed basically sound. He invited me back on another day to meet some of the traditional obstetricians he had trained over nearly 30 years.

The Yacht Club

On Sunday, there seemed nothing to do but work on my notes. But after a few hours, I decided to see how expatriates spend Sunday at the beach. The previous night at a Chinese restaurant, I'd run into Margaret and Peter, two Brits I met at the Yacht Club. They said everyone was going to Tarkwa Bay beach on a nearby island to swim in the relatively safe waters there. Margaret had warned me about the dangerous undertows at many beaches around Lagos, especially near the Eko Hotel.

After lunch I took a cab to a launch site near the American Embassy where one can catch a motorboat. We rode through the harbor for 20 minutes, rounded a point, and pulled into a partly protected beach with colorful sailboats. It had to be the hangout of the Yacht Club crowd.

I jumped off the boat into a foot of water and told my boatman he needn't wait, although I wasn't sure what I'd do if I didn't find anyone I knew. Tarkwa Bay is reachable only by boat. If I got stuck, I wouldn't last long in the intense, relentless, tropical sunlight.

I walked along scorching sands looking for a familiar face, while Nigerian boys called out, trying to rent me a place in the shade. Pink-skinned Europeans sat in an endless row under makeshift wood and thatch canopies, stretching to the far end of the beach. I strolled along the damp part of the sand and eventually found someone who directed me to Margaret and Peter. The Yacht Club had its own little open clubhouse, complete with fresh water shower, at one end of the beach. I found Margaret, and she invited me to leave my gear with them and enjoy the beach. They promised to give me a ride back to the Yacht Club at the end of the afternoon.

After a long swim in the lukewarm water—this was the Bight of Benin, I had to remind myself— I returned to the shade of the Yacht Club house. And there was the dark-haired Cypriot woman who had flirted with me last week. I said hi. She showed only a slight flicker of recognition.

I sat around drinking tea with older Brits, and listened to jokes about Aussies in the vein of Paddy the Irishman, or van der Merwe the Boer. Later I caught a boat to the Yacht Club proper with Margaret and her friends. The place was filling up with members—all Whites—and everybody was taking turns standing rounds of drinks for all those at or near their table. I learned about this custom at a comparable British club in Swaziland. In fact, only the presence of sailboats distinguished this place from the Swaziland Theater Club. After a couple of beers, I began imagining I could recognize some of my old British friends from Swaziland.

This club had Americans as well, mostly men connected with oil companies, some with wives. One such wife seemed different from the Club crowd. She and her husband had spent seven years in Nigeria some years ago and she had seen a lot of traditional rural life—and to my surprise, she loved Nigeria. She observed that most Whites in the Lagos area huddle together in places like the Yacht Club to keep from going mad. "As the expatriate population of Nigeria dwindles," she said, "Whites feel like an endangered species."

Solving the Columbia Mystery

The next morning, still in Lagos, I met with an official of the Ministry of Health. He was said to favor using traditional healers to distribute contraceptives in communities. I began to outline my idea for instructing herbalists in family planning and general maternal and child health, noting that it might be worthwhile to train urban as well as rural healers. The official, a doctor, interrupted me and explained that traditional healers are just that, *traditional*. Therefore they don't exist in cities such as Lagos where modern doctors are available. Moreover, healers should not be taught modern contraceptive methods. "They should only use birth control methods they are familiar with." If healers had condoms and such to sell, they would mark up prices so high that their condoms would be unaffordable.

I decided I shouldn't be the one to inform the doctor that the Lagos State government had been successfully training urban traditional healers in this activity for the past two years. After all, I was a foreigner who had been in Nigeria for just a week. And I had clearly been misinformed about this doctor's interest in "training" traditional healers.

Back in my car, I recounted the conversation to Alhaji. He wasn't surprised, but he still raised his voice in indignation. "These doctors and professors sit in their air-conditioned offices, and they don't know anything! They tell rubbish to you foreigners! They want to throw away our own heritage and only copy English medicine!"

Dr. Ejiwunmi was waiting for me at his clinic that day as we had agreed. We talked a bit about delivering babies while he got ready to leave. In Yoruba, those who deliver babies, but don't use herbal medicines or do any sort of healing, are called *agbebi*. After a number of years of successful practice, they may also be called *bababiye* if they are men or *iyabiye* if they are women. The stem *-iyabiye* apparently means "safe deliverer of babies."

Women prefer to go to herbalists, *onisegun*, for deliveries, and they are almost always men. Herbalists, especially those who specialize in childbirth, are said to offer effective medicines for dealing with the considerable hazards of childbearing such as breached birth or hemorrhaging. Many believe sorcery or witchcraft cause some or even most of these problems.

The doctor went off in his Mercedes, driven by one of his apprentices, while Alhaji and I followed in our car. We left Mushin and drove through similar neighborhoods: poor, congested, with kids spilling out onto sidewalks and streets. I noticed several signs advertising herbal health services.

We pulled up in a quieter, more suburban area in front of a large building complex still under construction. We joined Dr. Ejiwunmi and toured the facility. It was to be a 200-or-so-beds, traditional maternity hospital, paid for by the doctor himself, and to be run by one or two of his former herbalist trainees. After half an hour, some ten former students of his arrived and he suggested we begin the meeting with a prayer. We all stood and bowed our heads. According to Alhaji's translation later, the doctor called upon Allah to bless the meeting and to help our efforts to cooperate with physicians. He then asked me to explain my interest in Nigerian healers. I went through my spiel, with Alhaji translating into Yoruba: Health for All by the Year 2000 (a UN slogan) was possible only if we all cooperate. Traditional healers do some things better; doctors do some other things better. Nigerians need health care that combines the best of both traditional and modern medicine (I was quoting King Sobhuza II of Swaziland).

The doctor and some of his old graduates then took turns agreeing with my observations and sentiments. One English-speaking healer told me directly that he and his colleagues have always been in favor of learning more about modern medicine and collaborating with doctors. They were already referring patients to hospitals when they thought a Western-type cure was needed. The doctor asked me to say a prayer to close our meeting.

I realized my findings about the Yoruba were at odds with that Columbia University survey data. The survey purported to show where Yoruba women in Oyo State have babies, almost always in "modern maternities" or simply at home with the inexpert assistance of a mother-in-law or another minimally-skilled woman who might be available. Hence the survey director concluded that Yorubas just don't have TBAs (Traditional Birth Attendants), despite all the prior evidence for them, and so a pile of USAID money that had been earmarked for primary health care training of TBAs in Oyo State was diverted to training female "volunteers" in the "community" who were willing to learn about midwifery, primary health care, and family planning.

Why had the Columbia University survey gone so wrong?

The American who designed it was evidently looking for *female* TBAs, just as I was at first, often calling them "midwives." Yet most Yoruba birth attendants seemed to be men, a proportion nearly unheard of elsewhere on the continent. For one thing, many Africans believe menstrual, and other female fluids, are mystically polluting to men. Now, of course, Africans tend to be polite and they often don't like to contradict foreign experts or their scientifically constructed questionnaires, so it was easy for the Columbia survey to ignore the males and end up with misleading information.

If I've learned nothing else in my African research experience, it's that there's no substitute for just sitting down and having friendly, informal conversations with ordinary people and local experts in a position to know what you are trying to find out. This insight would serve me well in Uganda a few years later, when I seem to have been one of the first outsiders to realize that HIV incidence was declining—long before there were nearly enough condoms in-country to attribute that decline to them (as if that were a valid indicator!). This initial perception would shape the rest of my professional career.

My findings—gained through informal methods—also suggested that traditional sector people assisted most Yoruba deliveries, whether they were herbalist ob/gyn specialists who provided pre- and post-natal care, or specialists who limited their practice to delivery itself.

Flight to Benue

Soon I was off to Benue State. The Lagos airport this time was quiet and sparsely populated. I got my boarding pass without delay or bribe, and found myself with two hours to kill.

After a while, I wandered over to a group of men of indeterminate nationality who were carrying exotic instrument cases. I asked one if he was holding an *oud*, the lute of the Arab world. He looked surprised and an older companion said, "Yes, an oud. We are Lebanese musicians on our way to Kano to perform. You are what nationality?"

Oops, I thought. They're going to be Druze militiamen or other America-haters. They'll slip a bomb on my plane. I thought of saying I was Canadian or better yet Swiss, but I found myself mumbling that I was American. I tried to soften the blow by adding that I played a little mandolin.

"Ah, American," exclaimed the older man. "We played a job in Detroit in 1967!"

The apparent bandleader invited me to try to play the *oud*, which he said was made in 1906 and was worth $5,000. As I carefully picked up the instrument, the Lebanese musicians all clapped politely. I fooled around a bit and tried to make what I thought were Middle Eastern sounds, using a little of Jessie McReynolds' mandolin cross-picking style that I learned from bluegrass musicians.

No clapping when I finished. The bandleader thanked me and politely explained that the fretless instrument was meant to be played in quarter-tones.

Later, after I went through the surprisingly relaxed security check, I spied a pretty young lady who looked American. I sat near her and struck up a conversation. She was a CUSA Canadian volunteer teacher in a small village in remote Gongola State in far eastern Nigeria, bordering Cameroon.

She told me she had been teaching English there for a year and a half and was the only White person in the area. I told her about my project and soon we were discussing the prevalence of abortion and female circumcision in her area. She believed both were higher than reported. Women in her area didn't know why foreigners opposed clitoridectomies; they remove the clitoris—or part of it—in young girls who don't even remember this later, "and they never even miss it." she said quoting her informants. This is not the kind of casual conversation I might have with a stranger in a US airport, where the topic of clitoris seldom arises.

The flight to Makurdi in Benue and the taxi to the Makurdi Plaza Hotel went without problem. At lunch in the hotel, I was seated with two Ibos who worked in town. The Ibo are sometimes called "The Jews of Africa" because of their intelligence and business acumen. They were the ones who attempted secession from Nigeria in the Biafran Civil War of 1967–70. Now one man was telling the other that the students in the anti-US demonstrations were either ignorant or hypocritical. "They know Qaddafi threatens Nigeria. They know he is meddling in Chad and that he is a terrorist, yet they call for resignations of our leaders who remind them of these things! *Students*!"

I got into the conversation at this point, and expressed interest in the extent of anti-American feeling after the Libya bombing. One man told me he received his master's in journalism from East Texas University and now works for the Nigeria news service. They both said there was no real anti-Americanism among most Nigerians over the recent incident, since most Nigerians knew Qaddafi was a troublemaker. Otherwise, the journalist asked, why would he be involved in all the crisis spots of the world, from Northern Ireland to Nicaragua?

Since these educated Ibos seemed pro-Reagan, I asked their views on his support of Jonas Savimbi's UNITA right wing in Angola. The one not educated in Texas quickly denounced this action, saying that the Angolan government was elected fairly and Savimbi was just a poor loser who went running to South Africa. If he managed to overthrow the government and run Angola himself, South Africa would have established a pro-Pretoria, apartheid-accommodating regime in a neighboring state. South Africa would then likely try to "destabilize" other neighboring countries.

On the other hand, the speaker continued, when Zimbabwean leader Robert Mugabe's recently moved to exclude Whites from Parliament, he was violating a promise he made to White Rhodesians at independence. This act would make South African Whites feel their fears were justified— fears that any agreement they arrived at with a Black majority government in South Africa would sooner or later make them a relatively powerless minority.

He Claims He Can Treat Any Disease

After lunch I met with two doctors from the Benue State Ministry of Health, whom I shall call Dr. A and Dr. B. I first met privately with Dr. A and told him I had come to Benue because of the innovative program of training TBAs in community-based distribution of contraceptives started by the Planned Parenthood Federation of Nigeria (PPFN) and the Ministry. I asked if the Ministry would now be interested in expanding its program to include traditional healers. And what would they think about having short awareness seminars in family planning for local leaders?

Dr. A was quick to answer: "We are working with TBAs because we know what they are up to. We don't work with traditional healers because we don't know what they do. They are secretive and some of their practices are very doubtful."

I told him about the program for training healers in Swaziland, and how we tried to change any "doubtful practices." Dr. A looked skeptical. "In the old days the traditional healer just practiced out of his home. Now he's building clinics and admitting patients and acting just like a doctor, except that he claims he can treat any disease."

I had been about to comment on how keen healers were to learn more modern medical practices. But I realized that was precisely what made doctors like Dr. A uneasy. He'd rather traditional healers not undergo skill upgrading because even without it, healers were competing successfully with Western-trained doctors, judging by their patient caseloads.

While I paused, Dr. A went on to say that "in principle" he was in favor of finding a way to "use" traditional healers. He said he'd like to begin by having healers submit their so-called medicines for proper pharmacological analysis. I heard this a lot.

Dr. B showed up at this point and, after I repeated my project idea, we made plans to meet the next day with the permanent Secretary of Health along with local Planned Parenthood Federation of Nigeria officers and others involved in the ongoing training of TBAs.

Just before sundown, I had a cab drive me to the large, sprawling market on the other side of Makurdi. I like to get a feel for a place by walking through the local market and absorbing sights, sounds, smells, impressions. I also kept an eye open for interesting handicrafts, namely old, authentic, not-made-for-tourists artifacts.

The next morning I had a key meeting. I met with the Benue State Minister of Health as well as with Drs. A and B, and state PPFN volunteers Phoebe and Felix. After hours of discussion, we agreed on a plan. We would hold workshops, but they would not initially focus on traditional healers since the State or Federal Ministries of Health did not officially recognize them. Instead, we'd have a workshop for "community health opinion leaders" which would include healers as well as TBAs and chiefs. The workshop would encourage two-way communication: We would learn what healers and others were doing in rural communities, and they would learn what we had to say about family planning and primary health care.

If traditional healers wished to integrate our advice into their practice, we'd move to phase two: workshops specifically for healers. We'd treat these as pilots before going statewide. Everybody was cautious, largely I think because of the fears and objections Dr. A expressed at every juncture.

At one point in our discussions, someone mentioned the Traditional and Medical Practitioners Association (TMPA) of Benue. This apparently jogged Dr. A's memory because he said his organization had sent a representative to meet me. As a matter of fact, a traditional healer had been sitting outside A's office for the past couple of hours. I asked that the man be invited in at once.

The author with Nigerian healers, 1988

This healer was named Apaki and he was a Tiv, a famous tribe in the anthropological canon. For one thing, they don't believe in an afterlife for ancestral spirits. He spoke passable English, and I asked a few questions such as whether Benue healers would like to work cooperatively with modern doctors. Apaki said the TMPA had always wanted to. Felix inquired if different factions claimed to represent the TMPA of Benue, as the permanent Secretary of Health had suggested. Apaki denied it, saying there was only one TMPA with organizations in every local government authority, representing every tribe in the State.

Dr. A and a nurse then asked Apaki questions which I thought were impolite under the circumstances. For example, the nurse curtly asked Apaki how much he charged for delivering a baby. Apaki seemed a bit embarrassed by this directness, but when pressed, said he charged about 5 to 10 naira (less than $5–10 USD in 1988). The nurse sniffed skeptically, then looked away without commenting. Since Apaki seemed to be getting uncomfortable, I thanked him for coming to meet us and fixed an appointment for me to meet with TMPA officers the next day. At this point Dr. A informed Apaki, "We don't need you any longer. You may leave." Felix, bless him, made a friendly remark in Tiv to Apaki as he slipped out the door.

The nurse then said, "The traditional midwives are a lot easier to train. We got them to admit they don't know anything. The traditional healers probably won't ever admit this!"

And I am thinking, "Why should they?"

The next morning, Felix and I met with eleven members of the Traditional Medical Practitioners Association: three herbalist birth specialists, two diviner-mediums, two general herbalists, one bonesetter, one Christian faith healer with Bible in hand, one herbal preparer and supplier, and one female birth attendant. Before the meeting formally commenced, the Ad Hoc chairman (as he was introduced) showed me around the TMPA Benue headquarters, actually a traditional clinic with evidence of modern influences here and there. They had laid out a variety of herbal medicines for Felix and me to inspect. The chairman described the therapeutic purpose of each one: madness, convulsions, malaria, river blindness, ensuring a male baby. On the wall hung framed photographs of respected Benue healers, a UNICEF poster urging mothers to have their children vaccinated, and a certificate of having attended a seminar on how to use oral rehydration salts, dated the prior year. A copy of Warner's *Where There Is No Doctor* lay on a table.

Like my meeting with healers in Lagos, ours started with a prayer, this time a Christian prayer. They asked me to say something about my purpose of meeting with the Benue TMPA. I gave a ten-minute speech outlining my ideas, goals, and motives, ending with observations about the barriers in the way of modern-traditional cooperation. Several healers then took turns making comments, a few directly to me in English, but most using Tiv, Igala, or Adoma, with multilingual Felix or the chairman translating. The healers were unanimous in their desire to work cooperatively with Western-trained medical practitioners. I asked about the claim that healers tend to be secretive and disinclined to work even with other healers.

The chairman replied: "We don't want to be secretive anymore. In olden days, fathers taught their sons about medicines and how to heal. What happens if there are no sons? What happens if the sons are not interested in learning the wisdom of their fathers? The information will be lost forever. We know that we need to share our ideas and make our knowledge public if we will achieve health for all by the year 2000." A perfect answer for this occasion!

The subject turned to family planning. The faith healer was the first to comment: "God is angry with us for having too many children indiscriminately and irresponsibly." I asked one of the non-English speaking older healers his opinion. After some thought he replied, "It is better to have a few productive children—even as few as one—than to have twenty unproductive or bad offspring." I looked forward to quoting this statement directly to the Population Crisis Committee. I could already envision it in one of their pamphlets.

I told the healers about the plan the State Ministry of Health had agreed to, and said that their association would probably be asked to help select healers to participate in the workshops. They all seemed enthusiastic. One elder told me that with enough advance notice, the Association could arrange its own transportation, and bring as many healers to the workshops as we wanted.

They were on board with the plan.

The Reality of Lagos

I arrived back in Lagos the following afternoon after a problem-free flight. I'd learned about saving a lot of money by flagging down group taxis on the street, the same yellow taxis I was warned against my first day in Lagos: "They will harm you and rob your money and throw you by the roadside!" The dangers of traveling around Lagos were greatly exaggerated. I felt as safe here as in Washington, and from my trips to Benue and Oyo States, and from Nigerians I'd come to know, the further from Lagos you went, the safer you were. That would change with the rise of radical Islamic terrorism, still far away in 1985.

I had taken to going over to the Federal Palace Hotel around 6 p.m. to drink a beer and watch the sun set over the harbor. It had a gazebo-style bar built out on the water, with an outside perimeter area lined with chairs. I'd sit there facing the sea and hear a local band playing African music about 100 meters away (making the decibel level about right), while the sky turned shades of crimson and then deep purple.

Nigeria has countless brands of beer, all of them good when served ice-cold. The bartender at the gazebo was the one with a brother at Morgan State University. Ever since I started going there a few days before my trip to Benue, he greeted me with a tall, cold, green bottle of whatever beer was on ice. Sometimes we talked, but more often I sat alone and watched the gorgeous sky. Really, Lagos wasn't half-bad. True, there were traffic problems and you might need a little dash to get something done, but I had expected to find a hostile, crime-ridden city where any foreigner was easy prey. Instead, I felt safe walking even the slum areas like Mushin. In Benue, Felix and I talked about the negative image Americans and Europeans have of Nigeria. We only hear seamy stories of crime, drug smuggling, runaway inflation, government corruption, and *coups d'etat*. We hear little good, such as the friendliness and hospitality of Nigerians, the beauty and diversity of some of the land, the fascinating mixture of languages and "tribe," and the great views like mine at the gazebo bar. Someone needs to do serious PR on behalf of Nigeria's image in the West. Nigeria's population is expected to surpass that of the US in 2045. My father, by the way, and with my mother's blessing, hoped later in his life that I would take on population issues in Africa (as he did in Asia, after retirement). So I was doing what they both wanted me to do by this stage of my life. Therefore I am not sure where my lack of self-confidence comes from–or what keeps it going.

A Spectrum of Amulets

The next day, I was back with my driver Alhaji and ready to visit "Dr. Piles," the herbalist I met last week who takes his name from a special cure he has for hemorrhoids. We arrived at his compound in the Mushin slum. Since I wanted to pick his brains at some length, I thought it fair that I give him a little business. So after we sat down in his consultation room, I asked the old man if he could make me an *owo* (protective amulet) to keep me safe during travel. I would be especially interested in one that would keep me from blowing up in an airplane. Dr. Piles pondered this for a while, then told me I'd better have one owo for travel around my own country and another for foreign lands, since the latter has different hazards. He would make me two amulets, plus prepare two special medicines for me to take internally that would further empower the amulets. One caution: the amulets would lose potency if they came near a human corpse.

I agreed to return next Tuesday for my protection. It would all cost me about $12. I sensed, and got confirmation later, that I was getting a bargain rate. Alhaji told me Dr. Piles felt honored that I had come to him, and that I was trying to further cooperation between doctors and traditional healers. Such protection would have cost me much more in Swaziland.

As we drove off, I asked Alhaji to show me his protective amulets. In his glove compartment were three strange devices made of cloth, skin, feathers, beads, and other materials, each one different. One was to protect the car against thieves and bad drivers; another was to protect Alhaji from irate drivers who might want to punch him out. Road rage. "If anyone strikes me while this owo is near, his arm will swell up to a terrible size and it will not go down unless I release it. If he goes to a doctor and tries to operate on the arm, he will die at once."

I asked if most drivers carry these kinds of amulets.

"Of course, most of them do. Driving in Lagos is very dangerous!"

Belief in owo seemed to keep the kamikaze-style driving in Lagos from resulting in physical fights. Drivers, including Alhaji, were forever yelling insults and accusations at each other, and even threatening to get out of vehicles to fight. But I never saw a fight break out, and Alhaji admitted he never actually got in one. He said people sense his powerful owo and back off. I thought of Matawais who had been inoculated with snake venom.

Snakes sensed this and didn't bother to sink their fangs into the vaccinated, I was assured.

After I'd met so many doctors who adhered dogmatically to Western positivism and the scientific worldview—at least the current orthodox one—I found myself wondering if they weren't missing something important. Whether or not metaphysical forces actually operate in the world, open-mindedness to all possibilities at least predisposes the mind to learn about things beyond the narrow confines of current scientific paradigms. And who knows? Some degree of belief in things that are scientifically inexplicable, whether we call it magic or religion, may actually be a precondition for cultivating any psychic powers that might inhere in the human mind.

The Population Crisis Committee was happy with my work and it handed over my project design, and me, to Pathfinder, a Boston-based NGO (non-governmental organization) that implements family planning and reproductive health programs with USAID funding, all over the world. PCC is a lobbying organization that doesn't actually implement programs. Under Pathfinder, we started collaborative programs, with traditional healers and birth attendants on the one hand, and paid government health workers on the other. The program in Benue State was still going on many years later, under different funding.

The Voice in the Gourd

Let me mention an experience I had in Nigeria on one of my later trips (1988). The two programs I started a year or so earlier were up and running, in Lagos and Benue States. Keys McManus, the population and health officer at USAID, told me one day that she wanted to visit one of the healers "trained" in our workshops. Soon after, she and I drove a few hours from Lagos to make a field visit to Dr.—more precisely, TDr, for "traditional doctor"—Ejiwunmi in what looked to outsiders like a medical clinic, complete with female nurses in starched, white uniforms. Keys might have been a little disappointed, probably because he didn't fit an exotic witch doctor image. For the first several minutes, TDr Ejiwunmi seemed happy to impress her with his elaborate, modern-appearing operation. I am pretty sure we didn't tell Ejiwunmi anything about the complicated history of developing this project. I mean, why would he care?

He invited us into his special divination room. Okay, things were now looking up. What went on in this sterile-looking place? There were only the three of us in the spacious room, with Keys and I sitting on one side and TDr E. on the other. He then uncorked—if that is the word—a special gourd decorated with beads and feathers, situated against a third wall, and with no one near it.

Presently, a thin, high, mysterious voice began to call out, as if from a faraway place, such as in a telephone booth, underwater, door closed. At first, it seemed unintelligible, but it gradually took shape and we could make out the sounds. It was crying out, "Keys McManus... Keys McManus... Keys *McManus!*" Keys and I looked at each other with astonishment. Was our diviner-healer projecting his voice somehow, through ventriloquism? His lips didn't seem to move. We couldn't remember introducing Keys by her full name—that would have seemed very foreign to a Nigerian; we think we just told Ejiwunmi that "Miss Keys" was the director of national health programs, for a branch of the US government, based in Lagos.

Next, the faraway voice began to describe accurately the background of the project, to work with healers and involve them with Nigerian national programs. In fact, there had been considerable opposition to launching this project, and Ejiwunmi (or the spirit) somehow knew much about the background drama. Now, maybe Keys and I were witness to a parlor trick of the sort that Uri Geller performed back when he was bending spoons by mental concentration, before attempts by professional magician The Amazing Randi challenged this trick as mere sleight of hand. But I was impressed, and Keys was sold—truly enthralled—by an approach I had been pushing for years. How could the TDr have known about the background struggles to get this particular project designed and funded? The spirit of Keys McManus, at least the high-pitched, reedy voice we heard, revealed some of these particulars. On the drive back to Lagos city, Keys's excitement only grew as she thought about the epistemological implications of what we had both witnessed. She told me the US Ambassador happened to be throwing a cocktail party on his spacious back lawn that same evening, and if we hurried, we could make it before it was over. We *must* go at once and tell the ambassador what we had witnessed that eventful day.

Well, we showed up looking ragged from our field trip, having driven down dusty roads, plus we were dressed incorrectly for a semi-formal party. Keys walked right over to the Ambassador and interrupted his conversation with, as I recall, a visiting congressman. I stood to one side, since I had not been introduced, plus we probably needed more time to discuss what might have only been ventriloquism, and make logical guesses about its knowledge of our project's background. And now I was hearing Keys trying to mimic the voice in the gourd: "Keys McManus... Keys McManus... Keys McManus!"

As I recall, the ambassador seemed to think the population officer had either had too much to drink or had flipped her lid.

It would be almost another 20 years before I next encountered Keys McManus. I was preparing for an assignment in Southeast Asia, and we were all seated around a table at USAID Headquarters. But I had a chance to speak privately with her for a few moments. She told me that during her remaining years in Nigeria, she had funded a mini-family planning project that relied on traditional healers, and she paid for this out of her own private funds. Meaning TDr Ejizunmi and I had sold at least one USAID official on the approach.

I should mention that by 2021, Nigeria was being torn apart by Muslim extremists (Boka Haram) and kidnappers, especially in the northeast, as well as rebellion in the southeast. Parts of the country appear ungovernable. Nigeria might split into two countries, the predominantly Muslim north and the predominantly Christian south, as happened in Sudan. So as bad as the country was when I was there in the latter 1980s, things became worse. As would be the case in Palestine, discussed further on.

The Apparition in Santo Domingo

During roughly that time, I had another paranormal experience. I'd known Wayne since our friendship in high school in Korea. He later became a geologist and worked with the US Geological Survey. Then he discovered he had cancer. His health deteriorated as the disease progressed, and he underwent chemotherapy and radiation. They let him take home a kind of liquid morphine as well as methadone tablets. I don't know if this was standard treatment or if it had to do with Wayne's wife being a newly trained doctor.

We'd take walks while he was still ambulatory, and later we'd just sit around his house and talk about suffering, the human condition, and the possibility of life after death. I enjoyed the intimate conversations and self-disclosure we got into. Men don't ordinarily risk that kind of openness with one another. The morphine cocktails he occasionally offered me were stronger than anything in the opiate class I had tried before, but it didn't seem comradely to turn them down. Curiously, Wayne never felt euphoric on these; they just relieved his pain to a small extent.

One day we were walking near Wayne's home and talking once again about the possibilities of an afterlife. Wayne said in essence, "If all this damned treatment doesn't work, I tell ya what: I will find a way to get a message to you and tell you if there *is* an afterlife. And remember: we all die, all of us. It just looks like I'll be in the next life a little ahead of you."

I saw no point in denying that Wayne might soon know one way or the other, so instead of offering platitudes, I told him that such a message would be the greatest gift a friend could ever bestow. I'd be waiting for it if he left this life before I did.

Wayne's condition grew worse. Once they flew him up to Boston to try Interferon treatment, which some researchers thought might be a miracle cure for cancer. I went with him and stayed with him while he was in the hospital (or in a hotel nearby). After a couple of days on Interferon, Wayne told me might prefer to die than spend another day on it. It was his worst experience to that point. I noticed he was by then passing blood in his urine, although he denied it when his doctor asked him about it. Anyway, we came back to Washington, discouraged.

Then in November 1987, on the same day I arrived in the Dominican Republic for a short assignment, word reached me that he had died. I was not surprised. On my last visit to the Virginia hospital, I had a strong feeling that I would never see him again. After I said goodbye, my eyes filled with tears as I walked down the hospital hallway, averting my face from passersby.

That same night, I had a vision of Wayne floating in my hotel room in Santo Domingo, as I lay in bed contemplating my loss. There he was, I could *see* him. This couldn't have been happening, so I got out of bed and went to the bathroom and looked at myself in the mirror. Had this been a dream? No, because I had just turned off the light a few minutes before, and I was certain I had not yet gone to sleep. No drugs or alcohol in my system.

So I returned to bed, and a few minutes later Wayne's apparition —a less clinical term than hallucination—reappeared. I made a deliberate decision not to be frightened. Instead, I sent a thought-message to him, something like, "What's happening? You are supposed to be dead!"

He replied, or somehow conveyed to me, that he just wanted me to know that he was no longer in pain, that he was now at peace, and that he was just breaking the rules this one final time, since he was not supposed to be there communicating with me. Instead, he was supposed to be going somewhere else, right away. He reminded me that our friendship had its origin in breaking rules at our high school in Korea. He then communicated that he had to be leaving me, but he would try to find another way to contact me at a later time.

He asked if I had a modem. This was 1987, and I wondered—or asked— if it was a device related to the new Internet? Wayne said yes, and that I should get one and he would try to communicate with me again that way.

Then he was gone. I got out of bed at once, and again went to the hotel bathroom and looked at myself in the mirror. This was *not* a dream; I told my reflection. I had never been asleep. There had been no break in consciousness. And a modem! I didn't even know about these things. Wayne had been an early adopter of new technology. For example, he bought a CD player before anyone else I knew. And I supposed he was already using modems and email when he died.

I finally got a modem several years later and... well, no messages.

The Ineffable

This might be a place to pause and take note of the several supernatural, spiritual, metaphysical, mystical, or PSI experiences (as they say in parapsychology) I have related. When they first started, I had no vocabulary with which to describe them, nor framework with which to try to understand them. William James, in his 1902 *Varieties of Religious Experiences*, wrote that those altered states share certain qualities. One is ineffability: they are difficult to describe let alone explain. Another is transience: they quickly fade away. Upon learning about my ex-fiancée's wedding date through an astral message from Monica (not recounted in this book, due to space limitations), I was convinced this inexplicable revelation would change my life forever, if proven true. The date was proven accurate yet it didn't change my life. The more time that passes after such an experience, the harder it is to believe it actually happened.

But for a glorious moment, a person is transported to a non-ordinary, altered state of reality, or consciousness, to a superior realm or reality, often described as beyond human comprehension. These experiences are invariably positive, comparable to psychologist Maslow's Peak or Oceanic Experiences, and they are associated with positive emotions: joy, elation, awe, ecstasy. They elevate a person outside the realm of ordinary reality.

In James's synthesis, people in these states often feel like they are in the grip of a higher power. They often feel "one with God" or the universe, and the experiencers might suddenly be given profound insights that make everything else seem trivial by comparison. Yet these states fade away (that pesky old transience). In recent times, and in the English language, we have the example of Bill Wilson, whose classic peak experience while drying out in New York's Towns Hospital led to his co-founding of Alcoholics Anonymous. Probably millions of people have read about Bill W's experience by now, and many have probably wondered why they couldn't have a similar one. Such events provide deep insights and revelations inaccessible by every day "discursive" thought. They typically cannot be sought—they just *happen* to people. Of course, people might deliberately seek them with psychoactive drugs or alcohol. James himself experimented with nitrous oxide to achieve or mimic a mystical state of mind. While on this drug, he wrote "Oh my God. Oh God. Oh God!" I wonder how much more words would have failed him had he tried LSD. Ineffability to the 100th power.

I completely agree with the observation about the non-transferability of peak experiences or altered states of consciousness. Nothing I could tell another person will have any real impact, whether or not the person believes in the subjective truth of the experience I am trying to convey. James himself wrote that the quality of a mystical experience "must be experienced directly; it cannot be imparted or transferred to others." If I may paraphrase my brother Mark: "I believe that these experiences happened to you, but nothing like this has ever happened to me, so I don't know what to make of your experiences. I have no framework in which to place or understand them. But I am fascinated to hear about them."

Chapter 9
Tanzania: HIV-Infected Sex Workers
and "This Men Business"

Tanzania is a nation of natural spectacles. It borders three of Africa's Great Lakes: Victoria, the world's second largest freshwater lake; Lake Tanganyika, the world's second oldest and second deepest; and Lake Malawi, home to more fish species than any other lake. It contains Africa's highest peak, Mt. Kilimanjaro. Within its borders lie Nogorogoro Crater, a hundred square miles of classic African wildlife, and Olduvai Gorge, where researchers first found some of the oldest ancestors of our species.

Politically, Tanzania was then a kind of spectacle too, in an experimental sense. In many ways it was a fairly typical late-1900s African country in that, after ridding itself of the yoke of colonialism, it opted for a Marxist path to development. Its first president, Edinburgh University-educated Julius Nyerere, crafted a unique African version of Marxist-Leninism he called Ujamaa, which loosely translates as "pulling together," or "cooperative economics." He promoted agriculture via "participatory development" based on communal or collective farming. One of the nation's challenges had been the dispersal of its settlements. It's harder to provide services or form large joint enterprises when people are spread far apart. Nyerere, well intentioned, forced "peasants" into centralized settlements or collective farms. He justified the policy by reasoning that the provision of schools, clinics, and protected water supplies would become more cost-effective and logistically feasible, and services such as agricultural extension and literacy education would improve. But social engineering so easily backfires. "Villagization" often led to social strife, witchcraft accusations, violence, and other forms of conflict. It led to faster depletion of environmental resources in much of the country. Moreover, as populations concentrate, poor sanitation and contaminated water increase the incidence of diseases, and that happened with villagization and, indeed, throughout urbanizing Africa.

Once again I recalled Mr. Hervey's warning about the fatal flaw in Marxism: It tries to subdue self-interest in human nature. Before I arrived in Tanzania, most experts agreed that Nyerere's Ujamaa failed to meet his goal of creating successful agricultural and other cooperatives. To borrow from an article I wrote with Ray Isley, reasons included: a "natural individualism" that resists collectivism; ill-advised agricultural policies; failure to emancipate or sufficiently empower Tanzanian women; a refusal of bureaucrats and rural elites to share power with peasants; corrupt leadership, and the need to *coerce* peasants into villages. There was a one-party system, businesses were nationalized, the government became the largest employer in the country, private enterprise was squashed, government bureaucrats often went unpaid and had to take bribes to motivate livelihoods—you get the idea.

Despite the failure of African socialism, Nyerere put on a brave face as he left office and said if he had it all to do over, he would not change much. At the same time, as his *New York Times* obit reminds us, Tanzania enjoys one of the highest rates of literacy and primary school enrollment on the continent. It has avoided the civil wars and tribal conflicts that plague many other countries. Nyerere defeated the brutal dictator Idi Amin in neighboring Uganda, although this action was an added burden on the Tanzanian economy. He also made Swahili the national language of Tanzania, the most linguistically diverse country in East Africa. That helped engender a greater sense of national identity than in other African nations of similar size and diversity in 1990.

Nyerere retired and allowed a peaceful transfer of power, an act that brought him widespread admiration in Africa and abroad. The constitution of Tanzania was amended in 1992 to allow for multiple political parties, and three years later the first multiparty elections were held.

That is the bird's-eye view, the important context, but on the ground you always see much more complexity, a vivid motley of details and interactions, and surprises everywhere.

Dar

After I climbed into a cab to report to work on my first morning, the driver informed me, "I have accepted Jesus Christ as my personal savior. And you, sir?"

I had been told cab drivers in Dar es Salaam didn't speak English, so my mental dialogue gears were not engaged. This city is said to be more than 50% Muslim, so I figured I should express positive reinforcement, if not solidarity with a man who may have converted to the religion of my forefathers. I told him I was saved too. He said, "God bless you," and off we went.

My hotel, the Agip, must have been the one for literate tourists. In front of other hotels in Dar, one found trinket sellers. But, in front of the Agip, one saw itinerant booksellers who set up and tore down their stalls every day, loading and unloading hundreds of books, a few of a technical or scholarly nature. Most were in English or Swahili, although a few Robert Ludlum spy novels were available in German. The men hawking these books knew their trade. I picked up a volume on political economy, followed by another on the history of Africa, and within a minute or two a dozen other books on the same subjects appeared from neighboring stalls. I quicky found one on traditional medicine, based on a study conducted in Dar in the early 1970s. That seemed dated until I remembered that the early 70s is precisely when I did my own dissertation fieldwork.

The next day I again visited the bookstalls. A teen-aged boy remembered my interest in things cultural, so he offered me issues of a scholarly journal called *Tanganyika Notes and Records*, which aimed "to promote the study of ethnology, history, geography, natural history and kindred sciences." They dated back to the 1950s, although some contained ethnology that seemed to hail from an even earlier era, such as "The Defensive Measures of Certain Tribes in Northeastern Tanganyika," by H. Fosbrooke, M.A. At the end of each earlier issue, I saw a list of all the subscribers and their addresses, and perusal of them revealed quite a bit. Almost all the names were European, and others were connected with colonial government offices elsewhere in British Africa like Nyasaland or the Gold Coast. A few subscribers appeared to be nostalgic former District Commissioners who retired to spots like the Isle of Man, or Aberystwith, Wales. The missionary White Fathers seemed particularly fond of subscribing.

The journal sold for seven-and-a-half Tanganyikan shillings in 1953, one-and-a-half cents by today's exchange rate but, of course, bought more then. Local advertisers partially supported it. My favorite ad from 1953 was from BSA motorcycles, featuring a fine drawing of a severe, blond, colonial-looking woman atop a sleek 250cc machine, flashing a few decorous inches of dark-stockinged calves. Miss Johnson, my First Form teacher at Stockholm's English School in 1953 might have posed for it.

I read myself to sleep with this delightful journal, drifting off with images in my head from Ngulu folk tales, and wondering what the High-God of the Wasonjo might think of USAID-funded consultants puttering around his ancient land. Neolithic pastoralists expanded into Tanzania between 3,000 and 2,000 years ago, encountering Paleolithic folk already there.

The Road to Morogoro

I met up with my colleague Anne and we headed out to the field, to Morogoro, then a city of 300,000 about 200 km (125 miles) west of Dar es Salaam. Soon our Russian jeep started overheating and sputtering. Anne asked if I were mechanically inclined. I said no, I'm more philosophically inclined. Anne herself could do many, many things, but not, alas, fix cars or even diagnose their difficulties. In fact, she seemed impressed that I knew how to check the oil, and that I understood cars had something called a water pump (how manly that made me feel!). For the next hour or so we had to stop along the highway just about every kilometer to scoop muddy water out of a ditch and refill the radiator. But why did it need so much water?

Once, a couple of lean youthful Maasai warriors with distended earlobes glided up on old bicycles and asked if they could help. Later, a pair of identical-looking young men came walking down the road wearing a brand-new pair of shiny black-and-red sneakers. One wore the left one, the other wore the right one, while both of their other feet were bare. Under less trying circumstances I might have photographed this tableau of camaraderie and mirror symmetry.

We eventually made it to a truck stop of the sort that has spread the HIV virus up and down the Rift Valley. The place apparently was much larger several years ago before people started dying of AIDS in large numbers. Truck drivers fear infection, so they now stop further down the road. Anne told me a recent serosurvey (the testing of blood) here determined that 80% of women of child-bearing age are HIV-infected.

We hung out and tried to figure out what to do with our Russian jeep. It seemed we had blown a gasket. There were no Russian gaskets at the truck stop. After much discussion, we decided to leave the jeep and hitch a ride to Morogoro on a big trailer-truck. With four of us squeezed together in the high cab, the driver worked up through countless gears until we were cruising toward the western foothills of the Uluguru mountains at about 45 miles per hour. The driver had stopped to buy clumps of a weed described as producing an amphetamine-like effect when chewed—the Tanzanian trucker's equivalent of little white pills our truckers take for "white line fever" over long hauls. These guys had to drive all the way to Dodoma. It would take at least until midnight at our speed and there was no time for sleep. Besides, they told us, the weed gives you a nice buzz. I declined a sample. God, though, a beer would have tasted nice.

We talked about AIDS. The drivers said they had lost many friends to the disease. He had recently learned that having syphilis or gonorrhea makes one susceptible to AIDS, and he asked us if that were true. Both said they recently married their girlfriends to settle down to monogamous relationships and avoid the killer disease. I silently hoped they were not already doomed.

Anne was unusual among foreign aid workers here in that she spoke near-fluent Swahili. I sat back and listened to her talk animatedly with our overstimulated driver and his buddy. I caught occasional words that were similar to correlates in Swazi, also a Bantu language. My problem is that I seem to possess only two language chambers in my brain: English and Foreign. With each successive foreign language I attempt to learn, any new word blots out its cognates in all previously-attempted tongues—at least until I am ready to use the new word in the latest language, whereupon all the unwanted equivalents from inappropriate lingos flood my brain.

The Infected Sex Workers

In Morogoro the next day, I was led through a slum compound where some 200 prostitutes (now that we donor organizations need their cooperation, we say "commercial sex workers," CSWs) took care of local men at 200 Tanzanian shillings (about 40 cents) a tumble. Only eight days earlier, I had been in New Orleans evaluating an inner-city AIDS program there. Crack-addicted women were providing oral sex for only $2. The price had recently been driven down by the ever-increasing number of women willing to do anything to get money to support their habits. Young females preyed on old men in public housing projects on the day their social security checks arrived, hoping to trade sex for a few dollars. Some old guys who had had intercourse were getting infected with HIV. Women into shooting heroin could borrow needles from elderly diabetic gents and infect them that way, blood-to-blood.

Westerners often use "prostitution" loosely and inaccurately in reference to Africa. Much female sexual behavior in Africa can best be understood as strategies for economic survival and adaptation to patterns of male dominance in low-income countries. However, these Tanzanian women were pretty close to the stereotype familiar in the West: They sell their bodies for short-time sex, at a fixed price that someone else negotiates. They live and work in little alcoves that divide up long, barrack-like mud huts. I'm told that most afternoons and evenings, local men line up outside the huts waiting their turns. Truck drivers consider these women low-class and diseased, and prefer to park their rigs and "party" outside of town.

The truckers are right: almost all the women are infected with multiple sexually transmitted ailments, including HIV. Many have died of AIDS. My guide said the women, who are from the Haya tribe far to the west, at first thought they were being bewitched. Now they had pretty much accepted that they were in a deadly epidemic transmitted by sexual intercourse. But they had no other way to earn money to feed themselves and their children. None had any support from a man, unlike some women at truck stops along the highway who sometimes developed a long-term relationship with a driver.

My guide worked with a local female psychiatrist who had started a local Non-Governmental Organization—that magic acronym, NGO, which was starting to attract donor support back then—to assist the CSWs, among other causes. Our project would help the NGO aid these benighted souls. Commercial sex workers were a largely unstudied subculture in Tanzania and, indeed, in Africa—at least in the scientific literature. Our project sought to develop an information base for developing an effective STD prevention and control program, including counseling services for CSWs. In the final fieldwork phase, a Tanzanian doctor specializing in STDs would do physical exams, followed by laboratory analyses and treatment of the STDs that we had weapons against, such as syphilis, gonorrhea, and chlamydia. This phase would be available to all CSWs in the study area. I was glad we'd added this worthy component. Usually, researchers just grab the data and run, without interacting clinically with their "subjects."

After I walked around the compound this morning, some women summoned a man with a camera and asked if I would mind if they posed for a picture with me. In fact, would I just hang on a few minutes while they dressed up in better clothes for the shot? Africans from all walks of life have a highly-developed sense of occasion. After all, they learned that I had come all the way from America to learn about their lives, and the moment deserved to be recorded. Would we expect the same rection if a Tanzanian do-gooder, notebook in hand, showed up in a Washington whorehouse?

After my brief, pre-study tour of the research site, we had to get back to Dar, which meant dealing with the Russian jeep situation. We hired a car to drive us back to the truck stop. This part of the trip took only an hour and a quarter, half the time of last night in the truck. Our jeep was still there. After much discussion we agreed to pay 25,000 Tanzanian shillings to have another jeep tow our vehicle all the way to Dar es Salaam. However, when we saw that jeep we had profound doubts. It looked welded together from the parts of assorted, vintage military machinery, and it had to be jumpstarted. A team of young men produced a 5-foot long metal bar and linked the two jeeps. It seemed we were to be pulled, not towed. It occurred to me that if one jeep flipped over—say, if the wheels of the pulled jeep veered suddenly—we would both flip. So it didn't seem to matter which jeep Anne or I rode in. She chose her own, and I rode in the military surplus jeep.

The heating system of the pulling jeep was little better than that of our vehicle. We drove with the radiator cap off so that when steam began to obscure the driver's vision, we knew it was time to look for ditch or pond water to replenish the radiator. This meant stopping every 18 minutes or so. Travelling thus, we covered the 105 kilometers from the truck stop to Dar in a little over three hours. We never flipped, but my patience was wearing thin toward the end.

Little-Known Developing World Fact #3,017: It was cheaper to have a car towed between two Tanzanian towns than to rent a car or hire a taxi to cover the same distance.

Difficulties in Tanzania

Armed with my Swahili phrase book, I could now go forth into the world prepared for any number of eventualities. *Usifunge kitambaa jipu hili. Nitajaribu kumpa pumzi kwa mdomo!* (Do not cover this abscess. I will try mouth-to-mouth respiration!) Another useful phrase, perhaps from past days translates: "It is also declared that the principal means of production should be nationalized." I imagined a young recruit from Julius Nyerere's old TANU party pedaling up to a remote village on a bicycle and startling the elders with an announcement of the new economic order. Since the sentence contains "also," I wondered what this declaration is supposed to follow, perhaps "We are here to take your mothers and daughters."

In some ways it was harder to work in Tanzania than even in Mozambique. You could not make a phone call within the capital or between towns here. Of course, I could phone West Virginia if I so desired. Or Aberystwith, Wales. ("Sir, it has come to our attention that your subscription to *Tanganyika Notes and Records* is in arrears.") In Mozambique, right-wing RENAMO bandits kept the capital without electricity for a few hours every day, just to remind us they were still around. In Dar es Salaam, silted up hydroelectric dams, assisted probably by parastatal and statal inefficiency, keeps electricity off for even longer periods.

One thing I have noticed about African nations that follow the socialist path: They always lock the bathrooms in government buildings and make you ask for the keys, which are always hidden away. It's as true in Tanzania as in Mozambique or Ethiopia. Perhaps it's a control thing. Citizens with sphincters stretched tight as a bowstring are less likely to get uppity, democratic, anti-authoritarian ideas. It's humbling to have to ask for the toilet key every time you have to go. "It is also declared that the principal means of elimination should be nationalized."

The Promise of Herbs

Muhimbili Medical Center, Tanzania's major teaching and referral hospital, was teetering on the brink of financial collapse, according to recent newspaper headlines. The government was somehow not sufficiently overcoming cashflow problems to meet salaries and pay operating expenses. The last 100–200 yards of road to the entrance reverted from tar to dirt, and deep potholes crippled it. My cab driver complained that if he were driving a pregnant woman to the delivery ward, the delays and the bumpy ride would probably cause her to give birth in the cab.

Muhimbili has a Department of Traditional Medicine (DTM), just like some other countries in Africa. Mr. E.N. Mshiu, a Bachelor of Pharmacy yet called doctor, is the director. He gave me the standard rap: indigenous plant medicines are disappearing fast (he seemed to view traditional healers themselves as an endangered species); healers pull plants up from the roots rather than clip them, as more enlightened Chinese herbalists do; the DTM is trying to document and conserve useful plants, and it has set up "medicinal farms" in Arusha and three other locations to "cultivate plants known to be safe and medically useful." How much more the DTM could do if it had more money, vehicles, personnel! (I had noticed a nice Landcruiser with TRADITIONAL MEDICINE emblazoned on the side.)

Mr. Mshiu hedged when I asked him about herbal research in Tanzania. He found several ways to say that it can be justified, that medicinal herb teas are sold in Europe, that the government *should* promote certain herbs—but in fact it does not. It looked like the usual story: African governments could not officially promote plant medicines without a great deal of high-tech, expensive testing that they couldn't afford. If they made such tests voluntary, they would face charges of supporting a double standard by allowing "second-class medicine" for Africans, while the rest of the world enjoyed modern pharmaceuticals.

This didn't mean US and other large pharmaceutical companies weren't interested in discovering useful plant medicines. But they wanted profits. Mr. Mshiu told me of tantalizing preliminary findings from a small study in the Tanga district of Tanzania, an area reputed to have powerful traditional practitioners and medicines. Researchers created an experimental group and a control group. They gave the first a combination of herbs administered by a traditional healer as well as "modern drugs," including commonly available antibiotics and antifungals, but not AZT or other expensive antivirals. The control group received only the modern drugs. Of the 21 in the experimental group, one died within nine months and 20 "improved." Among the 27 in the control group, 14 died within nine months.

Improvement in the experimental group meant living longer, gaining weight, and scoring better in three clinical tests: hemoglobin, erythrocyte sedimentation rate, and white blood cell count (although the last tests were not done with all patients). The authors concluded, "Preliminary results indicate that taking the herbal regimen has a positive effect on people suffering from HIV disease." The methods and findings appeared in two papers jointly written by five authors—both Tanzanian and foreign—dated February 1991 and May 1991, and loaned to me by Mr. Mshui.

I wondered why the world had not heard of these findings. Even if all patients in the experimental group died soon after the May 1991 paper, the medicine still showed promise in slowing, or temporarily reversing, the ravages of the opportunistic infections of AIDS. Why hadn't AIDS activists dashed to the door of the Tanga healer who concocted the medicines? My colleagues Drs. Lwihula and Simali had never heard of this research, though both were active in the national fight against AIDS. Dr. Simali even worked in the Department of Traditional Medicine until 1992. All they could say was that Mr. Mshiu likes to keep things to himself.

An Empty City

Then it was Good Friday in Dar es Salaam. However Muslim the population of Dar might be, the city was pretty dead on Good Friday. Our research team members seemed to be the only folks working. We had a training session that morning during which we got into a productive discussion about STDs in Africa. I was again struck by the similarities among African beliefs related to spiritual matters, of which health is a part.

At lunch with Lwihula and Anne, I again mentioned the herbal AIDS treatment in Tanga district. Anne was surprised Lwihula hadn't heard of it. She told us that the study was continuing, and articles about it had appeared in the newspaper, and she in fact wrote one for her *Nature* column. The researchers wanted to move slowly and carefully, and the study director had departed, leaving Tanzania in a bad mood, but not because of any disillusionment with the herbal treatment. She said a number of infected local people were going to Tanga to get this cure. A local pharmacological researcher had "a pile" of this medicine, but had been "too busy" to analyze it, though researchers in Norway were doing so. The US sociologist on the team had an okay reputation, she said, as did the others, and the project may not have been better known because: a) the researchers were purposely keeping a low profile, and b) the press and the grapevine in Tanzania were full of stories of miraculous AIDS cures administered by traditional healers. Presumably the significance of a controlled study had been lost on many.

Late in the afternoon, I walked around the harbor. No one was around. I saw a fine old church that might have dated from the German colonial period. I heard African hymns from a block away, and approaching it, I saw it was so packed with worshipers that a hundred or so had to stand outside.

Later at the nearly deserted coffee shop of my hotel I spotted fish pie on the menu. Now fish pie in a developing nation was likely to be either very good or truly disgusting, with nothing in-between. I asked a pleasant-looking young waiter if he thought I would like fish pie. He smiled at being asked such a direct question and said he thought so, especially since as an Easter Special it came with an apple doughnut and three "Easter eggs." So I cast caution aside, ordered, and buried my head in *The Complete Works of Truman Capote*, which the booksellers across the street thought I needed in case I was getting tired of *Tanganyika Notes and Records*. I was completely absorbed—in fact, emotionally involved—in a long short story called "The Grass Harp" which Capote wrote in 1949. Brilliantly written when the author was only 27. The story would not appeal to everyone, in fact probably to very few. But they would be the few with whom I could share a roomette on the Siberian Express.

The fish pie was, indeed, good.

But loneliness be gone. Suzie was arriving the next day at dawn. Another assignment in Uganda had firmed up, and that would have added further separation time. So we decided it was worth the cost of a last-minute ticket for her to join me here and travel on with me to Uganda. Then Anne wanted me to return to Tanzania to start sorting through our research findings, which added more time.

Zanzibar

Suzie arrived and I had a free weekend. We decided to take a little trip. Nearby Zanzibar was where Arabs conducted the ivory and slave trade many centuries before the Portuguese ventured up the East African coast in search of a passage to India. It was best reached by sea, not air, and that meant taking a flying boat, or hydrofoil. Rain was falling in Dar while we waited for the boat on the dock, and the squall still hadn't let up when we pulled into Zanzibar town two hours later. But it couldn't dampen my mood. I was elated because just as I was leaving our hotel in Dar, I received a fax from my publisher with news that it had accepted my first book on African AIDS. Moreover, it would include endorsements from the reviewers of my manuscript. The first reviewer, a professor and a man I much respected, called it "a masterpiece that will have an immense impact on policy. The best synthesis I've seen so far." My brain flooded with endorphins. I was high on a euphoric cloud.

Five years later, I received news that another of my books *Indigenous Theories of Contagious Disease* was accepted for publication, just as I was leaving Cuamba, Mozambique, to catch a flight home. Finding a publisher for this book was more of a challenge than earlier books, because I was proposing a grand theory (or revealing an indigenous theory that I thought already existed), and I had to catch up on developments in anthropological theory over recent decades, long after I had left academia. My friend and mentor Russ Bernard helped me find the right publisher for that one. His email told me that my changes and my added chapter on anthropological theory had all come together nicely. Both in 1994 and again in 1999, I experienced the most wonderful feeling of self-contentment and it lasted for hours.

Back to Zanzibar. After the rain ended, we explored the narrow, winding streets of the labyrinth known as the Arab Quarter, or "stone town." It was set back from the harbor behind the fish market. The town is distinctly Islamic, aside from an Anglican church built in the 1870's on the site of the former slave market; otherwise I had no real sense of where I was. At times I felt I was in Nepal and at times in an Aegean village, but seldom did it seem like Africa.

Late in the afternoon, another downpour drove us to seek shelter under the roof of the fish market. A few elder men gestured that we could perch next to them, but we were beaten to the offered spot by a group of men who had to haul their cigarette stall out of the rain. For the next hour or so we waited out the storm with the local people, watching little human dramas around us. A madman was prancing around in the rain, shouting and threatening a person who had sloshed mud into a puddle he regarded as his very own. Everyone else seemed tolerant, bemused, relaxed, gentle, accepting. I felt relaxed and comfortable. These were the days before Islamic fundamentalism really spread in Africa.

Just two nights before, I had been feeling that Africa—and by extension, the world—was becoming an increasingly intolerant, polarized, sinister, and dangerous place. I tossed and turned most of the night, only falling into an uneasy half-sleep an hour or two before dawn. It wasn't my usual Accelerated Aging-Awareness Anxiety and Agoraphobia Syndrome that at times overcomes me when I'm traveling. It seemed more a combination of the religious sectarian violence starting to erupt in long-peaceful Dar es Salaam, the riots in South Africa over Chris Hani's assassination, the resumption of civil war in Angola, the continuance of civil wars in Sudan and Liberia, the newer civil wars breaking out in Zaire and Rwanda, and the collapse of the Nigerian economy. Was Europe a safe haven? I had also just read accounts of life in scenic Bosnia in which women graphically described being gang-raped by former friends and neighbors, including family doctors. Was America a safe haven? I brooded over the account I heard in the New Orleans slums a few weeks earlier. An 82-year-old crack addict sold his 100-year-old mother to prostitution to pay for dope. She died after a bout of rough sex, heavily bruised and infected with syphilis.

But one had to keep a sense of humor. I saw from the hotel laundry price list that it cost 600 Tanzanian shillings to press a wedding dress, whereas a kilt was only 50. So far, I had seen no one in Zanzibar wearing a kilt, nor did they seem likely to don one. Maybe the list was left over from the days of 19th century explorers Richard Burton and John Speke. I fell asleep that night imagining Mecca seen through the eyes of Burton, the first European to enter the holy city, in disguise, skin artificially darkened with natural pigments, speaking fluent Arabic, but trespassing.

Decadence in Hillbrow

We had also taken little trips elsewhere. In the early 1980s, Suzie and I occasionally went from Swaziland to Hillbrow, a neighborhood in Johannesburg. By South African standards of the time it passed for hip, Bohemian, even libertine. Prostitution and the gay life flourished there—and still do. It offered used bookstores, espresso cafes, pawn shops, health food stores, gyms, and movie theaters, in one of which I saw *Hair* as soon as it was unbanned. (Suzie and I chanced to meet one of the film banners when we happened to have lunch together on Christmas Day, 1981.) Vitally, to the weekend slummer, most of these places were open on Sundays.

By 1993, Hillbrow was becoming integrated even before the dismantling of *apartheid.* But it drew non-Whites disproportionately from the ranks of thieves, thugs, alcoholics, addicts, and derelicts. Drug dealers and prostitutes connected to the Nigerian mafia would be well established by the late 1990s. Over the previous three to four years, most of the resident and visiting White population had fled to the northern suburbs of Johannesburg, surrendering Hillbrow to its new claimants. This had the effect of lowering prices and pulling in more derelicts and criminals. Few *belungu* (Whites) among my acquaintances, including Americans, visited Hillbrow anymore, due, they told me, to the odds of getting shot or robbed.

But I liked staying in an area that was familiar, full of agreeable memories. In fact, I was attracted to the new ambience of decadence. On a stroll through the street vendor section of Pretoria one afternoon, I was drawn to a small group crowding around a stand-up table of weapons. An Afrikaner was demonstrating a super high-powered air pistol.

"It will shoot a hole," he promised, "through a thin piece of hard wood. It's perfect for target practice, small animals, and your next-door neighbor. And the beautiful thing is that you don't need a license!"

Apartheid South Africa was notorious for requiring licenses. People needed a license even to own a television. The vendor also had a mini-crossbow, the size and shape of a large pistol. It too didn't require a license. I tested the tautness of the rope that propelled a small, featherless arrow that looked like it could pierce a suit of armor. It would probably do more damage to your next-door neighbor than the air gun. An Indian youth came forward to buy lethal-looking pellets for the air pistol he apparently had purchased earlier. In fact, he bought all the pellets the vendor had left, prompting the comment, "After small animals, are you?"

Chapter 10
Mozambique: Descent into the Abyss

One day in 1994 I was living in the world's richest country—my own—and the next day I found myself in the poorest, in a sweltering, mosquito-ridden apartment on Avenida Vladimir Lenin in Mozambique.

Since 1990, I had been consulting there under the auspices of the EU, actually the European Commission. By law, they could only hire Europeans or people from developing nations. They were delighted to learn that I still had a bank account in Swaziland, so they could hire me as a Swazi—just like that! Rules were meant to be broken. This was all great, but EU bureaucracy was the most inefficient of any organization I would ever work for. It took nearly three years before I was finally paid for my multiple consultancies for them, by which time I was living in Mozambique, had a local bank account, and was paid in US dollars, cash.

I had been designing a national public health program for the EC that involved traditional healers—only recently decriminalized—cooperating with government healthcare personnel to achieve specified public health goals: reduced morbidity and mortality from HIV/AIDS and diarrheal disease. I wasn't super-optimistic that the Mozambican government, then slowly evolving out of Marxism and opening up to Western donors, would actually embrace my ideas.

Then suddenly Mozambican authorities found a donor, the Swiss Development Cooperation, for the program I proposed. But the Swiss insisted that I live in Mozambique full-time to run the program. I tried to change the terms—like, I would come to Mozambique as often as they wanted, but I needed to be based in DC. But they kept increasing my salary offer and incentives, and I finally caved in.

Culture Shock Redux

I committed myself to two whole years in this country, and all my transcultural experience did not soften the blow of culture shock, for some reason (older age?) I felt at first that I had made a mistake giving up my jet-set consulting life for this rootbound life. I found myself brooding over possibilities for escape. It was 1994, and I wished I had accepted a job I had been offered to work on the first bilateral USAID AIDS project in Uganda, where my destiny would take me, anyway, in a few years. But Suzie had not liked Uganda well enough during my week-long consultancy there in 1993, and so here we were in Maputo the following year. This happened to be the year of the great genocide in Rwanda, much of which was done by hand, up close and personal, often by machete, since bullets cost money. This started just a month into our time in Mozambique, and since Rwanda shares a border with Uganda, Suzie felt we were a little better off in Mozambique. Of course, we had our own brutal civil war going on, seemingly without end.

I did my first of three USAID consultancies in Angola en route to Mozambique (under the Congressional earmark called the "Displaced Children and Orphans Fund," also called "Children and War," or the UN designation Children in Difficult Circumstances), and they actually made Mozambique look comfortable by comparison. In Angola I had to take UN and International Red Cross flights to cities under siege by the right-wing rebel group UNITA. The food situation was so bad in places like Cuito that a few people resorted to cannibalism. Military officers typically ate civilians; any use of condiments was unreported. Surgeries were usually performed under battlefield conditions by barely-trained orderlies equipped with blunted saws. There was no morphine—just aspirin, and only when it was available.

I did witness MSF, or Doctors Without Borders in English, doing important, life-saving work under the most extreme circumstances. At the end of each gut-wrenching day, all the French doctors had for respite from non-stop surgeries was *vin rouge,* and then they would resume their amputations. But USAID'S focus was on the child victims of this brutal and endless-seeming civil war. For example, young children in besieged towns surrounded by UNITA rebels would be sent out to forage for food, because people were starving. They would sometimes step on land mines and be killed, or have to undergo amputations. Of interest to historians of US foreign aid, ultra-conservative US Sen. Jesse Helms (R-NC) was a relentless critic of all foreign aid, and as chairman of the Senate Foreign Relations Committee (1995-2001), he was in a position to cripple much foreign assistance. Yet I heard from reliable sources that he supported the Children and War projects that started in Angola and Mozambique in the early 1990s. Helms finally found an effort he could enthusiastically support, and he might have helped funding for all US foreign aid. I was lucky to lead the first mid-term evaluation of Mozambique's "children and war" project, the first under this rubric. My colleagues and I gave the project high marks. Mozambican schoolteachers (primarily) more or less invented effective methods *ex nihilo* to implement a type of project for which there was little or no precedent.

Once I reached Mozambique's capital, Maputo, fresh from two weeks in Angola, I still felt depressed, even though now Suzie was with me, and being supportive. Here we were, next door to Swaziland

On one of my first nights, I barely slept two hours. I just lay on our lumpy mattress with my stomach muscles in a tight knot and my teeth clenched and wished to God I had never committed myself—to this or to anything—for such a long period. I reflected that my cultural adjustment in Suriname 20-odd years earlier should have been more severe than this, since then I was experiencing it for the first time. Yet I don't remember it being so intense. It was a terrible feeling, and I suspected culture shock was far from over, since I had only been in Mozambique for several weeks. Plus, I had been working at short assignments there, on and off for three years.

My thoughts were: I was expected to initiate a new program in this country, and to achieve great results in a relatively short period of time. And I had to achieve them all using Portuguese, a language I was still weak in. I couldn't possibly succeed; the whole idea was preposterous, even if it had sprung from my own mind. How did I ever let myself be convinced to come to this country fulltime? I will fail, I will be exposed as a fraud, and so on, and so on. The old self-centered fears that I have carried around my whole life. Why the hell had I never taken any course in statistics! That was another reason I had not taken the job in Uganda: I would have been mentoring a counterpart in research, and the young man I met knew considerably more about survey research and statistics than I did. When I worked at the Futures Group a few years earlier, I was likewise offered the position of Director of Research across all of its programs, covering multiple countries in Africa and the Caribbean. I turned it down without revealing the true reason: I had no training in statistics, and by this stage of my career, I felt I could not reveal this.

I missed my friends in Washington. Now, all of a sudden, I was alone, coping with Portuguese. I was not involved with the American community in Mozambique at all, and almost never invited to any American home or event, except once to the Ambassador's Fourth of July party. And because the Swiss are insular people and don't typically reach out to non-Swiss, we were never invited to any Swiss event at all. So overnight I lost my social life after having a rich one in both Swaziland and Washington.

Is depression situational or organic? Do we ever know?

Meanwhile, Suzie was reading "Maputo for Newcomers," compiled by the United Nations Woman's Guild. She shared this tidbit: If we hang our clothes out to dry, creatures called fly maggots will get into the laundry and then bore into the skin, and we can be dead in hours. This revelation did little to lift my spirits. Then she said she had read the page wrong. It was actually cerebral malaria that could kill us in just a few hours. We could squeeze the fly maggots out from where they bored into our skin to lay and hatch their eggs.

One night I called a recent acquaintance, KC, in Johannesburg. I should have called him a few days before when I passed through Jo'burg, but Suzie didn't want to stay more than a half-day because we anticipated violence during a Zulu freedom march downtown. KC was concerned when I told him about my anxiety. As it happened, he had a female psychologist on hand who happened to be visiting him. They both spoke to me and tried to help me think through the sources of my despondency. KC wanted me to do a writing exercise in part, I think, to keep me awake until I became so tired that I would fall asleep without letting my thoughts push me over a cliff.

I appreciated their efforts, but didn't really feel the need to follow their advice. I was tired already, and went to sleep soon after the conversation. I slept most of the night, but woke up tired and still depressed.

What if I had never left the cloistered academic world? I would right now be jogging around the track in the coliseum at West Virginia University with my friend John Lozier, enjoying the spring weather. Security, peace, order, no anxiety, no fears, no worries, everyone speaking English. These doubts kept swimming in my head throughout the day.

Then it was evening. Suzie and I went down to the beach near Costa de Sol. We sat on the sand and watched the moon rise over the waves. Very tranquilizing. The things I worried about became downsized. We ate grilled prawns and chips within earshot of the waves.

Later, we looked at an apartment near the beach. The young, well-heeled Mozambican representing the family owning the house showed us around, then offered us a coke. I asked him if living right next to a police station made for any noise. He said, yes, as a matter of fact the police used to beat loudly on... how do you say in English...?

"A drum, a bell?" Suzie suggested.

"No, on prisoners. They scream very loud. I spoke to my uncle, the chief justice, and told him this was not correct. Now the police do not beat the prisoners much, and it is most quiet."

As the days went by, I recognized I had all the symptoms of culture shock: I wanted to cut myself off from everything around me. I wanted to transport myself to a place that was familiar and safe. I wanted to watch "Married With Children" on TV—but local offerings specialized in interviews with the government agronomist about new fertilizers and the promise of Russian tractors. I wanted to listen to a Bach concerto—but there was nothing resembling one on the radio. I wanted to play my guitar and maybe sing the blues—but my guitar was still in transit. I wanted to play one of my tapes— but no tape recorder. I wanted to visit one of the only American families we knew—but no car. I wanted to read the South African paper to see what was going on in the outside world, like the Rwanda bloodbath of ethnic Hutus I had heard about in Portuguese on local radio—but I had no way to get across town to the one hotel that sometimes had a foreign paper.

This was the pre-digital age, especially in Mozambique. No email yet. We could see an old Portuguese-built Catholic church from the window of our depressing, rundown temporary apartment. My mood seemed to be descending with the sun early one evening, so I decided to walk down our many crowded flights of stairs and cross a couple of streets to check out the church. I remember something simple and powerful I read in an inspirational pamphlet in Swaziland a few years ago: "God is near those who are discouraged." Maybe I did my part to move a little closer to the house of God just to make sure it was so. But when I rounded the side of the old colonial church, it appeared from looking in the smashed-in windows that the FRELIMO (Liberation Front of Mozambique) government had turned it into something else during its anti-clerical period. What else should I expect just off Avenue V. Lenin? On my trip to Cuba in 1985, the Castro brothers had turned churches into museums of the revolution, so why not here? When I went looking for a used car at a dealership on Avenue Karl Marx, I wasn't too surprised that there was no salesman and no one knew when one might be available.

But why was I getting culture shock after all my experience poking around in foreign cultures? And why hadn't I felt it for many years?

Maybe I'd just become spoiled by my comfortable life in Washington in between consulting jobs. Roughing it was a big adventure in my teens and 20s, but now at nearly 50 I'd gotten used to a certain comfort level, and—I must admit—having things go my way. But it was also true that I hadn't *had* to cope in a foreign language since Suriname. And I could remember how difficult things were there for at least the first six months—how inept, absurd, and just plain lost I felt. Later in the Dominican Republic, I got away with just being able to read Spanish reports and questionnaires when I worked; I didn't actually have to speak Spanish. And in Swaziland, I could sound better than most expat *belungu* working there by speaking a little siSwati. But I didn't need to speak that language well.

No doubt, I thought, I would feel better after we found a more permanent apartment, and after the initial confusion cleared up a bit and I could speak Portuguese better.

The Hunt for Basics

After several precarious dips, my mood swung, day-by-day, back to fairly normal. Suzie and I looked at two apartments one afternoon, both with sea views. The one I liked better, and which was available immediately, was unfortunately too small. Also, we were told that when the Portuguese left under fire, they took parting shots by, for example, pouring concrete down the shafts of elevators in apartment high-rises like both of these, making them hard to repair. So we'd have to walk up ten flights of stairs, carrying groceries and a television set if we ever bought one.

By April 1994, we were in our second temporary apartment. We had had no electricity there for more than 16 hours, and the fridge oozed strange liquid on the kitchen floor after defrosting itself. Unlike our water supply, which always came on for at least a few hours every day, the electricity seemed totally dead. I tried to imagine myself locating a presumed government Department of Electrical Affairs, finding the damned place, explaining my situation in Portuguese, and trying to describe where I lived. There were no numbers on most buildings in Maputo, nor for that matter names on the streets. Only our janitor knew the address of our 15-story apartment building, and he wasn't telling, lest his importance diminish. We also faced the question of how much of a bribe we needed to get someone to attend to the problem before the end of the year.

I wasn't up to handling this challenge alone, so I went to the Swiss Cooperation and found only Raphael, a Mozambican, to whom I had to explain the whole business in Portuguese, anyway. Still, he agreed to go with me to the right government department, and he was able to find an electrician civil servant willing to earn a little gratuity and slip away to my apartment. The problem lay in an external fuse box, reachable only by standing tiptoe on a chair in the apartment's hallway. The electrician explained that fuse boxes inside apartments are not the responsibility of the government, but of the building's owner. However, no one knew who actually owned this or many other buildings. Ownership itself was a complicated puzzle in Mozambique. It was better I deal with *him*. He said I had to take him to an outdoor market in a nearby neighborhood that sold surplus electrical equipment. I agreed. Fortunately, I had just bought a car to enable such back-and-forth.

On the way, the electrician asked Raphael, seated next to me, "Why is this man having trouble talking Portuguese?" To tell the truth, I'd actually been feeling pleased with myself for having coped so well, Raphael explained that I had only been in the country a short time, that I was an American. The electrician said, "Ahh," as if Americans were known to be mentally inept.

I finally got everything sorted out, paying Mt40,000 for an odd-looking device for my external fuse box, and Mt20,000 for the enterprising civil servant's time (a USD was worth MT31.21 in 1994). Raphael had told me that the presence of foreigners has so spoiled government electricians that they wouldn't leave the office to fix anything unless they were driven door-to-door. Not for the first time since arriving, I appreciated how relatively easy life was in neighboring Swaziland, and how good I had it there. And no bloody civil war was going on there, whereas in Mozambique it was impossible to drive into most rural areas.

Cars didn't last long in Mozambique without the help of more than one anti-theft device, and I only had one. Raphael had offered to take me to the guy who installed gearbox locks. So we jumped back into my car, but this time the thing wouldn't start. I had just bought it "newly reconditioned in Japan" the day before. Fortunately, we were outside the Swiss Cooperation and I got a jumpstart and a diagnosis: although my battery was brand new, the dealer on Ave. Karl Marx had forgotten to charge it up, and even new ones needed a charge.

So I took my car to the one mechanic in town reputed not to make copies of ignition keys for future larceny, left it there, and made the long, uphill trek back to my apartment.

When would I have time to work in my office?

The next day White rule ended in South Africa—the last country where it existed in Africa—with the inauguration of Nelson Mandela as president. October 5, 1994, was a holiday for us in Mozambique, as well as in Tanzania and no doubt many other former "front-line states" which had faced and opposed the apartheid regime. In Swaziland a few years earlier, Suzie and I had become active godparents to the two young kids next door. They traveled with us to South Africa, and once to Washington. Their father left their mother when the kids were very young, and married Nelson Mandela's daughter Zeni, and the two had lived in exile in Boston, which is where I first met Prince T, who was also a high-ranking royal in the Swazi monarchy. I mention this because we had a link to both the ANC and to the Swazi royal family. We were sometimes privy to stories that most White folks never heard.

Heroin in Government

Suzie and I spent three or so hours talking with a couple of Mozambican heroin addicts. They were friends of (new) friends and we had shown sympathy for their situation. The 46-year-old Carlos was said to be the most highly-trained professional in his technical field in all Mozambique. He had been a vice-minister before his life began to unravel. His 26-year-old wife Edwarda seemed to be from the local upper class as well. They had both recently snuck out of the country for a month-long drug treatment program in South Africa. A week or so after their return, Carlos started once again smoking heroin (the preferred method in Mozambique), while she tried to limit herself to lighter drugs like grass and hash and the odd methadone pill sent from friends in Holland.

I had spoken with her a few times after their return, but Carlos had been avoiding me, fearing that I might try to reform or brainwash him. He came home from a bar late one afternoon and found Suzie and me in his home, talking to his wife. He no doubt felt that politeness demanded that he put up with us for ten minutes or so. Our conversation that day went on for hours instead of minutes, by mutual consent. Perhaps they felt safe unloading their problems to sympathetic-seeming Americans. In fact, Carlos and Edwarda didn't want us to leave when I finally stood up to go.

In a number of ways, Carlos' story differed from that of the vast majority of addicts in America. In my country, addicts rarely complete advanced education or build up impressive resumes. Instead, they hustle and commit crimes to pay for drugs, though of course there are "successful" addicts who manage to lead double lives for years. Harvard professor Norman Zinberg

(Monica's old psychiatrist when she lived in Boston, as it happens) wrote in the 1960s that he had Harvard colleagues who would shoot up heroin no oftener than once a month, to avoid addiction. Yet generally it was different in this part of the world. In rich countries, addicts are mainly poor while in poor countries, it seemed to be the wealthy who first succumbed (this is before the opioid crisis in the US, which had not taken off yet). The situation in developing nations made sense: the people using narcotics were the ones with enough money to pay for them. The process seemed to not be left up to chance. When heroin first came to Mozambique, the Pakistanis and Tanzanians dealing the drug gave free, or highly discounted, samples to the local jet-setters, especially to youth from wealthy, urban, upper-class families. With not much private business or free enterprise in Mozambique in the early 1990s, this meant families in the upper tier of government.

After creating enough of a market ex nihilo, since there was practically no "demand" for heroin before a very few years earlier, dealers put a price on heroin and gradually raised it. First, there were periodic brown-outs ("brown" being the local nickname for heroin) when users could find no dope at any price. Then the brown would reappear, but cost more. After local addicts-in-the-making had a taste of withdrawal, they were willing to pay higher prices. Some turned to robbery, including hijacking cars at gunpoint, to pay for their habits. Crime rates soared after the introduction of heroin to Mozambique, and a number of criminals proved to be the addicted offspring of the best families.

Carlos was paying $2,000 a month in 1994, a great deal of money in the world's poorest country (according to the UN in 1990). Plus, it bought more dope than in most other countries: about three grams a day, he claimed. Heroin cost less here since the locals could pay less, a process known on Madison Avenue as "market segmentation." Carlos' dealers told him he was their best and most reliable customer in Maputo. They were dismayed when he went off to a treatment center. When he came back, the ever-attentive dealers waited a few days, then showed up and offered him free grams of heroin for weeks. In fact, he claimed he was still getting free drugs six weeks after his return. He knew how sinister and cynical his dealers were in attempting to re-addict their best customer, but he felt powerless to resist.

One day Carlos tried to call his favorite doctor at his treatment center in South Africa. This guy had been a heroin addict himself, and so he "really understood." Carlos was told that the doctor no longer worked there because, in fact, he too had relapsed. It seemed drug treatment along 12-step lines was so new in South Africa (and non-existent in neighboring countries) that few of the treatment center staff had more than two years of clean time themselves. (But I later read in a book that AA was actually established in South Africa around 1946.)

We now know the background of how this couple happened to go to rehab in South Africa. It has become part of the public record, which is why I can use their real first names. A South African television journalist had grown intrigued by the high political connections of heroin addicts he found in Mozambique. Some like Carlos actually held important offices. So after prolonged discussions, a deal was struck whereby the television station would pay for Carlos and Edwarda to go to rehab in South Africa, in return for the right to tell their complete stories and use their real names.

They were advised to go to different rehabs, and so they did. After Edwarda completed the in-patient phase, counselors strongly advised her to move to a halfway "sober house" where everyone participated in 12-step recovery meetings. She started doing well, found a job in a beauty parlor, and soon became financially self-sustaining.

Carlos however moved back to Maputo at the first opportunity, shortly before I met him. He quickly and predictably relapsed into heroin use. He began phoning Edwarda, telling her how much he missed her and begging her to return to him in Maputo. This turn of events alarmed Edwarda's new South African friends, and they strongly warned her not to go back to Maputo because she would almost certainly start using again with her boyfriend. It was an age-old pattern.

Alas, she did return and the story doesn't end well. They both died of heroin-related causes. Jacques Pauw, a South African investigative journalist and executive producer of a current affairs program on the South African Broadcasting Company, describes part of this story in his 2007 book, *Dances with Devils.* A few years after reading it, I found that the sad tale of Carlos and Edwarda (although for some reason her name appears as Dardinha) was on the Internet. Half the story is free, but to learn its ending, one has to pay for the complete video. I tried to do it, only to find that part two of the video was no longer available on the Internet. Here is the URL:

https://www.youtube.com/watch?v=NNgiTYhzdJI#action=share

It was through the book and the Internet that I learned of the fate of my two friends, who were still alive when I left Mozambique.

I should mention one other victim of the deliberately created heroin market in Mozambique. Nicole was a Swiss fellow anthropologist, also employed by the Swiss Cooperation and married to a husband who was willing to take care of their two sons while she worked. A nice multi-lingual family. They had arrived in Maputo a couple of months before we did, after a few years of work in Bolivia. In fact, our first temporary apartment was one they had just vacated, which is how we knew about it. We had become close friends, sometimes going to the beach together.

One day during the lunch hour, Nicole was driving back from one of the pro-bono language lessons she gave during her lunch break, teaching English or German to Mozambicans. She had a Mozambican colleague with her when she stopped at a traffic light, and gunmen suddenly yanked open the car door and demanded money and the car keys. Nicole complied. They shot her and her companion, anyway. Nicole died, but the companion lay in a coma for a week or so. When he regained consciousness, he related the details of the carjacking story. By cruel coincidence, Nicole's parents happened to be visiting from Switzerland, as was the Swiss Prime Minister. This senseless murder was an international incident, and great pressure was placed on the Maputo police to find the killers.

Getting Along in Maputo

We continued to discover how to get things accomplished in a neo-Marxist society, and were beginning to acquire items for our second temporary apartment. One night, I was frantically running all around a street noted for its electrical shops, trying to find an adaptor plug so I could try out a new (actually, used) electrical transformer that might make my Hewlett-Packard printer work again. No one had the damned plug, and every lead to a new shop proved fruitless. The next day we went to a private apartment sale and they had a *whole bag* of exactly the plugs I needed, at pennies apiece. I grabbed them all, just in case I might need another. And my printer worked again!

At the same sale, put on by a World Bank couple who were moving into a smaller apartment and needed to get rid of some worldly goods, we bought incredibly beautiful tribal rugs from Chad, with weird geometric patterns that could have been Navajo or Hmong, in haunting shades of faded dark red, orange, and black. We purchased three at $150 each (a bargain!), and they made a big difference in the ambiance of our place. Suzie had always wanted me to buy artful tribal rugs from places like Afghanistan or India, but I'd balked at prices like $1,000. These Chadian rugs were at least as good.

We took out membership at the USIS library at the corner of Kim Il Sung and Mao Tse Tung Avenues (anti-Communist crusader Sen. Jesse Helms would have loved this bit of irony), which meant we could now take home high-quality books. I borrowed an interesting 1993 text on the broad problems of Africa, and was flattered to see two references to my 1982 article about population policies among rural poor of Africa in the *Journal of Modern African Studies*.

By then I had a Portuguese tutor whom I liked a lot. He was a fiftyish scholarly gentleman from Lisbon who exuded dignity, and before our first formal session he showed me how to make circumflexes, acute accents, and other diacritical goodies on my computer (áàéúçóãíúêâ etc.) not to mention single keystrokes that produce the likes of -ção, -ções, and -idade. The trick was to customize one's keyboard. Soon I discovered how to print Greek letters (now to learn Greek.) Anyway, my mastery of Portuguese accents inspired me to write my first substantial memos in Portuguese, along with minutes of meetings, critiques of studies, and other documents. It was rather a giggle, as the Brits say. My Mozambican colleagues at work seemed pretty cool, and they were certainly patient with my plodding Portuguese. I felt we were starting to get real work done.

They had set up the Cabinet of Traditional Medicine Studies (GEMT in Portuguese) to study indigenous plant medicines, which was about all any Marxist-leaning African government was doing in this "superstition-ridden" sector back then. But a Dutch consultant at the GEMT read some of my papers about developing programs of collaboration with traditional healers, and I received a handwritten letter (written a month or two earlier) asking if the GEMT could hire me to show how to set up a program in Mozambique similar to the one we had established in neighboring Swaziland.

So now I was directing or at least advising on this program.

As mentioned, we didn't have much of a social or extracurricular life in Maputo, especially compared to ours life Swaziland, which in hindsight was the richest social life I was ever to have, anywhere. In Mozambique, the doomed drug addicts and the Swiss anthropologist and her family were just about our only friends, at first. And three of these were to die before long. Our temporary apartment building was full of Russian and Chinese doctors. They were not like doctors in the West. At home, they earned less than dishwashers in America. I happened to be renting the apartment of head of personnel at the Ministry of Health, and I came across a list of salaries of all foreign doctors working for the government. Living right above me was Dr. Deng, an orthopedic surgeon from southern China who ran a little private practice on the side, right in our apartment building, giving traditional Chinese massages based on theories of *chi* life force flowing along meridians. He came downstairs once and gave me a treatment in my living room. The Chinese don't seem to do so well learning Portuguese (like me). He only knew a couple dozen health-related terms, so it was a bit hard to communicate my medical history. I was able to show him my oversized magnetic resonance image (MRI) negatives, which I had brought to Mozambique. I wasn't sure he had ever seen these high-tech wonders of Western medicine, yet he appeared to have no trouble reading them.

Russians and Americans Are Exactly Alike

A family from Leningrad lived across the hall. The husband was a gynecologist and the wife was a speech therapist. They had been in-country about five years, and thus were away during the collapse of the USSR and the Soviet system. They had two kids and a long-eared beagle. We met them once when the electricity failed in our apartment for 24 hours. Alexander, the husband, fiddled with our fuse box and even managed to get an electrician to come to our apartment. Irene, the wife, offered to run extension cords from their own sockets across our balconies to our living room so we could at least have a light bulb. She even offered to feed us. This led to an invitation to "watch Russian TV" with them, whatever that meant. It turned out they had somehow gained a satellite hookup to a Moscow television station. We spent a few hours one Saturday watching an American sci-fi movie dubbed in Russian and interrupted by Russian ads for newly available consumer goods.

They seemed as lonely as we were. Most Soviet and Soviet bloc advisors had left Mozambique a few years earlier. Irene told me we were welcome to watch Russian TV any night: "We never go out." Their 13-year-old daughter was not attending school, but was taking a correspondence course at home so she could fit into the Russian system when they got home, several years from then. In the meantime, she hadn't learned Portuguese and I doubted she had many friends.

We talked a bit, in Portuguese and broken English, about the Cold War during a TV ad. Interestingly, they had never heard this term, but they knew what I meant. We agreed that it was all a lot of political foolishness. What was all that nuclear brinkmanship and paranoia about for a half-century? "Russians and Americans are *exactly alike*," Alexander assured me (by implication, not like our hosts, the Mozambicans?). The beagle laid his head in my lap and looked at me with big trusting eyes, and for some reason I recalled the image of Khrushchev banging his shoe on the table at the United Nations.

This friendliness reminded me of when I met and drank rum with ex-soldiers in Colón, in the interior of Cuba, during a mission to seek peace and improve US-Cuba relations. From my 1985 diary:

We struck up a conversation with four Cubans at another table. Three were men in their late 20s or early 30s, Gustavo, Juan, and Victor. They were surprised to meet Americans and they invited us to a house of one of them for rum after lunch. All three men worked in Havana. Victor was visiting his wife on his day off and had brought along his buddies.

Victor is some sort of maritime technician and he recently returned from two years military duty in Angola. He said he lost several comrades to

UNITA or South African gunfire, but otherwise he felt he had a good experience in Africa. I learned that Cubans who serve in "revolutionary" positions overseas, such as helping left-wing governments in Ethiopia and Angola, are regarded as heroes back home in Cuba. I commented that I have worked in Angola and I might have met some of the same South Africans he was trading gunfire with. Victor said, "To hell with all war and fighting and the generals who turn us against each other. The important thing is that we are now drinking rum as friends!"

I tried to get Victor to talk about the situation in Ethiopia (where I would work in 1999), but he was quick to say he really didn't know what was going on there. He went on to say that he believes in the Cuban revolution, but he likes North Americans, anyway. He took a photo of me with his daughter on my lap.

It is heart-warming that after generations of anti-American propaganda, my new Russian friends in Maputo and those ex-soldiers in Cuba wanted to look past politics and propaganda and accept "sworn enemies" as simply fellow human beings, despite demonization by governments on both sides. I would go on to later make special friends with a Cuban doctor in Maputo, and I credit him with teaching me the basics of DOS-based computer operations, and turning me on to great computer programs such as PC Tools and PC World.

This phenomenon of friendship trumping propaganda really hit home a few years later, in 1998, when I worked a short consulting assignment in Vietnam. The Vietnamese had suffered so much under American bombs, defoliant chemicals sprayed from the air, rape and torture of its women, and the list could go on. Yet they didn't hate Americans as a group, a nationality. They in fact were so friendly and interested in America that I sent for Suzie and, as already mentioned, we got married in a great, much photographed wedding ceremony in Danang, where my Vietnamese counterpart happened to have special relations with the Communist Party. The government quickly granted the necessary permissions for a pair of foreigners who for some strange reason wanted to get married in Vietnam. People said this had never happened before. An ex-GI marrying his Vietnamese girlfriend, yes, a few such couples got remarried, but never two Americans.

Later, work in places like China and Ukraine further solidified my belief borne of person-to-person interactions that people are basically friendly everywhere, and curious about people from elsewhere. I remember an elaborate toast at a hospital in Odessa during two assignments in 2000 when a doctor remarked that urban civilization began millennia ago in the Black Sea area. It had only been for part of the 20th century that Soviets and Americans were instructed by their governments to hate one another. "But we are all the family of mankind, and so I raise a toast to our new American friends!"

There Comes a Time in Every Mozambican's Life

We finally found a house we liked in the beachfront neighborhood of Bairro Triumpho. And there we discovered that old friends from Swaziland lived just up our street. We also became friends with a South African woman whose tiny dog would run on the beach with our new puppy, Carla (a new incarnation of Karl). And we adopted a baby vervet monkey, which I knew was not a good idea because how did we expect baby vervets became available? Their mothers are killed. But Suzie was lonely and really needed a pet, well, two or three pets.

Suzie and I had some friends over for a meal for the first time. She experimented with New England fish chowder, and it turned out... not bad. I suppose this is newsworthy only because Suzie almost never cooks. The first (and nearly last) time we had a guest for dinner in Swaziland, in 1981, the macaroni was a disaster. Now in Mozambique, we began eating better as we learned where to buy cheap papayas, pineapples, and other fresh produce, as well as special goodies like raspberry juice from South Africa, pre-made Indian samosas, and granola ingredients, including dark honey. We also began to find the restaurants that offered tasty grilled prawns, steamed clams, pizza with real mozzarella, and peri-peri chicken. Naturally we looked for post-Marxist waiters who would serve us in less than an hour in response to a corrupting tip.

Speaking of Marxism, more and more decadent Western consumer goods kept popping up as Mozambique moved toward a free-market economy. Q-tips and dental floss, those harbingers of a fully democratic consumer society, appeared in a few upscale stores. And speaking of capitalism, a newly arrived

American guy told me he wanted to form a little group of people interested in keeping up with investments in the US stock market, the idea being to meet once a week and share investment tips. It would balance the weekly meditation group Suzie and I started attending, where we tried to practice transcendence from all earthly desires, including stock market temptations.

I was still feeling depressed often in my early months in Maputo. At these times nothing seemed worth the effort. I did not want to go to work or see anyone socially or even leave the apartment, or later, leave our house. Everything around me seemed slightly sinister. I tried to find something to read that would make me feel better. I tried an Eric Newby travel book, a spy novel, an anthology on the writing craft, but everything seemed to point to the futility of existence. Life is nasty, brutish and short—and then we die. But not before our kids abandon us to homes for the aged where we might suffer in failing health for years—and *then* we die.

I realized that I needed to get away from the damned city, back to the countryside where Africa as it was meant to be prevails. The vicious RENAMO-FRELIMO civil war was still going on, and most of rural Mozambique was under the brutal, anti-communist, pro-apartheid RENAMO party.

Diviner-Medium healers in Tsitsikamma, South Africa, 1991

Europeans and Americans living in Maputo, who tend to be sympathetic to at least Marxist ideals, at times develop negative perceptions of local people because their main contacts consist of servants, street vendors, beggars, cripples, and other poor folk trying to get a buck out of the foreign do-gooders. Through my work with indigenous healers and chiefs, and local elites, I have maintained a genuine respect and admiration for African culture and people, in whichever country I find myself. But I felt it getting frayed living in an upper middle-class urban neighborhood whose houses were regularly robbed. I was getting paid in cash, and before I could figure out what to do with all of it, our cook Felix, who came highly recommended from other Americans, found out where I'd hidden part of it and took off with $3,000. The apparent cost to him was abandoning his wife and children.

Now it happened that I had brought in a South African traditional healer for a few of our workshops, a sangoma spirit-medium named Noktula. I picked her up at the airport and she stayed with us for a few days before we went upcountry. The word among Mozambican servants circulated that she had put a protective spell on my hard-earned money and when Felix stole it, it was just a matter of time before he would get sick and die. And so it came to pass. Except that Noktula hadn't really put a deliberate spell on my money.

When caught, and before he died, Felix told my neighbor Fion, "There comes a time in every Mozambican's life when he must go bad," anticipating the future TV series *Breaking Bad*.

Thrown to the Wolves

I was finally getting used to Mozambique, and settling into a routine, punctuated by field trips to, and stays in, towns such as Inhambane, Chimoio, Cuamba, and Nampula.

One day in 1994 I was flown from Maputo to Baltimore for a job interview with Johns Hopkins University. It began as a very different experience from my last academic job interview. That took place in 1979, for the position of Assistant Professor of Black Studies at the University of the US Virgin Islands. I discovered on the second day of interviews that the college had already essentially auctioned off the slot to the son of a local Islander businessman who coincidentally had just donated two million bucks to the college building fund. But the feds needed evidence that the college had made a fair search. This meant appearing to seriously consider a living, Black or White, credentialed candidate such as myself. Students and faculty alike held me up for public humiliation for two fun-filled days. Student radicals in a packed auditorium demanded to know, "What makes you think you as a White oppressor could teach us anything about Black culture?" The fourth time I was asked this, I replied that yes, they were exactly right: I was the wrong color for this position. I turned to my host and asked to be driven to the airport. I tried unsuccessfully to achieve drunken oblivion immediately after this ordeal, and I vowed to never again apply for an academic job. I had my sights set on other goals, anyway.

But now they had flown me to Johns Hopkins. A departing Hopkins faculty member, a man who had worked many years as an independent scholar and consultant, suggested me as a replacement. So it felt very different. This time a university was reaching out to me. And I was treated almost like royalty. After years toiling in relative obscurity, it turned out (I was told) I had more academic publications and relevant public health experience in diverse countries than many other applicants for this much-advertised position, not to mention many faculty members themselves. My self-confidence was boosted by learning that my book on AIDS and traditional medicine was then the fourth best-selling title out of the hundreds of books from Westview Press, which publishes in a number of disciplines. I got a further boost from what I consider my breakthrough in understanding the ethnomedical code of STDs and other infectious diseases in Africa. And then the previous week I was asked to advise a committee of the National Academy of Sciences. Yes, I felt I had come a long way from the frightened, insecure, powerless, struggling, bottom-of-the-heap academic hanger-on—the marginal character I had been in the 1970s. Fifteen years later, a premier university was enticing me to join it.

I had actually sent them a fax turning down the opportunity for a free trip home for Christmas, explaining I had thought the job was a nine-month appointment, not a tenure track position as associate professor, and that I didn't want to give up control over all my time. They phoned back and basically let me name my terms and conditions. "Okay," I said. "I want to work at home two days a week. I want to keep two months free to continue my Mozambique work. I don't want to teach very much. I don't want to begin until July first." They granted me my wishes on all points. The job carried a light teaching load (one 8-week course per year), and consisted mostly of the type of applied health research that I was already doing. In the memorable words of the Chair: "You have managed to carve out the interesting science from all of your weird assignments in faraway lands, all over the world." With all this encouragement and accommodation, I agreed to come for the interview as long as there was no obligation on my part.

I had to go through the requisite ordeal of a two days of individual and group meetings at Johns Hopkins. These all seemed to go very well. I felt that I had skills and experience lacking in the Department of International Health, which boasted more than 80 faculty members. I spoke candidly about my weaknesses (statistics), and objectively about my strengths (discovering important, broad patterns that others miss). The finale would be my "performance" (their term), which was described as an hour and a quarter lecture. The chair told me that the position was now mine, "assuming you don't really blow the lecture, heh-heh." Johns Hopkins was prepared to talk salary and make me a formal offer. And so we discussed these matters. But hmm... I thought it strange that he would talk about "blowing the lecture." In fact, I had been led to believe that at most I'd be giving a seminar, an informal affair during the lunch hour, mostly Q&A. So I didn't need to prepare much, I had told myself. No one had told me anything about a formal lecture!

Suddenly I felt rattled. In fact, I felt the stirrings of an old-fashioned panic attack of the sort I used to sometimes get just before "performing" in public lectures and job interviews. Here was the Real Test coming up. I was facing my one chance-in-a-lifetime to join the ultimate establishment team in the Elite World of Big Science. And I might blow it! Did the chairman in fact have a premonition? I thought of concert pianists who practiced one étude or sonata for years, and then, during their make-or-break performance, they hit one wrong note due to a sweaty finger. End of career! Condemned to a lifetime of giving music lessons in Peoria!

I had 20 minutes left before my Final Performance, and I told the chairman I had to go out to my car and get materials for the talk. In fact, I had no materials, but I thought the time had arrived to take my emergency 5 mg., long expired Valium that I have carried around in my wallet for years for just such an occasion. *Why wasn't it already in my pocket?* My rental car was parked in a weird, nautilus-shell-shaped multi-level parking lot a block away, but once there, I couldn't find my damned car! I was getting desperate. There was only seven minutes to go, and Valium needs at least 20 minutes to take effect. I knew it would do me no good during the crucial opening minutes, but at least it would kick in later.

I finally found the car, popped the trunk, retrieved the pill, and swallowed the damned thing dry. No water to wash it down. I found an old piece of dirty candy on the floor and stuffed it in my mouth to help force the pill a bit further down my parched throat. My mouth was completely dry from fear.

Five minutes later, heart pounding, I was led into a large classroom set up like an auditorium. They brought me to a lectern and handed me a microphone and a pointer, and I turned to face 65 to 70 expectant faces from various departments of perhaps America's most prestigious medical and public health university (Hopkins and Harvard routinely trade places as Number One). They asked me for my PowerPoint.

In 1994, I was not even sure what a Powerpoint was... something like an overhead projector and transparencies, and if I had been prepared, I would have had one of these presentations put together. I had been working in Africa, and all I knew was I didn't have a PowerPoint. I was screwed!

It was a professor's worst nightmare come true: You wake up facing an auditorium full of severe-looking, scowling, judgmental faces and you are not prepared *at all*. You find the notes in front of you are a shopping list from your wife.

Appealing for sympathy, I explained to the crowd that I had not been expecting to give a formal lecture, so I hoped they would bear with me. I proceeded to give the highlights of my research in Mozambique, and I tried to show how I felt I had achieved a breakthrough in understanding STDs and other infectious diseases in Africa, from an African viewpoint.

But my voice was trembling, and I was fighting a persistent voice that was asking: What happens now, if you forget what you're saying and your mind goes completely blank? Inevitably that happened. About four minutes into my halting presentation, my mind suddenly *did* go blank. I just stopped talking. All those faces began to look a little puzzled and worried, as the seconds crept by. God, I just wanted to run out of the auditorium! Fight or flight? Gimme flight!

After what seemed like three minutes, but may have only been scarcely one, I commanded my voice to pick up on the general theme of what I had been talking about, but now my voice was quavering even more, trembling audibly, I was sure.

But then... the Valium kicked in! I experienced an abrupt mood change that the audience might well have picked up on. I slowed down, my suddenly unstrangled voice descended a few pitches to a warmer, more resonant baritone. I spoke more easily and confidently. I even became a bit witty and ironic.

I continued for the required hour, and then answered questions for about 20 minutes. Weak applause followed. A number of students came up to meet me and tell me about their research. The famous emeritus professor of public health Carl Taylor also spoke with me, and told me he had enjoyed the lecture. But I knew it had been ragged and disorganized, and there was that embarrassing mini-panic attack that stopped me dead in my tracks early in the lecture.

I knew I had blown it. Why did that damned chair have to say the job was mine "if you didn't *blow* the lecture, heh-heh!" Was this public shaming actually *planned*? Or else why the prescient "heh-heh"?

In the remaining couple of minutes I had alone with the chairman, he commented, "I guess you weren't expecting something so formal, and I guess it threw you a bit." *A bit*? "Yes," I agreed. He then asked for my street address in Mozambique so the department could DHL his letter of formal offer. He said my salary would be higher than any other associate professor's, and I should not mention this fact to anyone.

During my first night back in Mozambique, I got a call from the chair informing me that the committee had met and changed its collective mind.

The job offer was off. The reason given was that my lecture was disorganized, and since "teaching is such an important responsibility in our department," they were concerned I might not prepare routine lectures adequately for students. He said something about a part-time, adjunct appointment as an alternative, but I was stunned and couldn't really focus on what he was saying. They had spent nearly $3,000 bringing me to Baltimore, and each of the search committee members had told me privately that the department had already decided that it wanted me at any price. They had me so snowed and hyped up that I had become convinced I actually wanted the job. And now they were rejecting my ass! That old castigating voice that dwells in my head, and that doubtless comes from early experiences with my ambitious if neurotic mother, was quick to tell me, "you really fucked up!" It gloatingly reminded me that I was no damned good, that I was a bum, a juvenile delinquent, a beatnik, a hippie, a failure. I'd disgraced my family by being kicked out of the very boarding school where my father and brother had excelled. And here I was thinking I could be a Johns Hopkins professor! Unmitigated hubris! The university had seen through my pose of professionalism and perceived me as I truly was—a fraud.

I decided then and there it's my unalterable destiny and innermost nature to be an outsider, a non-team-player, a loner, a marginal character, a maverick, a renegade, an expellee. I would not risk being denatured by an establishment-type job. Hell, if my guardian spirits had wanted me to do that kind of work, they would have arranged for me to stay with my ex-wife and my secure job with the DC government.

A decade later, to the very week if not day, I gave a lecture to a large audience in the same auditorium at Hopkins. I was debating Dr. Doug Kirby, a leading applied sociologist, about why Uganda appeared to be such a success story in AIDS prevention. The audience was full of USAID and World Bank officers as well as professors from Hopkins. This time I over-prepared for the lecture-debate and, of course, came armed with a well-packed PowerPoint. It happened that Doug and I actually had Thanksgiving dinner together in California a couple of weeks earlier, and after much discussion, we discovered our views had come to converge quite a bit. My opening line was, "Doug Kirby and I, having reviewed the evidence carefully, found we are now largely in

214 On the Fringe

agreement, so I guess you can all go home." Even though I was arguing the unpopular position, the event went reasonably well.

By this time, I was at Harvard, as a senior research scientist. Of course, I dragged along all my self-defeating neuroses that I was an imposter. Not all of it was mere neurosis. With my glaring knowledge gaps—for example, missing one year of high school (remember Korea and the wayward principal?), and completely untrained in statistics—I couldn't *think* or reason my way out of feelings of inadequacy. Or not yet.

The Society of the Fringe

In his 1976 Presidential address to the 75th Anniversary Meeting of the American Anthropological Association, Walter Goldschmidt reminded us that anthropologists tend to possess special traits rooted deep in our psyche. We distrust all sources of power, influence, and wealth. We loathe authority— indeed, we shrink from the prospect of finding ourselves in positions of authority. (Yes!) Our "escapist tendencies" find expression in xenophilia, the romanticization of all things foreign and exotic, along with the belief that emancipation from our oppressive culture lies in adopting another. We are unfit for most kinds of employment because the usual passions don't motivate us. In short, we are marginal. Alienated from our own societies, we seek a place in the sun—as Ruth Benedict, a lesbian, put it—in societies we hope are as different from ours as possible.

But alas, we fit even less into our adopted societies. In fact, we don't fit in anywhere. So most of us join together in a society of fellow-sufferers, a community of the socially and economically marginal, and call ourselves professional anthropologists. Most of us develop covers by becoming professors. We join the American Anthropological Association. We are no longer lonely misfits as we have strength in numbers as well as a respectable social identity. We may even overcome our ambivalence toward power by becoming departmental chairs or deans. It is much to Walter Goldschmidt's credit that he dared remind us of ourselves.

But perhaps we pay a price for the safety and respectability we gain by herding together. The loss of marginality may impair our ability to view cultures and societies including our own with a perspective normally denied the socially well-integrated. Perhaps the true anthropologists of today are the ones who have not been domesticated or denatured by gentility or deanship. They are instead the ones who choose to live in countries like Mozambique.

In 1992, a Berkeley friend sent me an article by a "mad" doctor she introduced me to: Jerry. He suffered a mental breakdown years ago and apparently hadn't worked as a physician since, so I was surprised to see his name in print in a serious magazine. He had written an essay on multiple sclerosis, and I found it interesting for more reasons than the author intended. It made me think that part of Nature's Plan must be that some of us resemble Jerry—marginal characters who view issues from the fringe. Otherwise, human thought would have progressed at an even slower pace than it has done. The history of science is full of stories of how outsiders and even amateurs— fringe elements—explode comfortable but faulty understandings, and usher in new, often radically different ideas that better explain the data. If one occupies a central position in a disciple and within a community of scholars, the pressures toward conventionality are great. I know, for I once had a fairly mainstream job in my field; now I seem to be regarded as a marginal scholar.

By "conventionality" I mean tinkering around with minor aspects of the dominant paradigm. The closer one is to the center of a field, the harder it becomes to challenge its broader framework of understanding and look at issues in a substantially different way. After all, one has one's own legacy of assertions in print to protect, one wants (or *needs*) to get other articles into print in journals with standard review processes, one has a job to keep and bills to pay, and one has colleagues one dares not alienate, confront, or insult. All these pressures fall away if one is a marginal character. Our marginality allows us—*impels* us—to see things from a novel angle or even a new dimension, to show those lemmings how they have been locked in fallacy for their entire careers. Sweet revenge on the mainstream! This is what I did to a degree in my first book on African AIDS. My subsequent books on AIDS would consign me to marginal or even pariah status.

The Question of Big Sur and Missing Link

Back in Mozambique I read Psychiatrist Peter Kramer's *Listening to Prozac*, then a best seller on the new anti-depressant drug. It's a serious book disguised through its first chapter as another pop psychology offering by a shrink. Perhaps this was part of the author's strategy to get the book into the hands of as many people as possible. Once they had paid good money for the damn thing, some might actually read further and find themselves in the heart of the hottest ongoing debate among behavioral scientists: nature versus nurture.

I had been thinking about the panic attack, or acute loss of self-confidence, I had just before my unanticipated Johns Hopkins lecture. Then there were the anxiety attacks coupled with insomnia I sometimes got at night, lying in bed where I worried about old age, failing health and death. Where did they come from?

Kramer begins his book with case histories of his own patients who are depressed (or mildly so: "dysthymic") and who then try Prozac. Not only does the depression lift, but profound changes can take place in the personality. Shy, inhibited, introverted people may become self-confident and outgoing. If the solution is biological, Kramer suggests, the problem can originate biologically. But aren't shyness and introversion, along with lack of self-confidence, produced by unsupportive parents or other early childhood experiences? The reader then sees the latest research in brain biochemistry and neurophysiology, as well as primate studies and the child psychology of Jerome Kagan, all of which point to the fact that basic personality ("temperament") traits come from the genetic roll of the dice in both baby humans and monkeys.

Some monkeys are born introverted and others extroverted, as tested on traits similar to those with human children, such as heart rate when exposed to a strange group of peers (or a frowning Johns Hopkins audience). Interestingly, when researchers allowed all monkeys to self-administer alcohol, the shy ones drank much more than the outgoing ones. What if they could self-administer Valium or Prozac? As a matter of fact, I then had two pet monkeys, Big Sur and Missing Link. Big Sur seemed self-confident to the point of recklessness. Quite the opposite of the other monkey, who technically belonged to an autistic boy up the street. This boy could never remember that he could not simply reach out and grab Missing Link, so he kept getting bitten. Finally, his exasperated parents asked us to take the hyper-alert, over-reacting simian. When brought to the front of our house, to face the big, wide world as it were, Missing Link often had what I can only describe as panic attacks. True, we didn't know about their early upbringings, but we treated and fed the two vervets exactly the same.

The theories of Freud and the now-disputed findings of Margaret Mead represent the extreme of environmental determinism, Freud in the psychological sphere and Mead in the sociocultural. I suppose John Watson, the founder of behaviorism, is a better example than Freud, but the latter has had more influence on psychiatry and psychotherapy, and Kramer, as noted, is a shrink. Anthropologist Mead told us that human behavior is "almost infinitely malleable." In fact, she argued, there is probably no biologic basis to behavior differences that seem gender-linked. One of the first things I remember from my introductory sociology course in 1963 was that Margaret Mead had discovered a tribe in New Guinea where the women hunt and carry on political life while the men sit at home gossiping and developing elaborate hairdos by which to charm their wives. The implications were staggering. Given the right upbringing, I could have grown up to be a woman, behaviorally.

Derek Freeman has since shown that Mead's fieldwork was highly flawed, and that her "findings" were distorted to fit the uncompromising cultural determinist beliefs of her mentor Franz Boas. In fact, the extreme "nurture" position of the popular psychologists and anthropologists of the past half-century fit nicely with the values of a liberal, egalitarian society. It meant, basically, that anyone could grow up to be a Johns Hopkins god, given the chance. A stammering, pathologically shy kid could, through behavior modification, become a self-confident stand-up comedian in Las Vegas. There was equal opportunity for all of us as long as our mommies and daddies were pleasant and supportive, and we were not molested by our scoutmasters.

Speaking of molestation, Kramer tells us that there was now (by 1994) irrefutable neurophysiological evidence showing that early trauma does affect us profoundly, but not in the way that Freud and his followers believed. Early trauma changes the biochemistry of the brain, affecting our mood as well as personality, perhaps permanently. It reconfigures our hard-wiring, so to speak, and brain neurotransmitters function differently.

We have all heard those who admonish, "Stop dwelling in the past. All this self-analysis is keeping you sick. Put it all behind you and get on with your life!" They are only partly right: dwelling in the past won't heal us. In fact, psychotherapy, especially psychoanalysis, cannot help the person who was sexually molested as a child because it cannot touch the core of the problem, which is biochemical, Kramer argues. I use the example of the sexually molested child because it illustrates how childhood experience can impact our genetic endowment, but through brain chemistry rather than solely psychological or "super-organic" processes. I also use the example because molestation cases were prominent in Freud's early case load. As Jeffrey M. Masson has hypothesized, to be accepted by anti-Semitic Viennese society, Freud had to pretend that children never really suffered molestation; instead, their claims represented fantasy or wish fulfillment. Freud went about collecting and destroying his early scientific papers which abounded with evidence of genuine child molestation, including post-mortem examinations conducted by himself. But that is another story.

Peter Kramer descends for a while from the academic clouds to appeal to the reader's common sense, to what "every parent knows," namely that children in the same family treated as equally as possible are nevertheless quite different from one another. No mention of sibling birth order theories. I only have one child, but as he grew up, I had to admit that he seemed to arrive on earth with a pre-determined personality. I had mostly taken the nurture side of the nature-nurture debate, truth to tell, because I was relatively ignorant of biology, but my son's kind and empathetic temperament seemed fixed from the beginning, and it appeared almost independently of any attempts at parental modification.

There is an evolutionary dimension to these brain chemistry ideas. When our ancient ancestors lived as hunter-gatherers on the African savanna, and a band of disreputable *Paranthropus robustus* heavies came up to the campfire to ask for a bone, there may have been a genetic advantage to being mistrustful (shy, introverted, socially fearful) and telling them to fuck off. But shyness and visceral mistrust confer no advantage these days; instead, self-confidence, chutzpah, and a touch of the old blarney pay off (recent research with rodents has challenged this idea). Introverts therefore experience social rejection and pain from at least pre-school. Depression often follows. In this view, introversion and social fear underlie and even cause depression. And so we take up with booze. Our vervet monkey Missing Link could not self-administer alcohol, and so he had panic attacks. Or bit Suzie for no apparent reason.

Suppose all this is true. Where does it leave us? Could I take Prozac, and sustain a state of hyperthymia indefinitely? A state in which I am energetic, outgoing, creative, robustly self-confident, expansive, magnanimous?

Chapter 11
Palestine: The Garden of Eden
and the Land of Checkpoints

Much happened later, in the 1990s. Both my parents died and I found myself orphaned. I published three scholarly books. I had worked in Southeast Asia and Africa, and by 1999 I was in the occupied Palestine territories for what would become five consulting assignments. I designed and supervised a "national qualitative study" of maternal and child health among Palestinians. It came at the request of Jack Thomas, the same USAID officer for whom I had done such a study in Bangladesh in 1985.

In my background reading, I absorbed statistics about, for example, just how many Palestinian children under 15 had been shot by Israeli soldiers and "settlers." There were quite a few even back in the relatively peaceful mid-1990s, especially if we include the wounded (figures are disputed by Israel, predictably), and it was unsettling to learn that the Israeli Defense Force policy was to aim at the head, to inflict maximum damage.

Such facts conflicted with the political views that I as a typical American brought with me. If I had any bias, it was pro-Israeli, going back to my childhood friend Yakov and his kind father. I was in many regards a typical American exposed only to pro-Israeli, increasingly right-wing propaganda from lobbying organizations like AIPAC and the Jewish Defense League. As the next two decades unfolded, younger Jewish Americans increasingly felt dissonance between their often-progressive views on most topics, and those on Israel. They could see that expanding the Jewish homeland appealed more and more to the Republican Party, and eventually to Donald Trump. So-called Christian Zionists nowadays donate more funds to Israel and the

EDWARD C. GREEN 221

expansion of its "settlements" than do Jewish-American communities. In fact, the consequential comment that "Palestine is a land without people for a people without land" came not from Theodor Herzl but from Christian "Restorationist leaders" in the mid-1800s, in the belief that the Second Coming of Christ only awaited the full control by Jewish Israelis of the Greater Holy Land.

On my second day in-country, Jack Thomas, his Palestinian partner, and I traveled to the Gaza Strip to introduce me to the authorities and explain the purpose of my health research. What I saw in my first 24 hours there really began a 180-degree shift in my political viewpoint. Just driving to the Gaza Strip showed the stark inequities. For starters, Jews had their own roads and license plates. Non-Jewish homes had water tanks on their roofs because, I learned, Israel routinely cut water and electricity for Palestinian houses. After passing several military checkpoints, we arrived in Gaza to find open sewers in the gutters and streets.

And this was in 1999, before a couple of highly asymmetric wars during which Israel let loose F-16 fighter jets and advanced tanks on a largely unarmed civilian population, one with little power to fight back with. Palestine had and has no formal military, although Israel "allowed" Palestinians to have an anemic police force that seemed mostly for show. Yet policing was highly dangerous work for Palestinians. On one Easter Sunday, also Passover, Israeli defense forces dropped a bomb outside the police station in Ramallah. I have a photograph of Christian kids, Quakers, all dressed up in bunny costumes for finding Easter eggs. It's hard to miss the trauma on their faces from the recent Israeli bombs. Eighteen years later, I would visit a school in Nablus which Israeli tanks had attacked directly. They had preserved an unexploded tank shell to show visitors, and its legend read: "Made in the United States."

On a happier note, I hired a Palestinian who worked at the American Colony Hotel. He had no research experience, but he spoke excellent English, having attended junior college in California for two years. I somehow sensed that this guy would make a good field assistant, even though he thought he couldn't measure up.

We haggled over salary. I wanted to pay him *more,* and he said, "No, no, I am worth far *less!*" I said "Listen, USAID has authorized me to pay an assistant up to $400 per day, so let's start negotiations there."

He said "No, no! Maybe $50 per day!"

This is not the way Middle East haggling is supposed to go. I said, "What about $350?"

He said, "What about $75?"

I eventually forced him upwards, to accept $200 per day. And my instincts were right: he proved extremely valuable. He served not only as a translator, but also as a culture broker, explaining many points of religious and cultural sensitivity that I would have missed. I am withholding his name lest he become investigated all these years later, but he and I went through many humiliating checkpoints together, and the experience taught me what it felt like to live under military occupation of one's own land.

Checkpoints

I remember an Israeli soldier at a checkpoint who, after seeing the address on my passport, said in American English, "Oh, cool! You live in DC near Wisconsin Avenue? I bet you know my uncle's deli near the DC line! What are you doing with this Arab?" (Referring to my translator.)

It would be so easy for me to see the world through this American's eyes. He knew my neighborhood and had even grown up near it. He was one of thousands of young Americans who chose to serve in the Israeli military. In the bombing of Gaza for weeks in May 2021, an estimated 5,000 Israeli soldiers were American citizens. It would be so easy if one had no regard for human rights, justice, and international law.

I will relate one other checkpoint tale, and then try to refrain from making further political commentary and observations. My Palestinian colleague K worked for an American agency. One evening, his brother had a heart attack. He was only several blocks from a hospital, but between him and it stood a military checkpoint. Two soldiers checked K's brother's papers... delaying him for hours. The brother was going into cardiac arrest.

Now, it was only because K worked for a US agency that he could finally get the US Ambassador to phone the Foreign Minister, and have him call the checkpoint and let K's half-dead brother pass and reach the emergency room. Had he been a regular Palestinian, the brother likely would have died at the checkpoint. Many did. Pregnant women often had to give birth on the street while young soldiers—sometimes from the United States—scrutinized their papers endlessly.

While working there, I realized there was at least one back way to enter Jerusalem without going through a checkpoint. How could there be such a hole in Israeli security? I happened to read an interview with the Israeli general in overall charge of checkpoints, in the liberal *Ha'aretz* newspaper. He acknowledged that there were circuitous routes by which "Arabs" might enter Jerusalem this way. "You miss the point," he explained to the reporter. "The reason we have checkpoints is to constantly remind the Palestinians that they are a defeated, occupied people." This kind of story almost never makes it into the US news media. And of course, Americans bear responsibility for the whole set-up, as without massive military and other US aid every year, the system probably wouldn't exist, or last.

These few anecdotes will have to suffice. But as I quoted in the Goldschmidt address to anthropologists earlier, "Anthropologists distrust all sources of power, influence, and wealth. We loathe authority." He might have added that our sympathies go automatically to marginalized people on the wrong end of authoritarian systems, to the "defeated, occupied (and second-rate?) people." To my many Jewish friends I can only say, "You have probably not seen up close how the occupied Palestinians are treated. They are usually out-of-sight, out-of-mind. Israel-Palestine has become an apartheid society, as Jimmy Carter declared unambiguously in the sub-title of his controversial book, predictably provoking outraged cries of "anti-Semitic!"

Since my experience in Palestine, I have joined Jewish Voice for Peace, which accepts participation from non-Jews. I feel in my heart that my Israeli childhood friend Yakov would approve. He disappeared soon after the 1967 war. I saw him just a couple of weeks before this event, and he confessed to me the anguish he felt—his crisis of conscience—dealing with powerless

Palestinian civilians. David versus Goliath, but this time David was the Palestinians.

Research Quick, Cheap, Yet Valid

My assistants from the Bureau of Statistics and I carried out basic qualitative, anthropological research using rapid methods, mostly interviewing representative key informants. In Palestine—the West Bank, Gaza, and East Jerusalem—we conducted interviews with a range of informants, and in a variety of settings, to capture differences that might occur along lines of geography, gender, socioeconomic status, age, West Bank or Gaza residence, refugee camp or non–refugee camp residence, degree of religious conservatism, and rural or urban residence. While we interviewed Palestinians who represented the range of opinion and behavior found nationally, we did not have precise percentages or numbers of interviewees preselected within these categories. However, as in my earlier rapid research in Swaziland, the Dominican Republic, and Bangladesh, we produced results that seemed as reliable and valid as those from expensive random sample surveys. When we tabulated and quantified our results in all four countries, our quantitative findings—derived from non-random sampling, so technically non-generalizable—were surprisingly similar and sometimes within the margins of error when compared with results from costly surveys done around the same time. For instance, these findings closely resembled those of a survey in the West Bank and Gaza by the Palestinian Central Bureau of Statistics in 1997.

Of course, our study was quick and cheap compared with the national survey—or with virtually any national random sample survey. I felt I was on to something major that could guide future "quick and dirty" research in... well, perhaps anywhere. It might only work in the health domain where we already know that KABP—knowledge, attitudes, beliefs, and practices or behavior—vary by socioeconomic status, age, gender, and rural versus urban residence. So we deliberately set out to interview informants whose viewpoints represented all these different groups, just as we had in Swaziland, the Dominican Republic, and Bangladesh. I published our results in the journal *Field Methods* in 2001, using only three countries as examples, to keep the article within length requirements.

Unfortunately, there was a struggle over ownership of the study. USAID had financed it so they expected ownership, but the Palestinian Authority felt they possessed it. As a result, the study—my study—was never "published," which meant that the contractor, ICF Macro, did not mass-produce my/our report on West Bank-Gaza. Therefore, few people read it outside Palestine and neighboring countries. Nor have I seen it posted on the Internet.

The Good Samaritans from the Garden of Eden

One day at the Bureau of Statistics in Ramallah, I heard mention of a Samaritan fieldworker on our team who was taking that Saturday off because it was his Sabbath. Okay, we had Muslims, Christians and... *Samaritans?* Samaritans, as in the Good Samaritan of biblical fame? They had survived until modern times, and were living in violence-torn Palestine?

My colleagues in statistics explained that Samaritans considered themselves Jews, the real and original Jews. The ones who never left the Holy Land, who never changed their ancient beliefs and practices. Other Jews adapted their religion to local cultures in the Diaspora, so Samaritans believe. I was told the main group consists of only about 450 people. They were mostly living in the Mt. Gerizim area, just outside Nablus, the biblical city of Sechem. Mt. Gerizim is a holy place for Samaritans, the site of the Garden of Eden, and the place Abraham is said to have brought his son as a sacrifice to God.

I did quick reading in the Albright Archeological Library in East Jerusalem. An unpublished paper by a Swedish missionary doctor reported that Samaritans were once numerous and widespread. Yet they had almost disappeared by 1927, following an earthquake and plague (the G-d of Vengeance of the Old Testament?). I learned Samaritans had the "highest inbreeding coefficient in the world," and for this reason often had physical deformities such as polydactylism, that is, excess fingers or toes. Samaritans

226 ON THE FRINGE

still carry out Passover's sacrificial ceremony in a meticulous manner, using live sheep, just as described in the Old Testament. A January 1920 *National Geographic* article found in the library provided photographs and a description of such a ceremony.

Relations between Samaritans and mainstream Jews have been somewhat strained over many centuries, according to one Christian scholar. In the New Testament, John (4:9) observes, "Jews have no dealings with Samaritans." The first small crowd attracted by Jesus are said to have been Samaritans. But what interested me most was how in the midst of the Second Intifada, "the authentic Jews" lived in apparent harmony with their neighbors in the middle of Palestine. They spoke Arabic and some worked for the Palestinian Authority, as did my fieldworker from the Department of Statistics. Yet most of the world had no idea they still existed.

This background whetted my appetite to meet Samaritans. One other inducement: my Palestinian colleagues said they had magical powers. Muslims were forbidden to use magic or consult magicians. Yet such use was "known to happen." One Samaritan magician was said to own a shop near the campus of the University of Nablus. Students flocked there near exam time to buy medicines and amulets to ensure academic success. Business was reputedly booming. Another Samaritan worked in a bank by day, but concocted love medicines by night, to help capture the hearts of reluctant lovers.

A Palestinian friend finally took me to a bank in East Jerusalem to meet my first non-team Samaritan. It was a letdown at first. The banker appeared to be a business-as-usual guy in a suit and tie, sitting behind a desk. He had red hair like me, and his name was Naveh Kohen. (Does that mean that all Cohens originate in the Garden of Eden?) When he heard of my interest, he dropped his formal banker demeanor and invited me to Mt. Gerizim on the following Friday. That was a free day for me—Good Friday, in fact— and a time when most of the Samaritan community would be at home, since it was in the middle of Passover holidays. Kohen would introduce me to a local leader who spoke good English.

The day arrived and I hired a Palestinian taxi to drive me, Suzie, a Palestinian friend, and a Norwegian tourist we happened to meet to Mt.

Gerizim. We found Mr. Kohen drinking traditional Passover wine at an outdoor café. He took us to the "summer house" of Benyamin Tsedaka, described as the unofficial foreign minister of the Samaritans. He lived most of the year in the Samaritan community of Holon, a suburb of Tel Aviv. Tsedaka was anxious to tell us the "true story" of the Samaritans, and did so for the next two hours.

Here are some things I learned on our visit to Naveh Kohen's village, on the side of Mt. Gerizim, that Passover of 2001. The population of the Samaritans was low and falling further. The Holy Land had always lain at the crossroads of Africa and Asia—it's at the "mouth of the Middle East"—and had therefore been a hot spot. Outside superpowers—the Greeks, Persians, Babylonians (those pesky Babylonians... don't you just hate it when they invade?), Chinese, Russians, the EU—all wanted control. The Samaritan people are few in numbers. Their population sank to a mere 146 in 1917. The Spanish flu was a factor. Though perhaps only 20 succumbed to it, that was a lot for this diminished group. A June 2021 online check with Samaritans.org (not to be confused with the Christian charity Samaritan's Purse) indicated that issues such as unemployment, isolation, mental health, family concerns, and possibility of suicides seemed to be about the same as how Israelis, but not Palestinians, were affected by the global coronavirus pandemic. Samaritans fled the Ottoman draft in World War I. Because of reprisals for draft dodging, Samaritans who did enter the Ottoman military received assignments few others wanted, and were soon dying in hospitals of infections they caught there.

Turkish rule had almost destroyed the Samaritans due to forced conversion to Islam, and some Arab Muslims have Arabized names of Samaritan ancestors. However, two "miracles" helped the Samaritans: The 1920 establishment of the British mandate (that is, its administration of Palestine) and the renewal of the Jewish settlement. The mandate brought back liberal Jews, and there were happy reunions of a sort after a 2,000-year separation. For instance, Issak Bulzui was a returned Zionist, but he wanted peace between Arab and Jews. He believed that learning Arabic would make for good communication and inter-group relations. All Samaritan families in greater Jaffa moved to Holon in 1955. Since then, their numbers had grown as

Samaritan men married Jewish women, and the latter had to convert to Samaritanism. Samaritans living in Palestine do not, or at least *had* not, married Muslims. According to a 2007 self-report by Samaritans, there were still only 705 of them total, half living near the West Bank city of Nablus on Mt. Gerizim, and the other half settled in a compound in the city of Holon, near Tel Aviv. Following the Oslo Accords, Samaritans in Nablus hold dual Palestinian and Israeli citizenship.

For seven days each year, all the Holon Samaritans return to Mt. Gerizim for the three festivals: Passover, Pentecost, and Tabernacle. The Samaritan newspaper was established in 1969. My informant insisted that Samaritans had kept their traditions unchanged for at least 3,000 years. All men wore simple white cotton robes to show equality under the eye of God. The appealing theme of equality permeated Samaritan religion and tradition.

Samaritans emphasized education. All boys and girls had 30 to 60 minutes of religious education, five days a week after their regular school hours. It was brief because "we don't want to force too much on the kids, and they need time for homework after school. Reading of the Torah requires 100% participation. Jews are called the 'People of the Book' ...and we really *are* these people." There was no illiteracy. "Our version of bar mitzvah occurs at an average age of seven or eight. Our boys are always better readers than non-Samaritan boys in the community.

"We foresee a good future," my informant Benyamin commented, speaking in 2001. "The Palestinian Authority helps Samaritans, but the PA's economic resource is very weak. Therefore, most help now is coming from the government of Israel. The main problems now were political.

We sit on the border between Palestinians and Israelis. There is violence and shooting, and we are caught in the crossfire. We have three festivals per year, but the Samaritans are now afraid to come to Gerizim. In fact, the Israelis are now warning against it. The two Samaritan communities are broken off from each other. The festivals ordinarily attract thousands of people; now there are none. However, there has been a Japanese TV crew on Mount Gerizim for the past two weeks. We welcome them and the opportunity to meet Japanese people."

Nowadays Israeli authorities advise American Jews and pretty much everyone of any nationality against venturing into Palestinian territory, and, of course, Gaza is almost entirely sealed off from the outside world. Journalists need approval by Israeli authorities to work in Palestine, ensuring that nothing too embarrassing to Israel gets reported.

My informant had led delegations to London's Foreign Office and to Washington, D.C. in 1995 and every year since. He wanted the Samaritan community to survive, and survival required peace. "No one thirsts for peace as much as we do," he said. "On the other hand, no one knows or cares about us. We are the smallest nation in the world. I call us a nation because we have our own language and distinctive written script, two things that constitute a nation. At the other extreme are the Chinese." (Think about that: fewer than 800 souls versus over 1.4 billion.)

"God says the Samaritan people must help themselves to be helped by God." He then told a joke to further explain. There was a poor man who needed help. He wouldn't ask for help and he wouldn't accept the slightest aid from his neighbors. The neighbors went to God and asked him to please help this man to win the lottery. God said he would, but the man remained in poverty. The neighbors went back and asked God why. God said, "To win the lottery, he has to buy a lottery ticket!"

"Samaritans is the name outsiders call us. We call ourselves 'the Israelites.'" (The low, seductive voice of Desmond Dekker's catchy reggae song, "The Israelites" began to play as mental background music for the rest of the interview.) In this community I noticed several redheads like myself, at least among men and boys like me and Yakov in the 1950s. I mentioned it, and Benyamin said that the Israelites had always had redheads. He said the Biblical David was known to be a redhead, and that's what gave him his strength. (Maybe that is how my old friend Yakov was able to handle that bully at school!)

We went to Mr. Kohen's home, next to the Passover sacrifice park. His wife invited us in for juice, nuts, and both fresh and dried fruit. Benyamin mentioned that photographers and cameramen like to shoot film from Kohen's rooftop. During festival times, family and friends drop in to one another's house, so everyone keeps trays of snacks ready for visitors. The next day at 4 a.m., the men and boys all dress in White robes and wend their way up the mountain to perform the final part of the Passover ritual, stopping at each of nine sites. The sun breaks as the procession goes up the mountainside. The Samaritans welcome anthropologists, tourists, filmmakers, and any other outsiders who want to accompany the procession.

We talked about religion. I explained that as an anthropologist, I couldn't escape the nagging thought that one's religion seems to depend so much on geography, on where one happened to be born. Benyamin went on to express his own modern-seeming, non-dogmatic views. He surprised me by commenting that he doesn't care whether a person is a believer or non-believer so long as he follows the Golden Rule: Treat others as you would wish them to treat you.

We discussed Samaritan-Christian relations, which seem always to have been good. He was aware that Jesus was always fond of Samaritans, and that Samaritans were among the first who listened to Jesus. He said that people did not need to take the stories/myths of the Old and New Testament literally. He himself did not. He said it was the messages behind the parables that mattered. I asked if the messages came from God or from, say, elders handing down collective wisdom? He said that they had to come from God because when you think about the perplexities of life, human agency cannot explain them. Note that Benyamin is an educated Samaritan who studied history and Biblical studies at Hebrew University. He observed that all creation myths differ from one another. He took this to mean that none were literally true. But he went on to refer to the opening sentences of Genesis, saying that God created heaven and earth and all that is upon it. He described God as a creator and a prime mover. He said creation was achieved by a great *external* force—and that must be God.

When this trip concluded a few weeks later, and I was at the airport in Tel Aviv about to leave, Israeli security agents questioned me at length. They had established during my comings and goings that I was a consultant for CARE International. Yet this time they discovered I possessed a Samaritan book in what appeared to the agents as ancient Hebrew. Who was I, really? Did I actually not speak Hebrew?

At the end of another trip, I had to fly on to the Philippines for a consulting job, which meant Suzie had to depart the airport in Tel Aviv alone. The security people became suspicious of an American woman traveling by herself and they went through her story—and her bags—so thoroughly that she was in tears, she later told me by phone.

The Walls

I was later called back to Palestine for other work. In the field of development, consultants who gain experience in a country or a niche are often invited back. Now I had earned Palestinian chops.

Then in late 2015, I was part of a delegation of philanthropists and entrepreneurs that traveled to Israel and Palestine with a quixotic view toward finding a peaceful solution. We were a rather high-powered bunch. For instance, we had the Apple co-inventor of the iPhone and the Siri language, and so we got to chat with people like ex-President, ex-Prime Minister Shimon Peres, Likud party members, Palestinian Prime Minister Salam Fayyad, leading Palestinian spokespersons from the PA and the non-governmental sector, as well as ordinary people from all levels of society, on both sides of the Israel-Palestine issue. Even before Trump unilaterally moved the US embassy to Jerusalem in 2018, life had grown considerably worse for Palestinians. "Settlers," often from New York, had taken over more and more of their land. High walls surrounded towns like Bethlehem and Nazareth, and most of rural Palestine fell under Israeli military control. Israelis had, indeed, built "facts on the ground" in their relentless appropriation of Palestinian land, believing literally that they are on "a mission from God."

Since I had been there 15 years earlier, the separation of Palestinians and Israeli Jews had grown steadily. The "Separation Principle" seems very much like the old apartheid practice and thinking in South Africa. Israelis and Palestinians lived separately, and their children attended separate schools and so did not mix. At least 42% of the West Bank was by then effectively off-limits to Palestinians because of the settlements and the Separation Wall, largely hemming in rural areas known as Area C, under Israeli military control. Opportunity has increasingly dwindled for person-to-person interaction and hence for friendship, or at least mutual understanding, and the capacity to place oneself in the shoes of another and to develop empathy. Scholars of the region were now speaking of a paradigm shift from an assumption that the Occupation was a temporary phase toward the sense it is permanent, with accelerated efforts to appropriate Palestinian land and remove or quasi-imprison its people.

Wall now surrounding Bethlehem, 2015

"War" periodically erupts, typically triggered when the government forces Palestinian families to leave their homes and neighborhoods in East Jerusalem, and there is interference with Muslims worshiping at Al Aqsa Mosque. It happened again in May 2021, leading to yet another "mowing the lawn," as cynical IDF officials call it. The term refers to the bombing of civilian targets and news media headquarters in Gaza, causing hundreds of deaths and the destruction of infrastructure. The "international community" always regrets the lives lost—on both sides—but the kill ratios are usually 20 Palestinians to 1 Jew (or guest worker from, for example, Thailand). Israel records Jews who suffer cardiac arrest during rocket attacks from Gaza as civilian deaths. Outside money rebuilds the destroyed infrastructure, only to have it bombed again the next time the "lawn" needs to be "mowed."

Of course, in such an asymmetrical power situation, the word "war" is not appropriate. It implies both sides have an army. When the misnamed wars erupt, the US and the West condemn the violence "on both sides" and urge Israel to work toward a two-state solution, even though the window when this might have been feasible has long passed. Israel's right to defend itself is always front and center in the Western media. There is no mention of a parallel Palestinian right to exist. Hamas, which came to power in Gaza though a 2006 democratic election that Israel and the US tried to throw in the direction of more moderate (and malleable) Fatah, was quickly branded a "terrorist organization" by Israel and the US. Even the liberal Western media almost never mention the fact that Hamas was duly elected to govern not only Gaza, but the West Bank as well.

As it happens, the Middle East envoy that President Biden sent to Israel in May 2021 is an old colleague of mine, Hady Amr. We last worked together in Palestine in 2000, and we stayed in touch for a couple more years by email. As a Lebanese American, he has always been careful to not appear biased in favor of Palestine, to have a career in the State Department, where as I conclude this memoir, he is now a Deputy Assistant Secretary of State. We happened to be together in Ramallah in July 2000, speaking with political insider Dr. Mustafa Barghouti, when he received notice that the Camp David peace talks organized by President Clinton had failed. We heard this news a couple hours before the story went public, and a strong reaction from Palestinians was anticipated. In fact, the Second or "Al-Aqsa" Intifada was about to erupt.

Chapter 12
Montenegro: "Gypsy" Refugees

I had several good experiences in Eastern Europe, once my consulting work expanded beyond Africa, but one in Ukraine ranks among my best, one that made me truly glad I had gone into applied anthropology. It happened in Odessa, in a hospital ward for women with breast cancer. I was with my friend, the late Dr. Barbara Pillsbury, who herself was a breast cancer survivor. It was a ward of doom and despair. Women of various ages had all said their farewells to loved ones. Breast cancer was a death sentence in Ukraine in 2000. In 1996, the US Congress established an earmark to provide funding through USAID "to screen, diagnose, and treat victims of breast cancer associated with the 1986 incident at the Chernobyl reactor in Ukraine." Basically, the US funded the project because the wives of Congressmen, not to mention several actual Congresswomen, felt profoundly sorry for victims of the Chernobyl disaster. The money supported treatment for two types of cancer related to major radiation exposure: breast and thyroid.

USAID had selected two hospitals to equip with the latest drugs from the West, one being Tamoxifen. Barbara and I were sitting in the cancer ward at the hospital selected to represent the south. And we were the ones to give gave good news to these women: They had all been diagnosed with Stage 1 or 2 cancer, and Tamoxifen was now to be available for them. They would all get the drug(s), and they would all live! This news was slow to sink in. I looked around the room: I was the only man present in a room full of women. What a privilege to be among these women at the moment they learned they would now survive, by the luck of the draw and their Stage 1 or 2 cancer status—and, of course, the financial assistance of USAID. Slowly the smiles and joy spread around the room. I remember a skinny, elderly women lacking teeth. She was one of the first to absorb the news, and I saw a radiant smile develop on her face.

World Vision and Montenegro

I dropped by a conference of the American Public Health Association in 2001, without being a paid or registered participant. That's the kind of thing one can do in the large hotels in DC, which are always having annual conferences. For instance, once I crashed a conference of the AAA, the American Accordion Association, with a workshop that seemed devoted to Gypsy tunes played in minor keys. This time I chanced to pass by a woman I knew in a busy hallway. She worked for the Christian nonprofit World Vision, and she seemed to have an *aha!* realization that I would fit nicely into World Vision's plan to evaluate a health project in Montenegro. Another advantage of living in DC is that after chance encounters like this, you might get a job regardless of previous regional experience—if you can leave, like, tomorrow.

And so it was that a mere week later, I was working in a new part of the world for me, the former Yugoslavia. I was with the Gypsies of Montenegro, evaluating a comprehensive health project designed and implemented by World Vision, the largest Christian humanitarian organization in the world. In fact, I think it spends more money annually than any other nongovernmental charitable type organization in any country.

This was my first, but not my last experience working for a faith-based organization (FBO). I would find I almost always liked the people and the work atmosphere of an FBO. The staff and consultants tended to be idealists, not cynics. It is easy to fall into cynicism working in "development." After all, billions of dollars are poured annually into poverty reduction, yet there is often little to show for it beyond dependency and corruption. But public health is one of the few areas of development that has achieved genuine, sustained results. My experience with FBOs was that people of faith tended to be working for more than a paycheck. They were willing to work in far-off countries to spread, in the case of World Vision (WV), Christian beliefs and values. When the US government began to designate "failed states" as special targets for critical assistance, the question arose: Who can be persuaded to work in these dangerous places where zealots might videotape do-gooders getting beheaded? Why, FBOs! They will work anywhere where Bibles are in short supply. This observation was articulated by my old friend Ned Greeley, who worked in a senior position at the USAID regional office for East and Southern Africa, in Nairobi. Marginal, unstable countries such as Somalia, the Democratic Republic of Congo, Eritrea, and Sudan were in his bailiwick. He had also gotten me my first USAID consulting job in failing-state Sudan.

World Vision first had a taste of my work in Mozambique, when in a report to USAID I singled out one of WV's community-based programs in central Mozambique as an example of the right way to plan and conduct a health program. I pointed out that rather than creating a new health project from scratch, it had brought back a WV officer who had run a project in the same part of the country, thereby harnessing her expertise and avoiding wasteful time in project design. She was also aware of the many ways a project can go wrong under prevailing circumstances. I made sure WV/Mozambique got a copy of my report, as encouragement. Many of my secular colleagues derided organizations like WV and Catholic Relief Services as mere vehicles for proselytizing. They seemed to forget that the NGO sector in Africa consisted primarily of FBOs, and that most Africans are happy to work with Christian or Muslim FBOs. They may prefer them over secular NGOs.

So now I was tasked with evaluating a World Vision health project for Gypsies expelled from Kosovo. I was told these people are Muslims. They did not speak Roma, the European lingua franca for the people most of the world called Gypsies. These expelled Kosovar "Gypsies" or "Egyptians" claimed descent from the builders of the ancient Egyptian pyramids. So I will use the name they prefer. In one of my first discussions with a Gypsy leader, he commented spontaneously that "World Vision respects us. They have never tried to change our culture." I had told him that there is considerable opposition in America to giving government funds to Christian organizations, for fear they might use the money to seek converts.

The Gypsy leader seemed unaware that WV was even a Christian organization. After all, the project manager was Muslim. The idea that people were criticizing organizations like WV for promoting Christianity annoyed this leader. "Who is saying such things!" he demanded. "It saddens and embarrasses me to hear that Americans can be saying that a group like World Vision would be trying to convert people! Let these liars from the media come and talk to me! Let them ask anyone in this camp. Anyone here can expose this lie!"

It is worth noting that WV was using no US government funds, but paying for this project itself. Therefore, World Vision would have had a right to proselytize, but apparently it didn't.

We later conducted systematic interviews to measure knowledge and behavior several months after the project ended, adding an item to our questionnaire about whether they perceived WV as respectful of Gypsy culture, and whether it had ever interfered with religion or culture in any way. People were surprised at such a question. Their answer was, "Of course not." People were unanimous, unequivocal, and emphatic about it. Many wondered how anyone could even think of such a thing. They saw WV as a humanitarian organization.

It was too bad evidence like this did not find its way to the *New York Times*, I thought. There had been too much discussion about US taxpayer money going to the Scientologists, and how the Constitution would unravel once we go down the slippery slope of funding any FBOs.

One day I was talking with a group of Gypsy women in a camp near Nicsik, Montenegro, about how hard life had been since they were expelled from Kosovo. They were Albanian-speaking, and Muslims, just like the people now in charge of Kosovo. But that didn't help. The ethnic Albanians kicked many or all minority peoples out of Kosovo. Yet, since Montenegro had not yet been recognized as a republic, these Gypsies were considered merely internally displaced persons (IDPs), not refugees. So international agencies like the UN High Commissioner for Refugees could not help them.

A Soothsayer of Coffee Grounds

The Gypsies were speaking in Albanian. My translator came from the obscure mountain people called Guranians, known in these parts for their traditional candy-making. Kosovo had also expelled the Guranians, although they too, like the Gypsies, were Muslims.

The women told me that their men were desperate for money, but there were no jobs for Gypsies. Everyone looked down on them. Their only income came from begging, or picking up scrap metal, or recycling soft drink cans. It was not enough. The women were willing to work too, they emphasized.

"What can you do?" I asked.

One old woman (well, okay, she was about my age) said, "I can see the future."

I considered the possibilities for earning income from telling fanciful just-so stories. Maybe it would work in Northern California, I mused, but times were hard for everyone in Montenegro. So I asked what else she could do.

"I can also see the present and the past."

"How?" I asked.

By using coffee grounds, I was told, a mystical art taught by this woman's aunt.

Well, I couldn't dismiss this claim without seeming rude, and I had just finished a grainy cup of Turkish coffee. So I offered to let her read my past and present life, right there in front of everyone. The woman dumped out my coffee grounds and proceeded to tell my family secrets to all present. Some comments were of course general, such as that "you carry a major issue in your heart and have done so for a long time." But others were quite specific. She said I have had two wives: "Yes, two. I hope you are not embarrassed when I say it aloud!" One wife bore me one child, she continued, a son. I have always been very close with my son. And then about my brother: "He never married because he was bitterly disappointed in love at an early age. And he will never marry."

All true! Her comments were so specific that I felt exposed. I simply told the Gypsy she was "good." If I had confessed that she was 100% accurate in such a public forum, I would have revealed too much about my personal life.

The woman next read the coffee grounds of my translator, and of the two Serbian health educators on my team. Soon, all their family secrets were also out in the open, and they were blushing. Later in the car, my colleagues told me that all the information revealed was basically correct, and none of it was wrong.

Before we left, the soothsayer remarked that her sister who managed to emigrate to Germany once told her that only the lack of a German visa prevented her from becoming rich. A visa to America might make her even richer, I thought. Maybe she could use a manager. I could imagine her on *Geraldo*, on *Oprah*. Maybe she could become Deep Throat for the *National Enquirer* and a dozen other tabloids. And I wouldn't need to keep designing and evaluating health projects in remote countries for the rest of my life. Not that I was not having fun.

Later, driving through the Montenegro mountains in search of other Gypsies who had benefited from the World Vision project, the driver and I spoke of the horrors of ethnic conflict and mass murder in the former Yugoslavia. My two colleagues in the back seat spoke poor English, and so were not part of these discussions. But finally, the young Serbian health educator (whom the Albanians had expelled, like the driver) spoke up. I think he had been rehearsing the English required for this question for a while and he asked, in a thick Slavic accent, "Ted. You are Amerikanski and as old as my father. Tell me, what was it like to live in... in the Age of Aquarius? Was it truly, truly sex, drugs and rock 'n' roll?"

I thought about this briefly and solemnly replied that yes, it was truly, truly like that.

He looked at me with awe and said no more during the entire trip.

240 ON THE FRINGE

Chapter 13
Suddenly, The Ivy League

By 2001, I was taking assignments on all inhabited continents save Australia, as I was proud to say if asked, and I continued to publish scholarly articles as well as books. My mentor Russ Bernard, used to encourage me to keep writing and publishing, often saying that non-academic anthropologists like me who publish "can be counted on one hand," surely an exaggeration, but it made me feel special.

The Mystery of AIDS in Uganda

I had made my first trip to Uganda in 1993 as a side consultancy from my work in nearby Tanzania. Even back then, the world was beginning to notice that HIV prevalence in Uganda was not shooting up as it seemed to be in the rest of Sub-Saharan Africa. Why? That year I was traveling to Kampala to give one week's worth of advice to USAID's first bilateral AIDS prevention project, so I had a chance to look into the question. I was also being considered for a full-time job there with the prevention project, run by World Learning, one of the definitely better contractors I was familiar with.

During my week in Uganda, I did what I imagine most anthropologists would do: Gather as much information as possible from informants knowledgeable about HIV and current trends in behavior. I sat down with clinicians who treated Ugandans with STDs, with the heads of prevention programs or support groups for HIV-positive men and women, with clergy, and with countless nurses and social workers, sometimes chasing them down the halls of government offices or clinics.

An interesting picture began to emerge. The number of people with STDs of any kind seemed to be declining. But how was that possible? Colleagues who worked in AIDS prevention told me that Uganda's President Museveni was hostile to the US (and Western) plan to flood Uganda with condoms. Consequently, condoms had been relatively hard to get in the early 1990s, even compared to other African countries. Ergo, colleagues said, it was impossible for HIV incidence (the rate of new infections) to be falling: it must actually be rising.

This was a time when researchers literally quantified AIDS-related "behavior change" by number of crates of condoms distributed. They did not consider factors such as number of lifetime or current sexual partners ("partner concurrency"), or median age of first sexual intercourse ("sexual debut") particularly relevant. Nor was there interest in male circumcision. AIDS prevention became all about what I would soon be calling a "technological fix." Sexual behavior and ideas about trying to change it were almost taboo. There was a historical reason for this.

HIV first arose in the United States among groups that were marginalized, and which suffered discrimination and rejection by the wider society. Gay men were victims of stigma and discrimination, and they died in droves at a time when the governments of the United States and other countries seemed to care little about a new disease that seemed to primarily infect gay men. Some religious authorities even said that homosexuals were just getting what they deserved. A sense of victimhood and a strong and understandable aversion to anyone's moralizing judgement about sexual behavior still lay at the foundation of AIDS prevention, even a generation later and in Africa. Public health measures such as contact tracing (locating the partners of people found HIV-positive) were considered "stigmatizing," and were not carried out.

Then there is the stereotype of the hyper-sexed African male. As I wrote in my 2011 book *Broken Promises*, in the global community that is AIDS World, one routinely encounters variants of this sentiment: "Most Africans begin sex at an early age and then are highly sexually active, with a great many sexual partners." One heard this idea at USAID, UNAIDS, the CDC, the World Bank, the Global Fund, UNICEF, and many other organizations. I can't count the times Western AIDS experts have told me that "an African man's idea of fidelity is to be faithful to his current five (eight, ten...) wives or girlfriends." When I asked what percentage of African men actually had five or ten partners per year, I usually got no answer, or was told we couldn't believe surveys about sexual behavior because "everyone lies." Many colleagues were using AIDS-related studies much as a drunk uses a lamppost: more for support than illumination.

In fact, the stereotyping was a close cousin to racism. At a meeting of family planning experts and their Congressional supporters in the Capitol dome building, Rep. Chris Shays (R-CT) said, "Asking an African to abstain is like trying to repeal the law of gravity." When I consulted the actual data, such as about lifetime number of sexual partners or proportion of (unmarried) teenagers who were sexually active, Africans turned out to be more conservative than North Americans or Western Europeans! It seemed my colleagues were unaware of these facts, or just didn't believe them.

One day in 2001, while I was back working at the Futures Group (half-time by choice, so I could still consult for other organizations), it really hit me how all Western aid agencies shared the same distorted, myopic view that the only way Africans and other "less developed" peoples could reduce HIV infections was through constant and consistent condom use. In the pre-AIDS era, USAID family planning department head Ray Ravenholt famously recommended dropping millions of condoms from the sky, as the solution to over-population. I published a photo that captures condoms-from-the-sky via helicopter for AIDS prevention in Swaziland in my 2003 book, *Rethinking AIDS Prevention*. Yet here were the facts: In Uganda, if we considered all men aged 15–49, they used an average of four condoms per year (!), on the low side for Africa. The highest rate was in HIV hot-spot Zimbabwe (10) and the lowest in Ghana (2). Greater use of condoms was somehow associated with higher, not lower, HIV infection rates, probably because it was a proxy for sexual behavior outside of marriage. Yet all these rates were embarrassingly low for those who believed condoms were the primary solution to AIDS in Africa. But on that day in 2001, my subversive ideas about AIDS prevention were still developing. I could not know what lay ahead.

I decided my first step was to state my case in a book. I had already learned that journal editors—especially medical journal editors—do not take kindly to attacks on established paradigms, by anthropologists or anyone else. Besides, a full exposé was essential. I could not kick the props from under the prevailing paradigm in a single article, no matter how long. So on that day I dashed off a book proposal. It's probably not a good idea to write a book proposal in a pique of righteous indignation, but that's what I did. I decided to go with a new publisher for me, so since the Internet Age had dawned I simply googled "academic publishers." I chose ten among the names that popped up and fired off my hastily written proposal along with my full CV.

In the next two weeks, I got three acceptances, to my surprise. I decided to go with perhaps the best known publisher, Praeger. A week or so after signing with them, I got a (modest) check in the mail. An advance! I had never gotten an advance before, and it never occurred to me to try to negotiate for one. A book advance surely put me in the same category as Hemingway and James Joyce!

Off to Harvard

One day in late summer of 2001, as we packed up in our Maine house to return to DC, Suzie asked, "Why don't we try to live here year round. Why don't you get a job at Harvard? That's pretty nearby." It was a 90-minute drive in good traffic.

"Well," I said. "I'm a freelance consultant and that means I have to be in DC, where all the international action originates. In the belly of the beast, so to speak."

Suzie argued if I was going to try to expose a multibillion-dollar global AIDS industry as ineffective, it might be better to have an esteemed institution after my name. Well, sure, but how could I get to Harvard at age 56, after being a nonacademic, applied anthropologist for so many years? A month later, on a listserv dedicated to international health that I checked intermittently, I just happened to see a notice about applications for postdocs at Harvard's Takemi Program in International Health: "For those scholars in mid-career who already have an independent research program with potential to impact international health policy."

Well, I was clearly beyond mid-career, plus burdensome applications were due in just a few days. *Hmmm.* I dashed off a letter with a few words about who I was, and asking if I could have an extra week to get my application package together. I explained that I had just signed a contract with Praeger Press to write a book exposing the multibillion dollar global AIDS industry as Eurocentrically biased and ineffective, potentially accounting for *millions* of unnecessary deaths because experts considered fundamental behavioral change impossible among dark-skinned people. The standard formula (then) of condoms and testing had failed, I boldly declared, yet Uganda had succeeded by reducing multiple, concurrent sexual partners. I frankly stated that my theory was politically incorrect and had already met with strong resistance. A year at Harvard would be great: I could devote fulltime to writing the book I had just started, plus I would have the gravitas of a top university to try and influence AIDS policy.

The Takemi program wrote back to say that my idea sounded "interesting" and I could take the extra week to gather my application materials. The head of the program Michael Reich knew I might be an unusual character, he told me later, but a letter of recommendation by former Takemi Fellow Charles Good helped. I spent academic 2001 and 2002 writing *Rethinking AIDS Prevention* and speaking out about sexual behavior change as much as possible. I teamed up with Ugandan infectious disease specialist Vinand Nantulya, who had been a Takemi Fellow the previous year. The head of the Takemi program thought highly of Vinand, and so I ran my ideas past him. It turned out that we saw the situation in Uganda virtually the same way. It also turned out that Vinand had been an advisor to the then-new Ugandan President Museveni, starting in 1986. He and I would present together, including once on a Voice of America TV broadcast that went out to several African countries. USAID also funded my effort to conduct research on the relative merits of the elements of the ABC strategy—Abstain, Be faithful, or use a Condom—in six countries, with me as principal investigator. If this seems commonsensical, the radical thing was the inclusion of the first two elements. Virtually no funding went to either A or B, to any interventions that addressed basic sexual behavior at that time.

Western planners wanted to understand how most African parents felt about AIDS. To give one example, if prevention meant "condoms only" (or was perceived as "condoms mostly") African parents would not accept campaigns for their children and family members because condoms were associated with promiscuity. They were not used by married couples. Moreover, as mentioned, many or most NGOs in Africa were religious. Therefore, even if promoting the delay of sexual debut for young people and "fidelity" for adults did not work—though it did—you'd have to include something other than condoms to mobilize African support. I saw this as Anthropology 101, as something basic, when Western values were promoted in the traditional, religious societies of Africa, where most HIV infections were found, and continue to be found to this day (69% of all HIV infections are found in Africa.)

Yet in the early decades, AIDS missionaries tended to be gay American men who sought the relatively few gay African men they could find, not an easy task. Gay Americans treated them as long-lost brothers, to the point of often getting these men on antiretroviral drugs before these were available to the general heterosexual population. All of which might be laudable— except that HIV in Africa was not, and is not, concentrated among gay men (known in the biz as MSM, men who have sex with men). "Know your epidemic!" I, and my small, but growing number of "behavior change" colleagues began to scream out. It was Epidemiology 101 as well as Anthropology 101. The fact that there was bitter controversy over this issue seems to surprise most people outside the field of AIDS.

The Iconoclast

During my first year as a post-doc fellow in Harvard's Takemi program, Suzie and I typically spent Monday through Thursday in Cambridge, staying at a three-story wood-frame house on Harvard Street, built in 1875, which later became a bed-and-breakfast place. It came with free parking. From there we could walk to restaurants, museums, and theaters around Harvard Square and Central Square. Suzie would visit places such as the Peabody Museum. After work, she and I would often explore Cambridge, which is especially beautiful in the fall. We ate at places like the John Harvard Tavern or The Dolphin on Mass Avenue for fresh broiled bluefish.

My office was at the School of Public Health, near the med school across the Charles River in Boston. There was a free shuttle bus for people like me, and it ran between the med school and the main campuses every 20 minutes or so. Suzie was taking a painting class at the Boston Museum of Fine Arts, four blocks from my office.

The six other Takemi Research Fellows in International Health were all foreign—two from India, two from Japan, one each from Indonesia and Nigeria—and most had MDs along with their PhDs. I liked them all. My research fellowship had minimal responsibilities, by design, so I could devote most of my time to my new book. All I was doing was giving an occasional seminar on my work and picking the brains of people like virologists, epidemiologists, and economists on both campuses about global AIDS issues during one-on-one meetings. I was also taking full advantage of Harvard's library and other resources. I had already found gems by browsing the library stacks.

My book was coming along better and faster than anticipated. It was stimulating to deal with major current issues that stirred up controversy, with questions like:

- Does poverty (apartheid, racism, homophobia) cause AIDS, or at least drive epidemics?
- Should we (wealthy nations) raise $8–10 billion per year for AIDS, and should most of this go to providing antiretroviral drugs to the poor?
- Are condoms the answer to AIDS?
- Can sexual behavior really change? Can *African* sexual behavior change?
- Do "faith-based initiatives" have a role in AIDS prevention, at least in Africa?

It was all the more stimulating because I disagreed with virtually all of Harvard's AIDS experts on every issue. Yet I was surrounded by foreign postdocs, and I noticed that they were always receptive to, and supportive of, my ideas that challenged orthodoxy. So during my first year at Harvard, I was insulated from the disapproval—and sometimes the wrath—that would make my life difficult after my Takemi Fellowship year ended.

After my Takemi year, Michael Reich, the Director of the Center for Population and Development Studies at Harvard, secured a three-year, renewable appointment for me, to give me extra time to finish my book. He also thought that I, perhaps along with Vinand, could take leadership roles in establishing a broad, university-wide AIDS prevention initiative. This valuable project never really took off because we were going against the amazingly entrenched, passionately defended AIDS prevention paradigm; and because Vinand accepted a very senior job in Geneva before my first year was even up, leaving me to fight the fight alone at Harvard. I would have had so much more credibility with a Ugandan doctor at my side.

Michael also asked me to help address problems with a $50 million AIDS prevention effort in Nigeria, funded by the Bill & Melinda Gates Foundation. I was able to draw a little salary from that project, and give advice that I saw as Africa-friendly and Africa-necessary. My idea was to actively involve the many Christian and Muslim FBOs in the fight against AIDS. Since our partners in Nigeria were academics, there was enthusiasm to launch a feasibility study of the idea of FBO partnership. I felt we already knew the answer to that question: Nigerian FBOs like those in Uganda would be happy to be asked (and funded) to participate in AIDS prevention.

The Persistent Fraud Syndrome

There were days at Harvard when everything seemed charmed. I couldn't believe I was part of the scene. It is possible that for a while I was gliding along in a form of hypomania, or elevated mood state, taking on more and more responsibilities. For one thing, I was on two important national advisory committees—the Presidential Advisory Council for HIV/AIDS (2003-2007) and the Office of AIDS Research Advisory Council, National Institutes of Health (2003-2006)—and they required that I fly to

Washington for six meetings every year. In addition, I testified in Congress four times in person, and a fifth time in writing, because on that day I was running a mini-conference in South Africa.

But at times I felt completely out of my depth, and anxiety piled on anxiety. Something would shift, and I'd be overcome with profound self-doubt. I felt I was a fraud posing as a Harvard expert. Then I would effectively shut down for a time, hiding out from people, promises, and responsibilities. For example, the President's Emergency Plan for AIDS Relief, or PEPFAR, was a federal initiative to reduce the global AIDS epidemic. Once they asked me to give the keynote speech to the annual global PEPFAR conference, in Addis Ababa. The audience was restive and even angry at my audacity in telling them essentially that their condoms approach was not succeeding, while the quiet, under-the-radar behavior-change strategy of Uganda seemed to be working, in spite of the fact that international donors had not underwritten any such prevention approaches, and dismissed them as George W. Bush religion-inspired nonsense.

I was showing slides I had created directly from demographic and health survey data, considered the gold standard in international reproductive health and AIDS circles, yet people in the audience were not paying attention—some were even talking to each other—very off-putting for someone who doesn't like public speaking to begin with. Fortunately, on this most difficult of days, I had woken up somehow feeling unusually confident. Such was the unpredictability of my moods.

I left Addis sunk in depression and insecurity. I cancelled a workshop I had agreed to run—in Ethiopia no less, and I was already there! I also reneged on my promise to mentor a USAID officer. I just dropped out for a couple of weeks, until my mood (brain?) cycled back to a more normal—at least, functional—mindset.

One interesting thing happened about a year later. A friend from my board work in primate conservation had a personal connection with an award-winning, superstar professor at Harvard, outside Pubic Health or the medical school. He arranged a meeting between me and this professor to tell him about our project. I anticipated this with some trepidation. The plan was to have lunch together. About 15 minutes before the meeting, the young prof called me and said he could only stay about 10 or 15 minutes, so it wouldn't really be lunch. This was because he suffered from "a chronic disease."

Uncharacteristically for me, I asked, "Um... what disease?"

"Depression," he replied.

"I can really relate," I said.

We soon met and went on to have a deep, frank, enthusiastic, soul-baring conversation about depression and insecurities, feelings of inadequacy, the Fraud Syndrome, and related topics for a good two hours. I had found someone like me! It was a cathartic and affirming experience for me, and probably for the other man as well. I was reminded that during one of my earlier periods of depression and anxiety at Harvard, I had a session with a trained counselor whose job it was to keep students and faculty from jumping out of windows or swallowing poison. The counselor told me, "You'd be truly astonished at the number of famous Harvard scholars who feel exactly as insecure as you."

So just when my self-confidence should have been moving in the right direction, near the end of my active consulting career, I had suddenly, almost accidentally, found myself at Harvard. I began to see myself as a fraud once more. *I don't belong here with the top brains in the country! This is not where failures end up! There has been some terrible mistake.* I swung almost in bipolar pattern, from feeling okay about myself and my work on certain days, to low, depressive periods during which I was robbed of any self-confidence that developed from my happy (or hypomanic?) phases. These mood swings recurred with fairly regular periodicity, but I had no idea exactly when downswings would occur. So I might agree to give a public presentation, or to be someone's mentor, but as in Ethiopia, if the pendulum swung in the wrong direction I would have to cancel out and let people down, which would make me feel even worse about myself.

On one occasion, I was asked to give a presentation to Bill Gates Sr. about my exciting findings regarding a Gates-funded project in three

African countries. My findings were that behavior change really works, moreover rural Africans could support a prevention program that includes abstinence and "fidelity" as well as condoms, but not one that focuses on condoms above all else. So here I was. I could potentially influence how the largest private donor in the world spent its money on AIDS prevention—already a priority area of Gates funding. But the pressure in my mind rose to a feverish pitch, so as the day approached, I claimed that I had come down with the flu and so could not possibly appear in person. I carefully made up a PowerPoint, and a colleague of mine (who happened to hate public speaking as much as I do) was left with the task—and all the pressure. There was no discernible impact on the Gates Foundation. If I had been there, able to answer questions, there was a chance I could have exerted some influence on the father of the then-richest man on the planet, and thus on AIDS policies.

Making a deal with HIV

I had managed some interviews during a World Bank evaluation of AIDS programs in Mozambique, in 2002. One took place on our second day there, with the head of the HIV/AIDS group, the widow of Eduardo Mondlane, the first president of independent Mozambique. Our full group was meeting mostly to lay out the general plan and timelines for our mission. By then, I was having pneumonia symptoms that also stayed with me for the whole trip. Nevertheless, I had a memorable first encounter with David Ross Patient, a gay AIDS activist who, with his partner Neill Orr, both of Nelspruit, South Africa, was running probably the first NGO for HIV-infected Mozambicans. Mrs. Mondlane had urged me to meet with David and Neill to better understand AIDS in Mozambique. Their nonprofit had a modest grant from somewhere. I would go on to greatly admire David for his powerful message to fellow HIV sufferers, and for his courage and humor. For many years, people regarded him as an anomaly, a man HIV-infected at the earliest point of the global pandemic—probably the late 1970s, in the San Francisco gay bathhouse scene—and yet he seemed free from the disease AIDS.

The following is the story he would tell groups of HIV-infected men.

He had taken part in the very first clinical trial of the drug AZT in the early 1980s, and he came to realize that the first dubious "cure" available then might be worse than the disease. One day, sitting on a cliff near San Francisco and facing the sparkling blue Pacific, he addressed his disease, saying, "Let's make a deal. I won't try to kill you with toxic drugs if you won't kill me. Are we in agreement?" His anxiety level immediately plunged. Empowered with this feeling of truce, David went on to live nearly 40 more years. He did develop actual AIDS in the early 2000s (if I have his dates right), and his HIV viral load began gradually to increase. In spite of his earlier pact with his disease, he was persuaded to start taking antiretroviral drugs. He continued to spread his message of hope and means to take care of one's body and spirit with nutrition, herbs, and meditation. He died in 2017 of pneumonia after a surgery, in Port Elizabeth, South Africa. He was one of my prominent gay supporters of behavior change for AIDS prevention.

I had participated in the Geneva Global AIDS Conference in 1998, where I met and interviewed long-term survivors from around the globe. I published a journalistic style article in the *Journal of Alternative and Complementary Medicine*, where I observed:

"At least a dozen survivors I chanced to meet have chosen not to take conventional antiretroviral drugs of any sort, singly or in 'combo cocktails.' Instead, they rely on a range of other therapies, including herbs, nutrition, yoga, meditation, acupuncture, exercise regimens, homeopathy, massage, and movement therapy, among others. A number (but not all) had stopped smoking and drinking alcohol and had opted for generally healthy lifestyles. Many were of the opinion that their greatest strength was simply in not believing that an HIV diagnosis means a death sentence. They had positive attitudes and faith in the future."

They seemed to be following the advice in the widely circulated booklet for PLWAs (Persons Living with AIDS) written by David Patient and Neill Orr. Some of them had read this booklet.

Linda McCartney's Favorite Aunt

I gained an addition to the small team at Harvard working with me on my AIDS research grant. Rose Friesch was an "I'll never retire!" associate professor in her mid-80s, and she'd done all kinds of wonderful scholarly things during her more active days at Harvard, publishing books and articles in *The Lancet* and *Science*. She was also the favorite aunt of the late Linda McCartney. She and Linda were always very close, and so Rose had great stories about adventures with the Beatles. For example, she would stay with Linda and Paul on their farm in England, and from the first visit, she noticed there wasn't a single book in the house. Since Rose herself always liked to read before going to sleep, she mentioned this to Linda. Linda just smiled and said, "Oh, Rose you know I just never read anything." Rose mentioned this comment to Linda's father (Rose's brother, Paul), who promptly sent the McCartneys a complete set of the *Encyclopedia Britannica*. But she thinks they were never opened.

Jump ahead to when Linda was sick with cancer and knew she was dying. She asked her Aunt Rose to recommend the 20 books that she ought to read before it was too late, books that would be both edifying and enjoyable. The first two on Aunt Rose's list were *The Portrait of an Artist as a Young Man* and *Huckleberry Finn*. Linda McCartney spent some of her last days reading these books.

I gave Rose a lift to her home one afternoon because it was raining, plus she then lived not far from Harvard Square. She pointed out Linda's father's old house to me as we drove by, as well as Linda's sister's house. Her favorite Beatles album was "Abbey Road."

Linda's dad, Paul Epstein, changed his name to Eastman to pass unnoticed among *goyim*. Linda grew up with people thinking she was from

Kodak's Eastman family. This notion gained strength when she became a photographer.

Rose eventually did semi-retire. In June 2010, Suzie and I visited her in a nursing home a short walk from Harvard Square. She was still plodding to work twice a week, and still doing cutting-edge scientific research on leptin (body fat). She was having her 92nd birthday in a few weeks when I last saw her. Harvard—which never promoted her to full professor (I thought they never treated her well, from what I could see)—finally got around to awarding her a special professor emerita status. She believes "that nice man" Michael Reich was behind the award.

She told me another thing about Linda McCartney that saddened me: She said Linda could have saved herself if she had consented to a double mastectomy. But she was afraid Paul might not find her attractive anymore and she could not bear the thought.

But Rose and Paul McCartney stayed in touch after Linda's death. Paul would usually call her when he was in the US. He would invite her to concerts, but she was invariably too busy with her research... plus, she was proud to not have to wear a hearing aid, like almost all the others at her assisted care home, and she didn't want to start worrying about hearing loss in the presence of loud rock music.

Travels with Tommy Thompson and Anthony Fauci

In December 2003, DHHS Secretary Tommy Thompson invited me to join an AIDS-related junket to Africa to fact-find about AIDS. In addition to Secretary Thompson, the group included Ambassador Richard Holbrooke; Randall Tobias, the newly appointed AIDS Ambassador; the directors of NIH, CDC, the WHO and the Global Fund; a senator; a congressman; and the CEOs of Pfizer, Merck, and Gilead Sciences. And Tony Fauci, who was later to gain notoriety trying in vain to warn and advise Donald Trump about the Covid19 pandemic. Secretary Thompson had asked me along because I had been instrumental in persuading the Bush Administration to adopt Uganda's "behavior change" model of AIDS prevention for the 14 countries targeted in the President's Emergency Plan for AIDS Relief.

Not long into the flight to Africa, I walked up to the front of the plane to introduce myself to Ambassador Holbrooke, the semi-famous diplomat widely expected to become secretary of state in a Hillary Clinton administration. I knew he had worked for my dad just when his career began to take off. I am not one who usually interrupts bigshots when they are deep in conversation with a bodyguarded Cabinet member, just to introduce myself, but an impulse had me doing it. Holbrooke immediately banished any nervousness and told the group he was delighted to meet me, and mentioned to those within earshot that he used to work for my dad. I gained some gravitas at once. He commented that he was sad that both my parents died relatively young. Then he launched into stories about the infamous and storied Lisa Green, the woman who loved to "control everyone's lives!" With great flair, Holbrooke shared anecdotes about my mother's efforts to help or hinder the careers of foreign service officers she liked or disliked, to the amusement of those at the front of the plane. The stories were true— and, of course, was there any life Lisa tried to manipulate more than my own, her #2 son? But, wait a second, these strangers on the plane were laughing at the expense of... my mother! That didn't seem right.

Lisa Green did, indeed, try to control others' lives, starting with her sons and later, grandson. An example: In 1960 my older brother had announced to our parents his decision to attend college at Berkeley, not Yale, even though he had dutifully applied and been admitted there. My father, a Yalie, was perhaps a little disappointed, but my mother's face went deathly pale. That evening she came into my bedroom and warned, "Don't let your brother throw away his life!" She proceeded to remind me that a young man nowadays simply could not go into the world without at least one Ivy League degree. But Mark was determined. As it happened, *Time* or *Newsweek* ran an article a few weeks later that ranked universities by the number of Nobel Prize winners on their faculties. And wouldn't you know? Berkeley boasted about five more Nobel laureates than Yale! Needless to say, my mother went around to her friends—really, to anyone who would listen—and said, "My oldest son is going to Berkeley because it has overtaken Yale, his other option, in its number of Nobel Prize winners."

No second-rate dumps for #1 Son.

My book *Rethinking AIDS Prevention*, hot off the press at that time, had become a topic of conversation among delegates on this trip. Richard Holbrooke rapid-read it during our first few days together, and persuaded Ambassador Randy Tobias (Bush's new Global AIDS Coordinator, who later rose to be USAID Administrator) to read it. This led to spirited discussions about what does and does not work in AIDS prevention, and how the epidemics in Africa and the United States were different. During a bus ride between Kampala and Entebbe, Ambassador Tobias and I were midway in one such discussion when Dr. Anne Peterson, the leading health official at USAID, joined the discussion. It was the perfect opportunity and setting (no interruptions, informal dialogue) to explain the most compelling evidence for Uganda's unparalleled decline in HIV prevalence, to speak truth to power. And power seemed to listen, with the possible exception of Tony Fauci, top scientist for infectious diseases at NIH. Fauci had been very involved with America's early response to the newly arisen retrovirus. He confronted but eventually made peace with gay activists, and eventually earned their trust and respect. He acted formal and distant toward me, probably seeing me as a Bush appointee and therefore a religious conservative.

A memorable event for most of us was a field trip to remote rural villages in Tororo district, Uganda. We visited families there where HIV-positive patients had been receiving antiretroviral drugs for several months, delivered by health workers on motorcycles. Some of the HIV-infected had, in their own words, recently returned from the threshold of death, a phenomenon called the Lazarus Effect, referring to Jesus raising the dead, or in this case, the nearly dead. But was this high-cost approach replicable on an Africa-wide or global scale? Subsequent studies showed that HIV antiretroviral drugs could bring "viral loads" of the HIV-infected down to levels so low that the person could not transmit HIV to others.

So-called treatment-as-prevention has now become the most popular approach to AIDS, and has driven up the cost of prevention superexponentially. Uganda's early prevention program cost $21,676,000 over five years, or a mere twenty-five cents per person, per year. Meanwhile, we in the West were pouring *billions* of dollars into programs that were having little effect, if not a negative effect, before treatment drugs became widely available. To be unabashedly cynical, the problem with a low-tech approach based on simple behavior change is that there are no commodities, no condoms, devices or drugs, and therefore no AIDS industry.

But the HIV pandemic is not over. By 2021, with treatment-as-prevention, and rates of treatment of over 90% of patients, HIV prevalence in Swaziland (now Eswatini) stubbornly remained at 27% in spite of all the money thrown at the problem. Part of the reason for this figure of course is that HIV-infected people are being kept alive, and prevalence rates reflect this.

Back to 2003, I was invited to make a 15-minute speech to the whole delegation on our last evening in Africa. I made a plea that in our own excitement over finally being able to bring life-saving drugs to the poor of Africa, we must not neglect basic HIV primary prevention. One possible downside of providing antiretrovirals is that people may feel less need to avoid risky sexual behavior, as had happened in the US. This phenomenon is called "behavioral disinhibition," or "risk compensation" meaning a medical or technological "fix" becomes available, so why worry about getting the disease? My colleagues and I later did a study in Uganda published in journal articles between 2011 and 2015, where we documented this phenomenon in what had been the world's first and best AIDS success story. Since that early success, Ugandans were subjected to messages that emphasized drugs and condoms, and simple cautionary messages about changing or avoiding risky behavior were being forgotten. Antiretroviral drugs meant that HIV-positive people no longer appeared sick. AIDS prevention had become Westernized and infection rates were rising again. Of course, with fewer deaths from AIDS, one would expect prevalence to at least remain the same, if not creep upward.

I should mention, at least in passing, the work I did on PACHA, the Presidential Advisory Council on HIV/AIDS. Unlike a similar Advisory council for NIH (National Institutes of Health) which consisted exclusively of scientific experts, PACHA was made up of a balance of scientists and people representing communities impacted by AIDS, therefore leaders of gay and African-American or Hispanic groups. Gay or straight, I found non-Whites especially sympathetic to, and understanding of, my emphasis on sexual behavior as the primary driver of HIV infection.

One night, I was invited to dinner with fellow PACHA member Dr. Hank McKinnel, then the CEO of Pfizer. His message to me was, "In God we trust. All others, bring evidence." This dinner in DC began an alliance that led to a suggestion by Hank that we at PACHA undertake the following exercise: We would describe exactly what would be needed to bring down HIV incidence (rate of new infections) to zero, putting aside politics and concerns about funding. I had been trying to get the major donor organizations to focus on sexual behavior and not treat it as an immutable "given," or a taboo subject. And for that matter, I and some colleagues in anthropology (e.g., Priscilla Reining, Robert Bailey, Daniel Halperin) had also been trying to get male circumcision to be taken seriously as an important (and not taboo) factor in understanding HIV transmission. Promotion of "voluntary medical male circumcision" (VMC) became public policy in Africa several years later, after this intervention was found in three RCTs (randomized, controlled trails, one by Bailey) to reduce significantly the chances of HIV transmission.) I had tried to get USAID to consider at least studying VMC in 1991, because I discovered evidence of VMC happening on the advice of traditional healers in South Africa. The senior USAID official at the time in charge of HIV/AIDS recoiled when I made my pitch. He told me he would "not touch this issue with a ten-foot pole." My argument that some South Africans were already doing this, more or less on their own, failed to persuade him.

Back to PACHA, we published a book that contained our recommendations, a consensus statement of what was needed to defeat AIDS. Sexual behavior change and the urgent need for research into the promising factor of male circumcision were much emphasized. Decisive support of my views came from minority group members of PACHA, especially African Americans. And I was able to tell anyone who would listen that the CEO of the largest pharmaceutical company in the world found it simple-minded to think that condoms were the primary solution to AIDS, but that is what almost everyone thought before a pharmacological solution "Treatment as Prevention" became embraced. My new ally Hank actually commissioned a Pfizer study in Uganda, and its findings generally supported my own.

Our idea of bringing down HIV incidence to zero seems to have caught on because not long after our book *Achieving an AIDS-Free Generation* (2005), the joint UN program on HIV and AIDS (UNAIDS) began a policy of "getting to Zero" AIDS deaths (along with zero discrimination and stigma) by 2015. Other government and private organizations began to likewise speak of "getting to Zero" new HIV infections. Could this way of thinking have started with Hank McKinnel and my immediate and enthusiastic seconding of his idea when it was first formally proposed at PACHA?

At the time of our PACHA work, key scientists representing different viewpoints on global AIDS were able to publish a consensus statement in *The Lancet* (2004). This led to a least one memorable public debate I found myself in with Dr. Helene Gayle who was representing the Gates Foundation (a version of this debate was televised in Seattle.) She was arguing that "we" (the major donor organizations) had "always" promoted sexual behavior change (reducing concurrent sexual partners.) I was able to reply that this is not what "we" said in our publication in *The Lancet*, where she Helene Gayle was in fact a co-author. (She had only reluctantly signed on as a co-author when prompted.) There was no answer to this.

Among the Satan-Worshipping Cannibals

Applied anthropologists travel a lot, and when you do the kind of anthropological work I have done, for as long as I have, you cover a lot of the world's more exotic spots. Sometimes this gets me in trouble back home. Once in 2003 Suzie and I arrived a bit early for a meeting in Portsmouth, NH, so we joined a little anti-war demonstration that took place there every Friday afternoon. The demonstrators were middle-aged or elderly, like us, with serious demeanors, and dressed casual-chic. Perhaps Spiro Agnew would have characterized them as effete, intellectual Unitarian nattering nabobs of nihilism, or by Trump as radical, left-wing, America-hating, Satan-worshiping, pedophile cannibals. Or liberal peaceniks for short.

So Suzie and I showed up and joined the small demonstration, already in progress along the main street. An elderly couple stood aside to make room for us, and gave me a couple of SAY NO TO WAR placards to hold up. A matron standing to my left made some comments that showed me she was knowledgeable about Iraqi issues. When she mentioned the Baath party, I commented that my grandfather was US ambassador to Iraq just before the Baathists came to power in the mid-1950s. She told me that this was really most interesting. She then mentioned how Saddam was trying to link his nefarious activities with the Palestinian cause, to look better in the eyes of the world, so of course I mentioned that I'd been working in Palestine recently. She exclaimed, "That's really fascinating! I mean, here are all of us demonstrating week after week, and now along comes somebody who's actually BEEN to Israel and the Palestinian territories. I'm so glad you've joined us today!"

She then drew parallels between the Iraq crisis and the Vietnam War. And well, you know, I like to be personable, so of course I mentioned that I'd worked in Vietnam not long ago, and in fact I married my wife (yes, that woman standing right next to me) in a Buddhist ceremony in Danang. She again said that this revelation was fascinating, but I noticed a tone of doubt creeping into her voice. I added that we had honeymooned in China Beach, just like the place in that old TV show that was set during the Vietnam War.

She next asked me if the present situation was as serious a threat to world peace as the Cuban missile crisis. I couldn't stop myself. Even though my credibility was slipping fast with this woman (and why was it so important that she believe me?), I told her it just so happens I worked in Cuba for a couple of weeks in 1985... you know, with the former CIA head of Cuban Operations.

She then asked me what I thought about the petition drawn up by a group of Harvard professors to pressure the Harvard Corporation to divest from Israeli businesses. Well, I knew I was growing less and less plausible by the minute, but somehow I couldn't seem to respond without mentioning that in fact I just happen to be a research scientist at Harvard at the moment. This was all getting to be too much for her.

Suzie and I had only come to demonstrate for a short time and it was starting to get dark, so I told the lady we had to be going. She assured me it had been fascinating to meet me, but I could sense that she was growing nervous, that perhaps she was beginning to think I might be a madman. Then I realized that I could at least leave her with a little evidence that I had not been making everything up. So I reached into my wallet and gave her my business card from the Harvard School of Public Health. She looked at it and smiled thinly and said that she hoped we could meet again at another demonstration.

As I was driving home, I realized I'd given her the wrong card! It was from Harvard all right, but it belonged to an African colleague I had just met that day, someone with a thoroughly African name like Ndabazabantu Mbambabashambo, MD, Pediatrician.

After seeing that card with that name, I could imagine the woman telling her husband and the whole band of peace-loving Unitarians that there was some crazy man going around impersonating an African Harvard professor and claiming, like Forrest Gump, to have been *everywhere* of current topical interest.

I feel I can no longer show my face in Portsmouth, NH.

Chapter 14
China: Missionary Doctors
and Hill Tribe Minorities

In 2005, I gave a lecture to a large group of Evangelical Christians in Louisville, Kentucky. As I have already underscored, faith-based organizations are extremely influential and powerful in Africa. They pretty much *are* the non-governmental sector. Western AIDS prevention programs cannot ignore or circumvent FBOs. The Louisville organizers had tried to schedule me once before, but I opted out a week before the annual conference. A year later, in 2005, the group again beseeched me in the strongest terms to give a presentation about AIDS and the role of FBOs. So I felt obligated to say yes.

The presentation went well, maybe because I had a friendly audience for once. I had encountered so much hostile pushback from my peers since 1998 (when I did my World Bank evaluation of AIDS in Uganda), it was a welcome relief to find myself popular with any audience, and in fact this audience was extremely large, a packed hall with five or so balconies. After my talk, a tall, bald man came up to me and in short order asked if he could hire me as a consultant to come to his program in China and help them develop a behavior-change-based strategy for AIDS prevention. I replied that I was super-busy these days, but I would think about it.

In subsequent emails, I learned that a group of medical missionaries had secured permission from the Chinese government to establish a program in Yunnan province called Bless China International, BCI. They could work among tribal minority groups. The Chinese government did not object to foreign doctors providing health care in the poor, neglected areas of China. It relieved the government of that responsibility They could even try to spread Christianity, as long the dominant, true Han Chinese remained un-proselytized, un-Westernized, and unmolested by foreign influence.

I was to learn Yunnan has the highest concentration of Chinese ethnic minorities, who speak more than 60 languages or dialects. It appeared to be an anthropologist's paradise.

I told Rob C., the director of BCI, that I was overly busy. Rob next asked about my extracurricular interests, and I mentioned traditional healing and folk music. So he sweetened the offer by promising I could begin my consultancy with a trip through the mountains of Yunnan, the most southwestern part of China, abutting the Himalayan range. To the south, Yunnan touches Burma, Laos, and Vietnam, and in the northwest at high altitudes, we find Tibetan speakers. I realized I was being offered a rare opportunity to go where few outsiders have gone.

I accepted the offer and went to Kunming, China in April 2006, after giving speeches in Poland, arranged through the Ambassador's program. Ambassador Victor Ashe, as mentioned earlier, was in my form at Groton, and was one of the casualties of the scandal known as "Bugging the Headmaster's Study." Two other boys, Grenville Clark and Joe Alsop (son of the famous Stewart, or perhaps Joseph Alsop, one of whom was in my father's form), had enough technical skills by Third Form year that they could wire up the headmaster's study and record faculty meetings. The scheme was discovered soon after my expulsion, and the three of them were also kicked out.

Suzie and I stayed at the Ambassador's residence, in a guest room recently vacated by Condoleezza Rice, we were told. Victor's sons were visiting and they were eager to meet someone who could confirm that their square, ultra-Republican law-abiding dad had actually been expelled from Groton. They never quite believed the story.

Doctors, Devils, and Saints

This consulting job in China was not my first in Asia. Apart from Bangladesh, I had done more recent AIDS-related evaluation work in Cambodia, Indonesia, the Philippines, Thailand. I also worked in Vietnam, although that brief work came under the rubric Children in Difficult Circumstances.

The flights to China from Poland, (where I had given speeches about AIDS) were endless: Warsaw to Amsterdam (wrong direction, I know), then to Beijing, then on a domestic airline to Kunming, situated at 6,000 feet in southwestern China, in foothills of higher mountains. Before my AIDS work actually began in Kunming, I took that tour through the mountains to the west, as BCI had promised.

I had also been invited to present an AIDS lecture at a family planning conference in Nanjing. A Harvard colleague of mine had been a Bell Fellow two years earlier and was now on the National HIV/AIDS Committee, hence the invitation in addition to the policy work already planned. I expected much exposure in Nanjing. But for now: working with Chinese speaking missionaries who provide medical services to minority tribes who live at dizzying altitudes? I couldn't wait.

We found ourselves at the aptly-named Paradise Hotel in Shangri-La, right on the border of the Autonomous Region of Tibet. If Zhongdian can be found on a detailed map of southwest China, be aware that the government officially changed its name to Shangri-La. It is situated at 11,000 feet, and I felt some altitude sickness. I might need to take hits from the communal oxygen canister the hotel provided.

But the beauty of this place! The snowy peaks, forests, and chasms—one called Tiger Leaping Gorge—were spellbinding. The people were mostly Tibetan, followed by the Naxi and Miao tribes. Not many Han Chinese lived there, so I suppose that made it permissible to proselytize, in the view of the government. BCI brings medical care to the tribal minorities of Yunnan. How did I have the great fortune to make it to such an exotic area of China, where foreigners were forbidden to travel prior to recent times, and which the more adventurous Western tourists were just beginning to discover in 2006?

We dined at the local expat hangout, where we found a few Germans, Canadians, and Americans. The religion here is Tantric Buddhism with strong Taoist and "animistic" folk religion at its base. I am reminded that I had a pre-Mao era book about the Tantric-animist tradition years earlier, and had written down a appealing commentary from a Taoist "recluse" (holy man) from these very mountains, recorded in the 1940s[III]:

Men, animals, ghosts, demons—all deserve sympathetic consideration. Formed from the great Tao, Matrix of the universe, all are equally necessary to nature's purposes. If we destroy any being without good cause, how can we expect our fellows to treat us less belligerently? Let live, leave well alone, abstain from exaggerated reactions and one may be sure of remaining on good terms with all the hosts of heaven, earth and hell. Even corpse-devouring demons are capable of gratitude. In my youth, I befriended such a fiend who at that time inhabited a dry well in the Tung Yii Temple. Ever since, it has constituted itself my protector. Now and then it goes astray and devours somebody's chickens, but its sense of loyalty is too strong for it to permit its fellow demons to molest me or my friends. Once when I was passing the night in a bower close to the mountain peak where I sometimes go to gather medicinal herbs, a famished tree-spirit pressed upon me and began to suck my vital energy. Fascinated by its burning gaze, I could make no movement to save myself. The creature would have drained me of blood, breath and semen, leaving me dead, had not my guardian fiend intervened by recounting my poor little virtues in such terms that the tree-spirit, greatly abashed, begged my pardon and went off to hide its shame.

Alas, communism is not sympathetic to religion, spirituality, demons, or mysticism of any sort, and forms deemed backward such as animistic, folk Taoism were—and still are—particularly scorned and discouraged. For example, China's well-known barefoot doctors came not from the ranks of existing traditional herbalists, acupuncturists, or spirit mediums, but from peasants unconnected to the rich tradition handed down over the generations. These peasant farmers received minimal training in contraception, first aid, and preventive medicine. In fact, to study genuine traditional Chinese acupuncture, one nowadays has to look outside China. Within it, the tradition has been stripped from its supernatural moorings, from any parts that conflict with the ideology of Marxist materialism. There was really nothing "traditional" about the cadres of village health workers created in 1968 at the height of the Cultural Revolution. Western writers have depicted them romantically as shoeless revolutionary heroes bringing effective, low-cost health care to the rural masses. Prof. Xiaoping Fang, in his book on barefoot doctors, found that "rather than consolidating traditional Chinese medicine, as purported by government propaganda, the barefoot doctor program introduced modern Western medicine to rural China, effectively modernizing established methods and forms of care," to quote a summary of the book.

Countries in Africa such as Tanzania and Mozambique, at least during their Marxist phases, followed the Chinese materialist model and tried to legally ban traditional healers (spirit mediums and herbalists from African tradition) and replace them with secular village health workers. I confronted this policy in Mozambique. When I first tried to assemble traditional healers in the early 1990s, they remained secretive; indeed, many thought the government wanted to get them out in the open to arrest them. I of course was trying to develop a program whereby indigenous healers might cooperate with government doctors and health workers to achieve specific public health goals. The ruling FRELIMO party in Mozambique supported the program I developed because it concluded (I believe in its Fifth Party Congress of 1989) that Marxism was, after all, a European import and certain plants simply would not take root in Mozambican soil, in FRELIMO's metaphor.

The Miracle of the Newspaper

It was an unusual experience traveling with American and Chinese missionaries in the high mountains of Southwest China. One physician from Tennessee, whom I must call Dr. X to protect him from undue scrutiny by Chinese authorities, told me amazing stories as we went around together.

Here's one that I keep thinking about: There is a tribal minority in the mountains that are among the poorest people in China. For work outside their traditional area, all they can do is sweep trash off the streets. They are like a caste of garbage collectors. One middle-aged woman from this group fell ill with chest pains, constant coughing, and blood in her sputum. Her husband was anxious to get medical care for her. But hospitals would not accept patients without money. And garbage collecting gave them barely enough to survive.

Then the couple decided they would go to the army hospital. The thinking was: this is The People's Army, and aren't they themselves... well, the people? So they went to the hospital, but it immediately turned them away when they could not produce any money.

The couple sat in the park feeling lost and defeated. A newspaper blew over to the woman. Now, she had only had three years of education and she could barely read. She hadn't even tried to read a newspaper for several years. However, by sheer chance she scanned this one, and her eyes fell on a paragraph that mentioned an American doctor who saw patients for free.

For free!

The couple quickly found Dr. X from Tennessee. He realized this woman had advanced tuberculosis. He gave her the medicines she needed, and instructed the husband in very clear terms how she must take the medicine. He cautioned that her case was so advanced that a life-threatening event might occur to her. For instance, air might build up in her chest cavity, outside her lungs. If any such incident happened, Dr. X told the husband to call his cell phone immediately, though he'd have to find a person with a phone and pay to use it, and then swiftly take the woman to the hospital. Dr. X would call the head surgeon at the hospital, and the husband would explain to the hospital gatekeepers that an American doctor had arranged for an emergency operation, and this doctor would pay all expenses.

Six days later, Dr. X got a call from the husband. His wife was in terrible pain and her chest was swelling. Dr. X reminded him of what to do. He then called the head surgeon at the hospital. It took Dr. X about 45 minutes to get to the hospital. When he arrived, the surgical team had already inserted a tube into the woman's chest to release the air, and the crisis had passed. The woman would be okay.

Dr. X went to pay the surgeon, but he and his medical team waved away the money, saying, "You have done a good deed to help this poor, suffering woman, and so we want to do an equally good deed. Thank you for reminding us to be caring people."

At the follow-up days later, Dr. X asked the woman how she had happened to come to him in the first place, and she told about the newspaper blowing her way. Dr. X was amazed, because it was most unusual for his name to appear in the paper. The local medical college was constantly asking him to give a speech at one of its many ceremonies, but he didn't like to give speeches and he always declined. Yet recently the school authorities had asked Dr. X if he would just sit in the audience; he didn't have to say anything. In fact, they had an ulterior motive. They knew that the press would be attending and they wanted to show that they had an American doctor in their audience. It lent prestige to the event. And that's how his name happened to be in the paper that fateful day.

At this point, Dr. X asked the couple if all of this could have been a coincidence.

They said, "No, indeed."

And when you think about it: what are the odds that one of the poorest people on earth would meet one of the wealthiest, which in relative terms must describe any American doctor, at the exact moment of life-or-death need?

Dr. X said this strange set of circumstances must have been arranged by God.

The couple wondered aloud, "Who is this... God?"

So naturally, Dr. X had much to teach about God, and they soon converted to Christianity.

Now, I think this is a wonderful story. A lot of my friends—I guess most of them—would resent the fact that the doctor promoted Christianity along with critical health care. But I don't see it that way. A life was saved, and a husband who loved his wife did not lose her. And who has the right to say their lives are not better with religion, with Christianity? Is it better to venerate God or the Communist Party? And unless motivated by "spreading Bibles," as I put it earlier in the context of Christians working in failed states, this American doctor would never have come to this remote corner of China.

Dr. X had been in the high mountains on southwest China for 11 years. Everywhere we drove in newly-named Shangri-la, people knew him and seemed so happy to see him. And he seemed to know everyone in that small city. The people who took tolls and charged admission and served drinks never accepted his money. If he hadn't given them medicine or helped them directly, he'd helped a family member. And he contributed in many ways beyond medicine. International churches that gave to his mission knew their donations went straight to saving or improving lives. Some went to medicine and surgery, and others to school fees for the disabled, programs for deformed lepers, taking care of orphans, helping struggling artists, and more. A core group of American churches had already taken care of all ongoing overhead expenses. I remained on Dr. X's mailing list for a few years, so I gradually learned more details of his activities and funding.

It seemed to me that in many ways, this Tennessee man was a saint. He also spoke Chinese fluently, with no accent that I could easily discern, unlike other missionary doctors in his program. So do his American wife and two kids. Some people regard my late Harvard colleague Paul Farmer, medical doctor and anthropologist, as a modern-day saint. A book called *Mountains Beyond Mountains* actually suggests he is, documenting all of Paul's good deeds. The difference between him and Dr. X is that Paul's work is widely known and respected, while Dr. X labored in complete obscurity. I cannot even reveal his name.

Yet saints may be as complex as anyone else. For instance, once a week the local English teachers come over to Dr. X's house to practice their English. I joined the group one Wednesday evening. An hour or so into the conversation, one of the Chinese teachers mentioned a strange experience he could not explain rationally. This was probably prompted by something I had said.

Here's the story: George (yes, a Christian name), from the minority Naxi ethnic group, was sitting around with a Naxi family that had lost the head of the household. The Tibetan father had died suddenly, well before his time. A man in the room among the mourners suddenly began speaking in Tibetan, yet he didn't know Tibetan! It seems he was channeling the man who had died, and who was worried about the two fatherless children he had left behind. The people in the room were terrified. They implored the spirit,

"Go back! You don't belong here. But do not worry about your children. They are not orphans. We are taking care of them!"

And so the Tibetan-speaking spirit departed.

George said that he has often wondered about this event, yet he can find no way to explain it scientifically or rationally, or within a framework of Christian doctrine.

No sooner had Dr. X heard this story than he said it must be the "work of the devil." Dr. X continued along these lines, speaking of demonic possession to the mostly female teachers. George leaned over toward me and whispered, "Are you a Christian?" I answered noncommittally that, well, I was trying, and how about you? George was not.

Now, it would never have occurred to me that this man's utterance was the work of the devil. A departed father was simply worried about his children. In my previous anthropological research, I've often heard stories of spirit possession, especially in Africa and the Caribbean. This one in Yunnan didn't strike me as evil or anti-social; it was normal family responsibility expressed in an exotic manner.

I later tried to discuss this issue with Dr. X. He seemed to believe that anything strange—not easily explained by the Bible—was probably the work of diabolical forces. He felt demons tried to capture people's attention and fascinate them by pulling stunts like speaking in strange tongues (we anthropologists call this *xenoglossia*). I thought aloud, "Why would Satan send demons on such an errand?" Dr. X's answer was to lure people down the path of the occult, which inexorably leads to the Evil One.

I pointed out that there were Christian Spiritualists who were regular Protestant and even evangelical Christians in every way except that they believed that one might communicate with people in heaven (or elsewhere beyond the earthly plane). Dr. X dismissed these Christians as perhaps a dubious breed of "charismatic Catholics."

I searched my own heart and experience. I remembered the missionary in Suriname who said I probably *thought* I was merely doing anthropological fieldwork and just keeping an open mind... but that was exactly how Satan worked! He loved to jump into the minds of so-called "open-minded" people like me.

In 2021, I happened to see Dr. X's name as part of my network on LinkedIn. I got in touch with him and found that he had found a job in the US working with Chinese refugees. The Christian organization that recruited Dr. X was delighted that they found a doctor who spoke fluent Chinese, perhaps with a slight Tibetan accent. I found him in great spirits, and still doing God's work. He still had a burning purpose.

The Abbot and the Language of the Heart

The Old City of Dali goes back at least 2,000 years, and no one knows its true age. I am told the largest pagoda in China is found here. Apart from recent signs of tourism, the Old City could be the set of a classical period Shaolin martial arts movie. This place was completely different from how I imagine most Americans think of China, which in my mind would be Beijing swathed in pollution. Or perhaps the uprising in Tiananmen Square.

A range of mountains encircles Dali, and they rise precipitously at the edge of the city. With two missionary colleagues, Suzie and I drove a winding road up, up, up, until we reached a spot where we had to leave our car. Here spring water came bubbling out of the mountainside into a pool. We were told this water had great healing powers, whether you drank it or washed your eyes with it. Suzie and I did both, but the missionaries declined. We were to notice that day, and routinely, that they scrupulously avoided even the appearance of participating in anything they regarded as pagan.

We had arrived near the peak of a beautiful, wooded mountain to visit a Shaolin Master, whose calling card read:

Jing Kong, Quiet and Empty Great Teacher, Abbot of Wuwei Temple, Dali, Yunnan, Member from the 31st generation of Shaolin Temple, Songshan Mountain, China, Wuwei Temple, Dali Old City, Yunnan, China.

We walked 30 yards and entered the monastery. It's hard to describe the beauty of its courtyard. We heard that the designers positioned everything here to express the harmony between opposing forces, yin and yang. There was a side with an extended temple; a corner with a gigantic, ancient brass bell that must have weighed several tons (how could men have possibly hauled it up the steep mountain in centuries past?); and in the center of the compound a goldfish pond surrounded by a gorgeous garden in spring bloom.

The abbot was finishing a Chinese board game. We waited until it ended and he emerged. He looked, I suppose, exactly the way a Chinese abbot should look, thin and with a wispy black goatee, and though he seemed young, we found out later that he was 48.

Our hosts asked us to sit around the table with the abbot. My Chinese missionary colleague started off a bit aggressively with several questions that the "visiting Harvard professor" needed to know the answers to at once!

The abbot said very little. He seemed to be sizing us up. He finally said that, upon reflection, he wouldn't be answering any questions.

I suggested to my colleagues that we simply relax, go with the flow, and be satisfied with drinking tea and, if necessary, with silence. After all, "Quiet" and "Empty" were right on his calling card.

The abbot asked if we wanted red or green tea, and I said red. The tea arrived, and an elaborate tea ceremony followed while we sat in near-silence. They washed each small cup in tea to warm it, and discarded the first pouring. Of course, as a naïve foreign observer, I did not know why they threw away the first pouring. Finally, they offered us our cups and we started to drink.

The abbot was a 31st generation Shaolin Master, Shaolin is a form of kung fu, perhaps the oldest that incorporates Ch'an philosophy. Ch'an is the Chinese forerunner of Zen. As a "Quiet and Empty Great Teacher," he was devoid of human material desires, we were told. He trained students from all over, including overseas, in his martial arts tradition. Probably "disciples" was more accurate, at least for those who also came to learn Buddhism and seek enlightenment, as well as martial arts. He mentioned that he took in orphans and other poor or destitute people who came to him. A little boy and girl who were helping with cleaning and tidying up turned out to be orphans. The boy had first appeared carrying two small wild orchids he'd found on the mountainside. The abbot seemed pleased with this discovery. He said he would use the wild orchids in medicine.

We noticed a couple of young European-appearing people lurking about beatifically. We later talked to two Israelis and two Australians who were studying under the master. Disciples could come to study Shaolin and enlightenment at this temple, for a contribution of 300 yuan per week ($36 USD), which included three meals a day and a place to sleep. We were given wooden bead bracelets with Buddhist inscriptions signifying this monastery. Suzie and I thanked the master and put the bracelets on. I noticed the head missionary translating for us declined. The female missionary, a Chinese, accepted politely, but did not put her bracelet on. As soon as we left the temple, she asked if we wished to take her bracelet. Throughout our travels, we couldn't help but notice that the missionaries would not associate with any competing spiritual system. I don't say this critically, since they are doing valuable work that saves and improves many lives. It's just an observation.

I asked the abbot through our translators how he communicates with disciples from other lands. He said that the "language of tongues" was not as important as the "language of the heart." Communication in fact is more profound when not weighed down by words, he observed. We had a few more conversations like this, most of them through the language of the heart. The abbot believed in the value of silence and so we tried to practice it, which was difficult for your indefatigably curious anthropologist.

I had the nagging sense that the abbot spoke English and understood everything we were saying. Or maybe his understanding was metalinguistic, transcendent of mere speech.

We discussed his healing through herbs. He told us he collects them himself on the mountainside. The altitude varies greatly in this part of the China, and the different levels yield an exceptional variety of plants, many of which people use medicinally.

I asked about treating drug addiction, since believe it or not, I had read that Dali is the IDU (injecting drug use) capital of China, perhaps because of its location at the northern end of the Golden Triangle of heroin trade. The abbot replied that addicts sometimes come to him, and he treats them with herbs, letting them stay as long as they wish. The same thing is true for those who arrive with what I would call clinical depression.

My colleague reminded me we had a dinner appointment soon, so we politely took our leave from the abbot. He smiled and told us we could walk all around the compound and take photos if we liked.

Suzie and I went into the temple side and gazed at what our missionary guides would call diabolical idols, though they didn't enter the temple with us. There was also a box for offerings. The abbot had suggested that if we wanted to donate, we would "make merit" for the next life. I gave 100 yuan. We walked around and spoke with foreign disciples. They all seemed happy that they had discovered this magical place. The young Israeli guy and I spoke about Israel and Palestine, since I had worked in the occupied territory about five years earlier. He dropped hints that he was pro-peace; admitting that he'd only visited the West Bank once was when he was a soldier. I had heard him speak briefly to the abbot, and I asked him if he spoke Chinese. He said that he was studying the language every day and could now speak it, to a limited extent. After he left this monastery, he would be heading for Mongolia.

As we drove down the mountain, Suzie made me promise that we would return as disciples—or at least students—someday soon.

A Generation of Emperors?

We remained in the higher mountains until one Saturday when we began to drive gradually to lower elevations, heading back to Kunming (elevation 6,000). Before leaving the higher altitudes, I secured a two-month's supply of both Tibetan and Naxi indigenous herbal medicines for liver health. And Naxi medicines for non-Hodgkin's lymphoma. A quasi-famous healer, Dr. Ho, showed me a letter with supporting medical reports testifying that he cured at least one case of non-Hodgkin's lymphoma after Western medicines had failed. So I bought the herbal medicines for Millie, my 78-year-old neighbor in Maine, who was very sick with this same cancer. She did, indeed, take them, and later told me she believed they added years to her life.

Dr Ho from the Naxi ethnic minority, Yunnan China 2006

While driving three hours down the steep canyon road between Snow Dragon Mountain and Tiger Leaping Gorge, my Chinese colleague made an interesting observation. Since 1980, China had imposed a strict policy of one child per family, maintained not only by an advanced system of contraception, but also by abortion and female infanticide. She observed that this policy had produced a generation of spoiled kids. Consider for a moment, she said: each child has six doting adults competing for its favor, two parents and two sets of grandparents. The boy (much preferred) or girl lives in a shower of attention and can, in turn, manipulate all the adults to get their own way. Each child is made to feel like His Majesty the Emperor (Freud had a very similar concept). Anyway, think about it: a nation of 1.4 billion self-centered emperors.

I told myself I'd keep this insight in mind as I observed events in China in the future.

We later saw a show about this very topic on Chinese CCTV, the government-run English language channel. It was an amazing program about kindergartners enrolled in an accelerated program for little geniuses. Example of interview:

"What do you want to be when you grow up?"

"Oh, I think I'd like to be the one to find a cure for avian flu, H1N1."

The viewership was then told the emperor theory, and the interviewer asked the first little girl:

"Since each Chinese child now has, in effect, six parents, do you feel that you are an... emperor?"

"No, my daddy is an emperor. My mommy is an empress dowager, my grandmother is a queen, and I'm a princess."

And to a little boy: "Are you an emperor?"

"Yes."

"And if your parents were very sick, what would you do?"

"Oh, I suppose if I had free time, I'd go visit them."

This may sound a little odd, but imagine being a five-year-old intensively educated in Chinese, English, computers, art, music, science, sports, you name it.

Only one child sounded American:

"If you could go anywhere in the world, where would you like to go?"

Little girl with oversized dimples: "I'd like to go to Disney World, in Hong Kong."

"And why would you like to go there?"

"I could get chocolate there."

"What else?"

"Cakes."

"What else?"

"Sweet tarts."

"Is that all you want to do, get things to eat?"

"No, I also want to shake hands with Mickey and Minnie Mouse."

I hasten to add that all the (Han) Chinese I met were wonderful. No emperors, no "self-will run riot." And I had been meeting folks from exotic tribal minority groups. In that regard, I was in an anthropologist's heaven.

Phantasms of HIV

Back in Kunming, I attended meetings, read reports, and familiarized myself with the Chinese HIV epidemic. Top American agencies—the CIA, NSA, and DOD—had released apocalyptic projections that HIV would soon infect over 100 million Chinese. These agencies made the same kind of unfounded forecasts for Indonesia and The Philippines. I conducted USAID consultancies in both these countries, and assured USAID officials that these extreme projections arose from assuming that Asian nations would all go the way of a few countries in southern Africa. I had met Asian-American epidemiologist Jim Chin in the Philippines, who saw the data emerging from Asia much as I did, and together we tried to quickly reassure American and local officials that they were quite safe, based on "knowing your epidemic" and on data collected in Asia. Jim and I would soon be proved right.

As in many other Asian countries, injecting drug users (IDUs) likely drove China's epidemic (such as it was), even if the percentage of sexually transmitted HIV increased to a certain level that was natural in what we call "concentrated" epidemics. Yet the main intervention that the Western major donors offered IDUs was sterile syringes and methadone. Sterile needles are no doubt needed, just as condoms are to some extent, but donors needed to support a greater range of interventions and not overlook the role of behavior.

There were two programs in Kunming to help addicts get off of drugs completely: one run by Daytop Center, and one by Population Services International, or PSI. The local PSI American representative seemed to be a sensible woman. She agreed with me that abstinence from highly addictive drugs was better than needles or methadone, but that all three options were necessary. We agreed on that.

Daytop was modeled after Daytop Center in New York, which like almost all detox and rehabilitation institutions in the United States was based on the 12-step recovery program of Alcoholics Anonymous and its sister group Narcotics Anonymous. That is to say, it promoted abstinence from all mood-altering drugs and alcohol "a day at a time." We might say the Daytop Center focused on helping IDUs get off drugs ("risk avoidance" as distinct from "risk reduction," in the parlance of public health), and they were engaged in it until the large international donors began thwarting them by funding only needle exchange and methadone programs. The big donors insisted that it was completely unrealistic to expect any true addict to get off heroin, so why try?

However, I, and some of my colleagues at the time, argued that:

- The premise is false. Addicts can avoid relapse for a lifetime. There are many examples from around the world.
- Needles and methadone programs allow health official to produce numbers quickly, and satisfy donors that a large and expanding number of IDUs are using needles or methadone. But many methadone users still inject drugs from time to time, as researchers had discovered in China and elsewhere.
- Needles and methadone involve commodities, therefore commerce, therefore profits and an industry in condoms or opioid substitutes. There is no profit from drug abstinence for middlemen, marketers, or merchants, only for the addict whose risk for AIDS, drug overdose, hepatitis C, and death plummets dramatically.

Daytop Center staff members were very frustrated. They told me most clients came to them to get off drugs, to abstain, just like 57% of British IDUs in one study I saw. Yet Daytop could only get funding for risk reduction programs. The Chinese Director at Daytop Center had heard me speak in the previous year, 2006, and she wished she could talk to me about the relative merits of risk avoidance versus risk reduction. She and I both recognized that major donors funded only the latter.

The major programs for IDU prevention showed the same bias against "interfering" with risky behavior. It was a twist on what was once billed as

Plan B: if "abstinence" failed to work, you fell back on reducing the risk through distribution of syringes and condoms. But now that same Plan B was the only plan funded.

China expert Drew Thompson (from the Center for Strategic and International Studies) commented to me about how nicely methadone programs fit the Chinese government, society, and economy: It involved onetime big donations from well-heeled foreign groups, the distribution and sale of commodities in a social marketing-like system, and perhaps most appealing of all, a profit of about 80 US cents to local government on the sale of every dose.

Meanwhile, I had lectures coming up the following week, and since arriving in China, I had been fine-tuning them as I talked with my colleagues. They also helped me tailor each PowerPoint slide to have maximum impact in this country, and to not give offense in any way.

The BCI I was working with suggested that it would be a good strategy to mention that my father had come to China in 1970 with Nixon, and that he wrote a book about China and was regarded as a population and family planning guru. So I started off my Kunming presentation with two pictures showing my father, Nixon, and Mao. The audience seemed very impressed, even stunned. A few people jumped out of their seats and took pictures of the Mao photograph on the screen.

After my talk, the UNAIDS country representative, a Chinese, came up and said she liked my remarks. Moreover, when she gave her talk she repeated and reinforced several of my main points, including that China should not uncritically accept the West's offerings, but instead should develop its own AIDS program—because China knew what worked in China better than foreigners did. *Amen.*

They held a banquet for the honored guests at Kunming Medical College, and I seemed to be the main guest of honor. I was seated to the right of the college President. The conference was called "HIV/AIDS Prevention and Control: Sharing Experience and Rethinking." The last word came from my book title. I don't know if I was the guest of honor because of my book or the Harvard brand name, but probably the latter. Wherever I went throughout Yunnan province, people had heard of Harvard and seemed spellbound by the name. Even at altitudes of 11,000 feet, Tibetan healers, Shaolin masters, Buddhist recluses, and tribal Naxi herbalists apparently had heard of Harvard. The president of Kunming Medical had visited the college, and he was very proud of this. I gave him my card and said if he emailed me the next time he was dropping by Harvard, I'd arrange hospitality. In a final little after-dinner ceremony, the president gave me a gift of a lacquer tray with an engraving of Kunming Medical College, to take... you guessed it... back to Harvard.

Templeton

During my years at Harvard, I made occasional trips to southern Africa, including one when I evaluated a three-country AIDS prevention project funded by the Gates Foundation. I also made three research trips to Uganda to collect further evidence of the efficacy of that country's AIDS prevention program—and I showed evidence of how interference from the major Western donors (however well-meaning) diverted emphasis and funding from behavior change to condoms and testing. During the early stages of Uganda's AIDS prevention program, designed primarily by Ugandans themselves, people were made to fear contracting AIDS and dying from a new, poorly understood disease. They believed that their survival depended on their behavior, and behavior was something they could control.

In this period, Uganda became the only country in the world to reverse a generalized HIV epidemic. Our 2009 study found that Ugandans had come to view AIDS as a treatable, chronic disease not unlike malaria. They were no longer seeing visible signs of AIDS, such as alarming weight loss (the "walking dead"), and they didn't seem to fear AIDS as they once did. A colleague and I documented use of "fear appeals" as a deliberate, thought-through AIDS prevention strategy carried out a generation ago, yet this approach no longer seemed a noticeable component of prevention campaigns. Gone were the old messages with images of caskets, cemeteries, coiled snakes, skeletons—all aimed at limiting sexual activity to one and only one sexual partner (or "zero-grazing" in a locally understood metaphor... quickly mischaracterized as "abstinence only"). Instead, we saw feel-good, light-hearted, and humorous messages. I mean, the thinking probably went *why needlessly make people feel uncomfortable?*

HIV incidence and prevalence began to rise again in Uganda, the one standout AIDS success story in the world. Of course, the major international donors wanted to pitch Uganda as a condom success story. Yet studies conducted before HIV infection rates began to rise again in Uganda found that only four condoms per man, per year were circulating in Uganda, slightly lower than the Africa-wide average of 4.6 condoms.

Virtually no one wanted to hear the unwelcome news about Uganda. The major Western donors explained the rise in infection rates as evidence that behavior-based prevention never worked in the first place, and thank God Ugandans have learned the error of their ways and were now promoting condoms-testing-drugs instead of the antiquated "sex-negative" messages that led to fear of getting AIDS (and to changing behavior!).

In the current era of Covid-19, I have noticed considerable renewed interest in the article I wrote with Kim Witte about "fear appeals" in 2006. We found much evidence—including in a systematic review of peer reviewed literature—that fear is a powerful motivator of behavior change, even of entrenched habits. When I was 18, I saw a health education film of how human lungs looked after 20 years of smoking. After seeing this film. I was never again really able to enjoy smoking and I gave it up a few years later, even though I was highly addicted to nicotine by my early 20s and it took me many stop-and-go months of trying to quit. But Kim Witte and I faced great difficulty in getting our article published. It seemed that associating fear, death, and AIDS in the same piece of writing violated several taboos, at least in Western AIDS and medical journals. We were accused of promoting stigma and shame, and of course, "sex-negative" (anti-pleasure) messages. Who could continue to enjoy sex after thoughts about sickness and death had been implanted somewhere in one's mind?

At Harvard I had been limping along with scant funding, which I supplemented with occasional consulting gigs. One of these was for an AIDS prevention project funded by the Gates Foundation in three countries in southern Africa. In rural Zambia one day, I received an email from the John Templeton Foundation (JTF). Truthfully, I had never heard of them, but the assistant to a vice president informed me that her boss might want to support my work, and when could he come to Harvard to meet me? I would later find out that a great many hopeful researchers bring all kinds of ideas and schemes to JTF, but only rarely does it take the initiative to contact a prospective grantee. Anyway, I didn't think much about it.

On the appointed day, Dr. Charles Harper appeared in my office. He turned out to be an Oxford-educated astrophysicist who had once been on the Harvard faculty. He had read my *Rethinking* book and, given its controversial arguments, he wondered if I might be struggling along in an unfriendly world without much financial and moral support. Right on both guesses!

From a September 2006 article about me in *Anthropology News*, published by the American Anthropological Association (AAA) and written by the Director of External, International and Governmental Relations:

AAA member Ted (Edward) Green, whose work at the forefront of HIV/AIDS research has garnered wide attention in recent years. On June 27, Green made his third of four appearances before Congress, this time testifying before the House Committee on International Relations (Subcommittee on Africa, Global Human Rights & International Operations) on blood supply safety in Africa... Two days later, Green learned that the John Templeton Foundation had awarded him a $2 million grant—through his employer, the Harvard Center for Population and Development Studies—to extend his research on HIV/AIDS prevention. It is expected he will also oversee a second $2 million Templeton grant to support behavioral research of other scholars, including anthropologists.

And this is how I came to be Director of the AIDS Prevention Research Project, generously funded at Harvard for the next three years, with a modest staff to support me. My later struggles at Harvard, and with AIDS prevention orthodoxy, have been described in my other writings. But finally, I was no longer working virtually alone, in near obscurity.

Chapter 15
My Mother's Pride

It was my mother who I believe took away my self-confidence at a tender age, so the self-defeating thought of failure was never far from my consciousness. But she also motivated me to bestir myself, get rolling and achieve, to prove her wrong and make her proud of me. This is no doubt a gross over-simplification, but, allied with the theory of sibling birth order and some insights of cognitive behavior therapy (which I absorbed when I was in therapy a few years ago), it helps make some sense of my inner and outer life. I've described her in some detail in this book.

I had lunch date in 2006 with a Harvard professor, so I googled him and learned he was a Harvard PhD who had taught at MIT before getting tenure at Harvard. He was a MacArthur Genius grantee and had won numerous other awards. A *wunderkind*.

A year ago, I would have fretted before such a meeting. I would have worried about feeling adequate, about being exposed as a fraud, about not seeming as smart as this guy—all that self-defeating neurosis. But on this day, I was for some reason relaxed, natural, and engaged in the right level of give and take, of speaking and listening. At one point, listening to this genuine scholar discuss a fine point of methodology, I felt comfortable commenting, "Oh, I have no training in methodology; I'm just an old-fashioned anthropologist," or something like that. I am still not as a good a listener as I should be, but my self-confidence was all right, or about right-sized, as some say.

If this is normal social interaction, why was I crippled by low self-confidence, feelings of inadequacy, for all those years? (I hope I can use the past tense here.) These neuroses, well, they are classic symptoms of depression. Can they really have been caused by simple deficiencies of serotonin or another brain neurotransmitter? Just being a tad low on one chemical? They seemed such an integral part of me, part of my core being, for so long.

I tried to explain it all to my brother, in part because I recognized some of the same symptoms in him. If I had just listed certain traits in him without confessing that I had them too, he might have denied he had them. I reminded him that he—rather like myself—always tried *not* to get promoted to positions with authority over others. And if offered such positions, we would both turn them down. Speaking for both of us, I suggested it wasn't just because we preferred to work alone. It was basically a fear we shared that we were not really good enough to be others' boss. I mean, what if they knew more than us?

Mark agreed, at least in part, and he suggested spontaneously that our mother was always exaggerating our capabilities and accomplishments. *Hmm...* Did these exaggerations suggest that who we really were, and what we did was never quite good enough? I think Mark said they meant she had such high expectations of us that we could never live up to them, no matter how hard we tried. So why even try?

Mark perhaps had reasons for lack of great ambitions, for not trying to achieve conventional success. Whereas I was actually driven to achieve. I wonder why we were so different? In my case, it must be that I was trying to prove to our mother that I was a not complete failure, that I was as good as boys who were not kicked out of Groton.

Yet Mark shared something that came up when he was briefly in grief therapy after our mother's death. He was asked if our mother was proud of him. He thought about this and said, no, actually she mostly seemed proud of his brother Ted's accomplishments. She bragged to her friends about... me. I thought at the time—and now too—this was a remarkable thing for him to say, or admit. And to me, no less. And I whose psyche she had stamped with failure! I who had lived so long with it and battled it so hard— I was her pride.

Mark is a good man. And Frank Sulloway's theory of sibling birth order seems challenged to some extent here. Perhaps it even falls apart. My brother apparently resigned from competition with me a great many years ago, and he was not a "defender of the established order." In his less overt way, he rebelled against institutionalization by Groton as much as I did. He became politically progressive in later years, and would have nothing to do with his old prep school, where he was "supposed to make the friends he would stay with for the rest of his life," as our mother told both of us. Mark made his lifelong friends in the Peace Corps. He went out of his way to become the direct opposite of a Groton Old Boy. The school has no mailing address for my brother so for years, his *Groton School Quarterly* was sent to my address, meaning I received two copies.

Yet Mark seemed free of mental health problems that intermittently plagued me. Were my intermittent episodes of depression simply inherited, and to hell with theories of sibling birth order? Was I driven by inner demons that demanded I achieve outward success at any cost? Do my feelings of being a fraud derive solely from my mother telling me at a vulnerable age what a failure I was, and how I would always be one? At times this seems too tidy and simplistic. Maybe my depression was/is a mere epiphenomenon of a brain lacking a few essential neurotransmitters, and my explanation was a just-so backstory, needed to explain a cerebral and emotional deficiency.

In any case, Mark has been there for help in recent years, and he provided a steadying hand when I suffered through head and neck cancer in 2016, followed by my nearly three-year struggle to regain the ability to swallow food in solid form. We have grown closer in later years.

A Semi-Outsider at Beacon Hill High Society

Ironically, since I was in truth an expellee, the *Groton School Quarterly* interviewed me in 2012 about my anti-establishment AIDS prevention work, and ran a four-page article ("Unconventional Wisdom") about my career in Africa and AIDS. Then in 2020, and as already mentioned, the editors asked me to research and write a cover story for the *Quarterly* about the significant influence Groton had on World War II, published as "Uncommon

Impact" (seems I am still viewed as The Un-Grotonian). This article ran with photos I supplied of US Ambassador Joe Grew playing golf with my dad, the young Marshall Green, not long before the Pearl Harbor attack, as well as part of my maternal grandfather's diary about his receiving the formal declaration of war from the Japanese government. A surprising number of key players involved in the entry of the US to World War II were Groton "boys."

Nick, a Boston Brahmin friend of mine who had gone to Andover, Harvard, Yale, and Columbia— making him a preppy and a triple Ivy Leaguer—invited me to a formal dinner with a group of men my age and older, who belonged to a very exclusive private club in Boston. It turned out that the pre-dinner cocktails were hosted by one of my distant cousins, Jonathan Winthrop, a descendant like myself from Governor John Winthrop of Massachusetts Bay Colony.

The evening began with champagne which Winthrop served just as we walked in the door of his apartment, which sat on the top floor of probably the tallest building on Beacon Hill, a block or two up from John Kerry's multi-million-dollar townhouse. It was enormous, high-ceilinged, filled with antiques, and it offered a masterful, unobstructed of view of Boston and the Charles River. In fact, it might have given me views in *all* directions if I'd had the opportunity to fully explore.

After champagne, cocktails, informal introductions, and conversation in this vast apartment, we walked higher up Beacon Hill to an exclusive club founded in the late 19th century for dinner and elevated conversation. I will withhold the exclusive club's name so as not to betray the hospitality they showed. Tuxedos were worn. We got zonked on expensive champagne and vintage wines (I no longer drink, but I pretended to get into the spirit of the occasion), smoked fine cigars with brandy after dinner, and discussed issues of the day in historical context. Interesting that this kind of tradition still goes on.

I discovered later that one of my cousins was also a member. He had attended Harvard, where his dad, my great-uncle William W. Howells, was Professor and Chair of Anthropology. By the way, whenever I achieved a milestone in anthropology, such as my first published book, my mother would immediately call my Uncle Bill and report the news. His approval was very important to my mother, for some deeply implanted reason. I still have a letter he dutifully sent her, complimenting her about my writing style. That made her day, week, and month. There had been a second guest the previous evening (were they assessing us for possible membership?), and my friend Nick formally introduced me to the men around the table, establishing my breeding and lineage right away. I mentioned the village of Kittery Point, Maine, and several men said they knew the W.W. Howells family. When I commented that he was my great-uncle, someone remarked, "Ah! You must be the grandson of Lispenard and Ned Crocker! My summer home is right next to Adree and Fergie's old house" (referring to my great-uncle and -aunt.) Adree was the wife and, yes, the wife's name is normally mentioned first in my family and it's not because they're characters. It's because we tend to be matrilineal, matriarchal, and matrifocal, if I may use anthropological jargon (at least to speak of summer residences), and these men seemed to know that. It must be the women that keep many of these old New England families going.

Nick asked me to relate my saga of running away from Groton in 1957, early in my First Form year, in detail. So I told the tale of hitching to Fitchburg, boarding a Washington-bound train without a ticket, hiding from the conductor in the locked men's room, getting captured, and ending up handcuffed to an Irish cop in the South Boston police station—the whole story, percolating with captivating details developed over years of retelling.

Club members seemed to receive my story with enthusiastic approval, and a few expressed regrets that they had not run away from their own boarding schools and explored the great outside world. What opportunities lost, some cried out!

I added my older brother's plea to our parents at the time:

Mark: "It's not fair! Why does Teddy get to be expelled and I don't?" (This coming from a Sixth Former, a prefect, on the cusp of graduation.)

Mother: "But darling boy, you have been at Groton for almost six years! You have barely four months to go, and then you will have a degree from Groton! Think of that! You don't want to throw away something you will treasure for the rest of your life, after all your investment—and our own!"

He did want to throw it all away. But no cigar; he was compelled to stay. My parents probably should not have forced him, I told my audience. In later years my brother would affect a Southern accent and tell people he hailed from rural poverty in South Carolina. He makes sure there is no trace of Groton left in him. He might have turned out a different person without his lifelong effort to escape the influence of Groton. I feel I got out just in time. (But why do I sometimes wish I had a better secondary education?) Guests seated around the table seemed very interested in my tale.

It turned out the guy seated to my left at dinner was named... well, let's call him Smith. He had also attended Groton, five years ahead of me, but he did not actually finish there, so we did not overlap. He told me a long, convoluted tale, explaining why he did not graduate, which I heard in detail twice during the evening. Over-explaining, if you ask me. The man has issues, as no doubt I do, too. Smith and I went on to discuss each of the Groton masters of the 1950s individually, pretty much agreeing on which ones were eccentric but bearable, if not even decent (Mssrs. Strachen, who published a poem of mine in the school annual publication in 1958; Wright; Gammons; "Spag"-Getty; Sackett; and "Bongo" Murray, our resident Bohemian artist) and who were not just weird, but mean (Jack Crocker, Paul Abry, Corky Nichols, Hawks, and too many more.) Actually, despite the incident at the police station, Mr. Abry was not that bad. He assigned Alan Paton's *Cry the Beloved Country* in Sacred Studies, and he gave me the equivalent of an A that one semester when I worked as hard as I could. I later learned that headmaster Crocker joined his braver students who went on freedom rides, on busses in Mississippi. Muscular Christianity in action! That was a side of the headmaster I never saw.

I had forgotten that some masters were okay dudes, if one could transcend the broader totalitarian system for a moment. Many were eccentric, but not nasty, and Smith helped me remember this. When he finished college, he went to Poland for a few years to study art, of all things. He had to learn Polish, and he remains fluent in it. He had great stories of Poland in the Soviet era. I told him about staying for a few days in 2006 with our US ambassador to Poland, who had been a Groton classmate and who had also been expelled the same year as me. My form was distinguished in its number of expellees (five or six out of about 35, as I recall), and I cleared the path for them as the first to go.

Anyway, here I was at this exclusive, historic club, seemingly accepted by the very people I spent much of my life running away from, finding that I could probably be part of the Old Boys Network if I desired. Of course, I was the only guy not wearing a tuxedo ("It's at the dry cleaners, gentlemen"), just a dark suit and a clip-on bowtie borrowed from Nick. So yes, I was still a fraud, a poseur on the fringe.

All of this was most interesting, sociologically. But in the end, I don't especially like long dinners of any sort, especially since booze was consumed liberally and I was avoiding alcohol, which kept me from really getting into the celebratory mood of the evening. I could see how this experience could be more fun if I had been growing ever boozier with the rest of the men.

I found out later that one attendee listened with resentment to my tale of Groton expulsion. He himself had worked very hard to get into this famed school, he later confided to a mutual friend, and his parents sacrificed much to pay for his tuition. And here was I making fun of—*bragging about*—my Groton expulsion. I see his viewpoint. I probably seemed elitist in the extreme.

In 2021, the Fay School alumni office phoned me because I had been selected as one of the successful boys of my form to be interviewed for Fay School Magazine. I replied to the nice lady on the phone that I was a "most unhappy camper" at Fay and explained some of the reasons why. She said she totally understood and Fay school was quite different in my era, but could she interview me, anyway? This resulted in a pleasant interview that was mostly about my international health career. I suppose I did this interview for my mother, as well as the earlier interview from Groton, just in case she is still monitoring my activities from on high.

Satisfactions and Sorrows

Looking back over my life, I feel very fortunate that I went into applied anthropology and accumulated so many rich experiences in so many faraway corners of the world. In what other line of work would I have conceivably fitted in for the long haul? After Harvard, I ran a small nonprofit focused primarily on AIDS prevention and behavioral interventions, this time including IDU (injecting-drug-user) transmission and alcoholism, in addition to sexual transmission. I came to realize that precious few nonprofits were willing to work in the drug addiction "space." My nonprofit probably lost our pro bono lawyer, who had helped us get established as a 501(c)(3), because of our shift to include drug addicts and alcoholics in AIDS prevention.

I had a faculty affiliation with Johns Hopkins for three years post-Harvard, where I helped guide a PhD student who had already become my co-author when we were at Harvard. I continued to serve on several boards of directors or advisors. I was asked to join most of them when I was at Harvard, and no doubt that affiliation helped make me attractive to the subsequent boards.

After I went back to Suriname in 2016, I planned to write a book about the Matawai Maroons, and I had a publisher lined up. But then I discovered I had head and neck cancer. There followed a few years of suffering the side effects of radiation treatment, in particular —but not only—an inability to swallow solid foods. Then I had painful back surgery and other health problems that made me give up the idea of writing an updated Matawai ethnography.

When I began to finally, slowly feel better, I decided to work on this memoir, part of which covers my years with the Matawai when I was in my mid-20s, plus my return trips there, so that the reader can see how these descendants of rebel slaves seemed to have managed to adopt better—not to mention more quickly—than other Africans in the Diaspora. But of course, it covers many additional events of my life, the outer and the inner, the good, bad, and ugly, the paranormal, the epistemological, the ontological, and the downright embarrassing.

Given how common the Imposter Syndrome is at Harvard, and perhaps everywhere, I now know that behind their masks of professionalism, there are many fellow sufferers with low self-confidence and tattered self-esteem. I have learned that men often feel they have failed to live up to the expectations of their fathers, not mothers. In the end, I made peace with my mother and she was proud of me. But that did not put a complete end to some of my feelings of inadequacy. It seems nothing can dislodge them; they are there permanently.

As I finished this memoir, a book by Michael Knox Beren has recently appeared, called *WASPS: the splendors and mysteries of an American aristocracy*. It is about the descendants of the old New England families that helped create the United States. Once family fortunes had been secured, the ideal was to go into public service with a sense of *noblesse oblige*. I noticed that many of the people referred to in the last two or three generations are either people my father was connected to, or I myself was, especially if their bios included Groton or Harvard. According to the author, America's ruling class has been in decline for several generations, but especially after the "best and brightest" supplied LBJ with such bad advice about the Vietnam war. A surprising number of the American aristocracy have committed suicide over the generations, or were sent to "lunatic asylums"— McClean and Austin Riggs were mentioned. Or else they "languished in self-doubt and nervous debility, an affliction they knew as neurasthenia for which reading Dante was the only cure."

The WASP physician George Miller Beard described neurasthenia in more detail as a disease caused by:

"... lack of nerve force and productive of such symptoms as, but not limited to, insomnia, bad dreams, mental irritability, nervous dyspepsia, fear of society, fear of responsibility, lack of decision in trifling matters, profound exhaustion, and excessive yawning.

Some of these I mentally checked off, although my excessive yawning might be attributable to cancer treatment rather than ennui.

Other symptoms of social class in decline include lowness of spirit, hypochondriasis, hysterical distemper, ennui, and needless to add, a general sense of failure, of not living up to expectations of family, prep school headmasters, and society in general."

So it was not just me. I was part of a "dying race" (today we would say "social class"), the old patrician order collapsing all around us.

This same 2021 book quotes Averill Harriman as noting to Arthur Schlessinger, "the only recipe for success is to be unhappy at Groton." He might have been thinking of Dean Acheson, who was treated unkindly by his form-mates because he bucked the establishment and system at Groton, or even of FDR himself. The WASPS author notes, "That Franklin himself felt something of a failure at Groton was one of the saving features of his career... it played a part in stimulating the ambition that carried him on to future triumphs."

My Other Brother

I have mentioned my younger brother only twice in passing, in spite of introducing the theory of sibling birth order. Brampton Seabury Green hated his historic family name, but in later years decided it was cool to have a distinctive name that no one else had. Following is a synopsis of his tragically short life.

He had trouble in school from the very beginning. At the start of his senior year in high school, when our parents were living in Indonesia, Bram found out that he wouldn't be graduating with his class at the Maret School in DC. He had not passed enough courses, the principal explained to him, and so had not earned nearly enough credits for his high school diploma. Well, why had he been advanced through the grades to become a senior? The principal told Bram that the school had "an understanding" with his mother. That is when Bram confided in me that he "realized he was retarded." Since our parents were halfway around the world, I spoke with the Maret principal and found out that Bram had "dyslexia," and that educators had just arrived at a "consensus definition" of the condition that same year, 1968. But a literature on dyslexia existed. I did quick library research and learned about famous historical figures as well as notable contemporaries that were known, or suspected, to have dyslexia, and it had

nothing to do with "retardation" or intelligence level. I explained this to
Bram one night in a hotel room in Atlanta and he felt very much relieved.

That night was the high point of our relationship as brothers. I was then
a grad student at Northwestern in Chicago, and I had flown with Bram to
Atlanta to act *in loco parentis* and try to get him admitted to a special
tutoring high school in Georgia. The interview went well, but the
headmaster warned Bram that he would have to work extremely hard if he
wanted to make up three years of high school during his last year, and he
didn't see evidence from Bram's transcripts that he had ever really had to
apply himself. I too had my doubts this would work. Our mother spoiled
Bram, probably in over-compensation for his "little learning problem" that
was never explained to him, or to his siblings.

Sure enough, a couple of months into his new regimen, Bram somehow
found a car and with a fellow escapee from the school, fled to the great
American southwest where they were picked up speeding recklessly on a
highway in Arizona. For the rest of his short life, Bram bounced from one
menial job to another. He finally ended up with a high school equivalency
certificate, a wife, and he was finally doing well selling real estate in
Kentucky. He and his wife had become born-again Christians, right-
wingers, and aggressive anti-intellectuals. His politics, of course, rubbed me
exactly the wrong way. I think part of Bram's political posture was to stand
out from the rest of his family. For example, he read conservative, anti-
family-planning books to challenge my father in the population control
work he did after retiring from the State Department. Passive aggression?

But Bram finally seemed happy, and he had recently been honored as
Salesman of the Year by his real estate company when he died suddenly of a
heart attack. I can only speculate that stress had been wearing him down
over his 37 years living in the shadow of two brothers with PhDs and a
family that over-valued intellectual achievement. I still remember with pain
how I felt when that woman in Berkeley told me I was "really stupid."

With her youngest boy's death, my mother sank into a depression that
grew deeper and deeper. She died from suicide not too many years later,
suffering from Parkinson's Disease, exacerbated by depression and
dementia. Privileged people are not exempt from life's problems. One of my

mother's closest friends was the wife of a former CIA Director. Their daughter had anorexia, and spent the last year of her life hanging out and slowly starving herself at my parents' home in Washington, because her parents were then living abroad. I had left home by that time, so didn't know her very well, but she died of anorexia. I don't know, nor and have I ever read of, any people from Africa or the Caribbean, who have suffered from *anorexia nervosa*. It seems to be an affliction of the privileged. But it can be as deadly as diseases associated with poverty. And of course, depression and other mental illness, plus "substance use disorder," as it's now called, impacts all socioeconomic classes.

Up to the Present

In 2016 I received an invitation and a Wenner-Gren Foundation grant to turn over all my fieldnotes, photographs, tape recordings, and the like to the National Anthropological Archives, Smithsonian Museum. I was surprised and honored that I would be inducted into the ranks of an archive that included Franz Boas, Marvin Harris, Melville Herskovits, Colin Turnbull, and other giants in my field. There must have been some mistake, I thought. I think what happened is that there was—and still is—a special interest in "salvage anthropology," or documenting languages and cultures that were disappearing through urbanization, modernization, Christianization, and adoption of outside, national languages.

I would have taken far more fieldnotes, photos, tape recordings, and the like if I had had any idea my materials would someday be archived. I really believed at the time of my fieldwork that no one except my academic advisor would ever read my notes. The archive directors saw no problem that I went on to become a non-academic, *applied* anthropologist: the Smithsonian wanted all my materials from what grew to be over 30 countries by the time of my induction.

In October 2018, three Matawais were awarded a Smithsonian grant to visit Washington DC to study my archive. I knew they would be arriving, so I brushed up on the Matawai language from old interview tapes I had later digitized. I went to meet them—I had not known them before, the two women were born well after my time there—at the archive in suburban Maryland, along with the two interpreters from the Amazon Conservation Team, headquartered in Virginia. Three things stand out from this week-long visit. First, we together watched an ethnographic film from the 1930s made by professor Melville Herskovits, the famous anthropologist who did fieldwork in Suriname. I was asked in advance of this if I thought our Maroon visitors would be interested in seeing an old silent film from generations ago of a different tribe. I said they certainly would, and added that, in fact, the histories of both societies were intertwined, believed descended from an original mythical mother.

Second, we visited the Smithsonian Museum of African History, joined by the one Saramaka Maroon I know who was living in the US. So my friend of many years, Adiante Franzoon of Baltimore, made some new friends with whom he has stayed in touch since, via WhatsApp.

Third, the three visitors and the two men from ACT came to my home for dinner, and we had a chance to speak informally. I showed them my study, whose walls exhibited four enlarged photographs of Matawais from the early 1970s, including a legendary diviner-spirit medium and village chief. His nickname translated "Head like the back of a pipe," which my visitors had never heard before. I also showed them my modest collection of Maroon woodcarvings, from combs and staffs-of-office to paddles and pot stirrers. I knew who made the beautifully carved hardwood paddle: an elder back then named Kaubunu. I remember feeling guilty about buying this particular paddle. I justified what I saw as a very unequal exchange (mere cash for a unique hardwood paddle) by making a promise to myself that I would not simply hoard the wood carvings I got from either the Matawai or the Saramaka, I would exhibit them at universities, particularly traditional Black Land Grant universities such as Fisk in Nashville. This I was able to do. And they will all end up at the Smithsonian after my death. More immediately, some of my woodcarving pieces have been selected for a 3-continent tour with Smithsonian's National Museum of African American History and Culture, for a special exhibition on slavery and justice.

Back in 1971 it never occurred to an obscure anthropologist such as myself that people from my adopted rain forest society would one day be in my hometown, at my undergraduate university, and at a place like the Smithsonian. These realms seemed like different universes. Until recent generations, the anthropologist stepped into an environment utterly different from the modern Western world, and the presumption was that the two worlds would never converge. Of course, on one level, we knew that things would change and the people we lived among would modernize and urbanize and become more Western-educated, but still I don't think many of us imagined that those days would actually arrive, that Matawais would arrive in my world of TV, traffic, and skyscrapers (I can still remember trying to describe skyscrapers in the Matawai language. People had somehow heard about monumental buildings that went high up in the sky, but they had trouble wrapping their imaginations around the image.)

I have heard it said that the quality of experience an anthropologist has with the first people one does fieldwork with indelibly colors one's view of the entire non-Western world forever. That may be true. I experienced such a positive experience with the Matawai that when I went to Africa and then to other continents; I was pre-adapted to find good in others, in strangers. I could not help but feel—and think—that however different from me these new people were, if I could somehow get to live with them and learn their language, I would surely find that most were good people, like the Matawai. I imagine that those with initial negative fieldwork experiences would have perceptions and assumptions slanted in the opposite direction.

Of the three Matawais who were awarded a Smithsonian grant to visit DC to study my archive, a woman subchief (*bassia*... there were no female bassias in the 1970s) named Tina is now staying in touch with me via WhatsApp, and she keeps me up to date on who has died. She lives in my old village, Posugrunu. She had heard recordings I made of older women singing the timeless songs of yore when she was in Washington, and one day recently she asked if I could send her a few of these recorded songs via WhatsApp, which required me to hold a button down while playing old songs on my laptop's hard drive.

Tina was quoted on the Amazon Conservation Team website, commenting on her trip to Washington:

"The experience is so meaningful because I am a Matawai. I think that as a Matawai, you have to know where you come from. Today, we don't have many elders, and the stories are being lost. But then you have somebody like Mr. Green, who even my grandmother told me about when I was young. She told me that the people back then taught his wife to dance 'bandja' style. And then you can read all about these stories in his archive. It makes me feel so alive... it's an incredible feeling."

I can't think of a better summation of, and reaction to, the ethnographic enterprise by someone in the study population. Basically, she is saying that their culture is changing fast, so quickly in fact that much has been lost along the way. But an outsider happened to be there at a time when their grandparents lived and he wrote things down, and took pictures and recorded songs and interviews. It is therefore all preserved for history, instead of being irrevocably lost.

My adoptive Matawai brother-in-law Akukupaia died last year, and I was astonished to learn he was 94. I had thought he and I were the same age (I was 77 last year.) A few years earlier, there was another death that seemed unprecedented to me. A bassia of Posugrunu committed suicide by shotgun. I learned that there had been a controversial, disputed gaanman then serving in the Paramount Chief's village and this man had humiliated the bassia, who then resorted to suicide.

I happened to be starting my cancer treatment, and was walking into my oncologist's office when I got a cell phone call from my Matawai friend Oswald, who also found this social pathology unusual enough to feel he should call me with the news at once. It seemed like a call from another world, or dimension. I was unaware of any suicides during or up until the early 1970s. I vaguely wondered if the bassia's suicide could be classified by Emil Durkheim's typology of egoistic, altruistic, anomic, or fatalistic suicide. Perhaps anomic, as it seemed related to the breakdown of social equilibrium in my old village, which I have probably idealized over the years.

I have had the good fortune to work in many countries around the world, and as of this writing I have visited or lived in 101 countries or overseas possessions, and have served on a number of non-profit boards.

Moreover, by this late stage of my life, I have learned a few things about the Imposter Syndrome and what underlies it. *Psychology Today* reports research that suggests that "Around 25 to 30 percent of high achievers may suffer from imposter syndrome. And around 70 percent of adults may experience impostorism at least once in their lifetime." So it is practically epidemic, and it particularly messes with the minds of high achievers. Yet people don't talk about this because of shame and embarrassment. It is like removing our professional masks in the company of our peers, who may then judge us... and not take their own masks off. It occurred to me that if one never feels like a fraud, that person might be self-delusional, convinced that, "I know more than the generals, more that then State Department experts, more than the doctors at the CDC; the only expert I need to consult is... myself!"

I am proud of some of my accomplishments, and hope I have learned from my failures, several of which I have documented in this book. Among the former, two Praxis Awards for my research in Swaziland, and the Philly Lutaaya award for "looking at AIDS prevention from an African perspective," awarded by Ugandan President Yoweri Museveni. I know that both my late parents would also be proud, but far more important than their pride and mine is the knowledge that my work—and that of my supporters—in HIV reduction and childhood diarrheal disease prevention has had real-world impact, and may have saved a great many (especially) African lives. By about 2010, when I semi-retired, it was widely accepted that having multiple, concurrent sexual partners (MCPs) was what drives HIV heterosexually transmitted epidemics, which were and still are mostly found in southern and eastern Africa—not because Africans are more "promiscuous" (studies show they are *less* likely to have MCPs, or for unmarried teenagers to be sexually active, when compared to Americans or Western Europeans), but for reasons (such as rates of male circumcision) that are still not well understood. My participation on the Presidential Advisory Council on HIV/AIDS, and a parallel policy advisory group at the National Institutes of Health (Office of AIDS Research Advisory Council) amplified my message about the crucial role of sexual behavior change. Since my 1994 quick trip to Uganda, sexual behavior change was also the focus of many of my journal articles, books, speeches, and media interviews about AIDS. I believe that African lives might well have been saved, even though Western AIDS programs were stubbornly fixated on condoms and testing. But African governments began to follow the example of Uganda, whose prevention program I helped make popular among policymakers and the general public. By about 2010, HIV prevalence had fallen in Zimbabwe, Zambia, Kenya, Ethiopia, and Malawi, and before this decline, the proportion of men and women reporting more than one sexual partner in the previous year had declined. Condom usage was too low to seemingly have been responsible for HIV decline in the countries that followed Uganda, nor as discussed earlier, in Uganda itself.

I hope my earlier work, to include traditional healers in collaborative public health programs in combating cholera, schistosomiasis, childhood diarrheal diseases, and, of course, behavior change for HIV reduction, also contributed to saving many African lives, because traditional healers are the de facto primary health care providers for most Africans. I wrote earlier that I became something of a pariah in my field by taking an unpopular position on AIDS prevention. On the other hand, my earlier work with traditional healers has proved popular with students of anthropology. I happened to have seen about 20 textbooks of introductory or medical anthropology where my work with healers is described in one or two full pages. This means that new generations of anthropologists are exposed to the idea that the power and ubiquity of indigenous healers can be harnessed in programs of public health, which to me means providing the maximum health care to the greatest number of people in the least costly and most sustainable way.

On a more personal note, a multilingual Tanzanian woman who was educated in North Korea and the Soviet Union, and later earned her PhD in the UK, interviewed me for her dissertation. She believed I was a rare *mzungu*, White person, who really understood Africa and AIDS and was willing to take unpopular positions, such as challenging the Western stereotype of the oversexed, polyamorous, promiscuous African male. She loved that I presented survey evidence that shows Africans are actually more conservative in sexual behavior than North Americans or Western Europeans. She also asked me and my son for permission to use a shot of Piki Dungidungi being fed a piece of dry cassava bread by a Matawai chief's granddaughter, when Tim was one year old. My Tanzanian colleague heads a nonprofit dedicated to fighting racism, and this picture proves, to her mind and mine—no doubt quixotically—that kids, and by implication adults, would get along just fine if left to their own devices. Yet we learn to fear "The Other," and many of us absorb chauvinistic, prejudiced ideas and sentiments along the way, often unconsciously.

A few years ago, I remarked during an interview that I came to realize I had more or less "stumbled into bliss" when I left the academic world, and tried my luck at applying anthropology to the real world. I can't imagine any other career path that would have led me to so many adventures in so many countries around the globe, encountering so many different people. I may have felt like an imposter some of the time, and that might have occasionally interrupted my career arc, but it didn't deter me for long.

About the Author

Dr. Edward C. Green is a widely-respected anthropologist, former senior research scientist at Harvard University and member of Presidential Advisory Council on HIV/AIDS, and author of eight previous books, nearly 500 academic articles, book chapters, etc., and contributions to popular media (Washington Post, NY Times). He has consulted for a number of international health organizations and has testified before Congress five times. He has worked in all major regions of the globe, performed various types of field research, and led efforts to design and evaluate both local and national public health programs. He has served on several boards of directors. He has received professional awards and his fieldnotes, photographs and recordings are now archived at the Smithsonian Museum.

Note from Edward C. Green

Word-of-mouth is crucial for any author to succeed. If you enjoyed *On the Fringe*, please leave a review online—anywhere you are able. Even if it's just a sentence or two. It would make all the difference and would be very much appreciated.

Thanks!
Edward C. Green

[I] Some of this part on Sudan was published in Green, E.C., "Have Degree, Will Travel: An AID Consulting Job in Africa," Human Organization, Vol.40, No.1, p. 92-94, 1981.
[II] Green, E.C., "A Short-term Consultancy in Bangladesh." American Anthropologist, Vol. 88, No.1, pp. 176-181, 1986.
[III] J. Blofeld, The Secret and Sublime, 1973.

Glossary of abbreviations and foreign words

USAID: US Agency for International Development

Suriname
kapiten: village chief
gaanman: the paramount chief
womi mii: son
afibiti, (piki dungidungi): a fish known for its curiosity (and the diminutive form) gaan
sombe sondi: "adult things," or sexual intercourse
pandasi: horticultural plot
obzichter: (Dutch) a government functionary
ndjukas: a neighboring tribe of maroons vodun
santeria: Afro American spirit possession cults, or religions
hogi mbeti: jaguar
keeti: white kaolin powder
saafu ten: slavery time
pandaasi: plantation
dikitor: slave boss
bassia: assistant village chief
koopina: secret language
bila tongo: "turned language" similar to pig Latin, or coded teenager language. Synonym for koopina, secret language.
kumalu, anumaa, tukunai: three desired species of fish
deesiman, obiaman: traditional healers
ataapau: matawai greeting later in the day
soso koili: travel for no specified reason
foto nenge: town creoles
saba: week
sukumaoudu: fermented sugar cane beer

Swaziland ngwenyama: king, or lion
ndloviukati: king's mother, or she-elephant
nduna: a sub-chief
belungu: White person, plural form
Gogo: grandmother
batututeli: rural health motivators
lugedla: herbalist
sangoma: spirit medium
tilwane: a type of spirit medium (plural form)

Bangladesh

ICDDR,B: The International Center for Diarrheal Disease Control, Bangladesh nirog: disease-free, health-promoting, and "cooling"

Nigeria naira: local currency purdah: enforced female seclusion.
onisegun: herbalist (Yoruba language)
agbebi, bababiye, or iyabiye: those who deliver babies
owo: protective amulet
TDr: traditional doctor
TBA: traditional birth attendant

Tanzania
CSW: commercial sex worker
UNAIDS: joint UN Programme on HIV and AIDS
PEPFAR: the President's Emergency Plan for AIDS Relief,
PACHA: the Presidential Advisory Council on HIV/AIDS
BCI: Bless China International
FRELIMO: Liberation Front of Mozambique (political part)
IDU: injecting drug users
NGO: non-governmental organization

We hope you enjoyed reading this title from:

BLACK ROSE writing™

www.blackrosewriting.com

Subscribe to our mailing list – *The Rosevine* – and receive **FREE** books, daily deals, and stay current with news about upcoming releases and our hottest authors.
Scan the QR code below to sign up.

Already a subscriber? Please accept a sincere thank you for being a fan of Black Rose Writing authors.

View other Black Rose Writing titles at www.blackrosewriting.com/books and use promo code **PRINT** to receive a **20% discount** when purchasing.

Printed in the USA
CPSIA information can be obtained
at www.ICGtesting.com
JSHW012031101023
49711JS00008B/80

9 781685 132960